FREEDOM AND CULTURE

of the nation, the individual must be safeguarded against the subordination of his individuality to the anti-individualistic claims of robot efficiency.

But on the other hand, the more responsibilities that the State assumes in providing for the general welfare, the more it can claim protection for itself, or at least for the collectivity whose interests it is endeavouring to pursue, against the irresponsibility or the ignorance of individuals.

Thus in the spheres in which UNESCO is interested, the right to freedom of opinion might involve holding opinions which were contrary to established scientific knowledge and also dangerous to the health or safety of other individuals. To believe that death is always due to witchcraft, as is the case in many primitive communities, involves the punishment and sometimes the killing of people who on the basis of established knowledge cannot be guilty of any offence; and all colonial powers in point of fact do not permit this opinion to be legally held. Similarly the belief that epidemics are punishments inflicted by God and not due to bacteria or viruses is not only contradictory of established scientific knowledge, but leads to the neglect of necessary precautions and may cause the illness or death of others; and civilized societies, although they may not forbid the holding of the opinion, do have regulations which forbid its being translated into practice.

Again, once the State has taken on responsibilities in providing education for its future citizens, it can be argued that it has both the duty and the right to see that they are guarded as far as possible against palpable error, and that the education provided should deal in facts which are true and in ideas which are conducive to the general welfare. If the individual has a right to education, he ceases to have a right to ignorance, however blissful. And his right of freedom of opinion, though it involves the right to make mistakes, cannot include a right to palpable error: for instance the child cannot be allowed to persist in the opinion that two and two makes five.

In any case, once the State has taken over any large responsibility, of finance or of policy, for education, and *a fortiori* when it has taken over all responsibility, what becomes of the right in Article 26 of the Universal Declaration, namely that 'parents have a prior right to choose the kind of education that shall be stage. The 'worker' in most primitive societies cannot obtain, but does not require, protection against 'capitalist' exploitation. On the other hand, he has not to be on guard against infringements of his liberty by such organizations, as occurs when membership of a Trade Union is made compulsory for workers in that sphere.

The real problems emerge, however, when we consider the changes that have recently taken place in the nature and functions of the State, and in our general conceptions about them. In the last century the State was, in regard to internal affairs, regarded as an essentially passive organization, whose functions were limited to securing fair play according to accepted rules, and to preventing undue friction between individuals or private firms and organizations. In countries such as those of Western Europe and North America, this concept had in practice resulted in the establishment of various individual rights, notably in the fields of justice, religion, freedom of opinion, and elementary education.

Today, however, the picture has radically changed. The State has ceased to be mainly an arbiter or umpire, and has increasingly become an active organization, devoted (either directly or indirectly) to the improvement of the internal functions of society, such as health, education, culture and the arts, scientific research, social security, and often economic activities and general planning. This tendency, which leads at the same time towards the Welfare State and the Planning State, has proceeded at different rates in different countries, but appears to be inevitable in our present complex technological and nationalist civilization.

In addition, the State has become more powerful, partly owing to the very fact of its increasing intervention in domestic social affairs, and partly owing to the new methods of exerting power which the sciences and their applications have put into its hands, including heavy weapons, improved communications, and organized propaganda.

These changes have inaugurated a new phase in the relation between individual and State.

Protection is needed in the many new fields of life which the State has invaded, and against the many new forms of exerting power which it now possesses; safeguards are required against the desire for further and more complete power which the possession of power almost invariably begets; and, since the State is becoming increasingly concerned with the economic and technical efficiency given to their children'? It is like the right of the people to choose their representatives by means of free elections, in countries with the one-party system, and where therefore no choice exists.

In both instances there is or can be much freedom within a particular system or framework, but no freedom to go beyond the limits of the framework or to change the system. And this means the restriction or curtailment of certain rights.

There can be no final detailed answers to such problems. The task of defining in legal terms or in practical regulations the actual rights and freedoms which are to be enjoyed by individuals in any given society will be a continuous one, demanding adjustments to conditions of place, time, and change.

But there are certain permanent principles and basic facts which must be kept in mind in all further discussion of Human Rights and their practical implementation. The first and most important is what I may call the paramountcy of the individual. The Universal Declaration speaks of 'the inherent dignity and worth of the human person'. The Christian churches all lay stress on the intrinsic and transcendent values of the individual soul. The biologist reminds us that the appearance of increasingly individualized organisms had been one of the marks of evolutionary progress, that individual human beings are by purely scientific criteria 'higher' than the community or the State, and that well developed human individuals are the highest product of evolution to date. And the students of human nature, whether philosophers or psychologists, anthropologists, political or social scientists, all converge towards the general conclusion that the welfare and development of individuals is the real goal of social organization.

Furthermore, since no two individuals are alike, and since their differences provide a wider basis for social life, human variety must be protected against the powerful trends making for uniformity or, at least, conformity.

The Universal Declaration speaks of 'the full development of the human personality' as the primary aim of education. This is true: it should be the primary aim of education, but only in virtue of its being something more, namely the ultimate aim of human life on this planet.

The second point to be kept in mind is that an organized

society is necessary as the means of carrying on human life in general, and in particular of providing individuals with opportunities for development. This point has acquired its full force only through the emergence of the historical approach in human affairs and the evolutionary approach in science. For we can now see that, in addition to the short-range aim of attaining the fullest and widest development of human individuals existing at any one time, there is a long-range aim of improving the organization and working of society so as to lead to life, in the person of man, realizing new and higher possibilities: and since those possibilities must take the form of human individuals or their experiences or their creations, the future of society is interwoven with our ultimate aim of securing the fullest development of the greatest possible number of individuals. Thus the individual has duties as well as rights in the present, and must be prepared to accept limitations and make sacrifices for the sake of the future development of society.

The claims of the individual and of society thus stand permanently in the relation of Hegelian thesis and antithesis. Their reconciliation in a higher synthesis must in part be attempted in the present, but in part must be deferred into the unknown future.

Finally there is a third point to be borne in mind — the brute fact of history that power corrupts, or at least tends to corrupt; that authority tends to arrogate more authority to itself and to oppress those who are submitted to it, until they are reduced to what Aldous Huxley calls 'the equality of universal rightlessness'; that the State, in so far as an instrument of material efficiency, tends to degrade human beings to the rôle of machines or of cogs within a machine, to think of them not as ends but as means; and that the community tends to act as a herd and to ostracize new or unpopular opinions. Consequently, individuals in all their variety always need safeguarding against these tendencies of organized power: and one of the safeguards so far devised is the enunciation of Human Rights. Further, the oppressive tendencies of power have so far been so dangerous that it is better to go too far in our assertions of Human Rights rather than not far enough. For instance, it is better to proclaim complete freedom of opinion, even if this involves freedom for opinions which are demonstrably incorrect or pernicious, than or dead; or in the form of 'collective representations' or other expressions of thought which are diffused through the community; or by the efforts of our own intellect and imagination, either reaching something that is wholly new, or at least something that is new to us — a revelation to ourselves, though well-known or even a commonplace to others. Of course the different methods are combined in various ways. Individuals always enter into the chain of events to some extent; and the ideas of notable individuals will always have a certain degree of general diffusion. But the differences are real and significant. In any case the 'ideal community' differs from the other types of communities in that it is primarily a community of ideas existing essentially in mind and subject to psychological relationships, whereas all the others are groups of people, existing in human society and subject to social relationships.

The various groups that I have mentioned may overlap; one group may take on some of another's characteristics; and one or more may coincide. Thus in a theocracy, Church and State are one: in medieval Europe the Church was the religious community, but was also an instrument of power: the religious community may or may not largely coincide with the ideal community: in totalitarian countries the nation becomes, if not identical with the State, at least for most purposes merged in it (witness the present cultural nationalism of the U.S.S.R.).

We need not concern ourselves overmuch with primitive societies and others less (or differently) developed than our Western type. However, it is as well to remind ourselves of one or two points. First, that many people still live in societies which are organized in a quite different way from ours. Thus in many primitive societies religion and politics have not yet differentiated their separate organizations, but are inextricably fused in the life of the tribe or other unit. In such cases 'freedom of religion' is an empty phrase, with no real meaning, and religion merely ensures fuller participation by all in the life of the social group, and provided no separate refuge for the individual, no safeguard against temporal power. Again, professional and workers' organizations, apart from small and often esoteric groups of priests or medicine men or special 'professional' groups like smiths, do not exist: labour organizations such as Trade Unions will not develop until capitalism has reached a fairly advanced ideal has been publicly proclaimed, and through that fact the ideas have begun to germinate in the general mind in all parts of the world, so that it will be difficult to eradicate them, difficult to prevent their growing slowly to full fruition.

However, as I have already said, this is not enough. In addition, we need a reasoned and scientific analysis of the facts and relations which in the last analysis are the raw materials from which the formulations of Human Rights are distilled. Without this, the Rights which are proclaimed will be out of touch with reality, and will tend to fall into contempt or disrepute. Further, it is essential that the formulation of Human Rights should change with changes in social structure and economic conditions: and for this too scientific analysis is necessary.

A declaration of Human Rights is what I have called a distillation, an ideologically operative formulation, of the relationship between the individual and the group, as seen from the angle of the individual, and of his protection against exploitation or interference. From a slightly different angle, it is one aspect of the general problem of power within society.

It will, I think, be helpful to pursue this analysis a little further, paying special attention to the problem in those cultural and scientific fields which are UNESCO's special concern.

First of all, the human individual has no meaning or significance except as a member of a group: in total isolation, he could develop none of his truly human characteristics. The characteristics both of individuals and of societies are in considerable measure conditioned by the nature of the relations between them.

In the second place, individuals in any modern society are in functional relation with many different kinds of communities or groups. In regard to human rights, the most important of these groups are the family, the profession or professional organization, the local community, the State as chief instrument of power, the nation as a continuing and developing entity in history, the religious organization, the world community, considered both in space and in time, and, finally, what I may call the ideal community.

By this last term, I mean the pool of ideas, concepts, and ideals which are so general as always to transcend the particular, so abstract as always to transcend the concrete. We make contact with them primarily either through notable individuals, living

So in the political and legal field. To imagine that a declaration of Human Rights is all that is required to safeguard the individual in his relation with the State would be like imagining that one could subsist on brandy alone, and I do not suppose that anybody save a few cranks are guilty of any such stupidity. But there is a danger in believing even that a statement of universal Human Rights can be true in the same sense as can a set of equations describing a physical or chemical process, or a detailed and reasoned analysis of an historical event or a piece of social organization. Human Rights must to a certain degree be relative to the stage and form of society in which they have to operate, and there will always be exceptions to their universal validity. Thus the very first article states that 'all human beings are born free and equal in dignity and rights', when it is at once obvious that this does not hold for congenital imbeciles. Or again, when Article 21 lays down that 'the will of the people ... shall be expressed in periodic and genuine elections which shall be by universal and equal suffrage', or Article 26 affirms that 'elementary education shall be compulsory', it is equally obvious that this cannot hold at the present moment, and probably for a long time to come, for say the pagans of the northern Gold Coast, the Australian aborigines, or the pigmies of the Congo.

I repeat, however, that this does not matter. All sensible people know that human laws inevitably have exceptions to their applicability; that allowance must be made for what I may call historical and social relativism; and also that a general theoretical declaration cannot be a practical instrument for everyday affairs — for which are needed carefully drafted laws and regulations and detailed codes of practice.

Those who are not deluded by pure logic and undiluted rationality will look at Human Rights from the functional angle. A Declaration of Human Rights is a public assertion of belief and duty concerning the relations of the human individual to the political and economic forces with which he is surrounded, a proclamation of what the signatories believe *ought* to happen, subject to various inevitable exceptions, in the world's present stage of development. Its value lies precisely in the fact of its being a public profession of general ideas. The profession of belief will undoubtedly often not be fully honoured in practice, the reality will often not correspond fully to the ideal. But the

INTRODUCTION

I am sure that UNESCO has rendered a real service by its contribution to the question of human rights. The United Nations itself had agreed on a Universal Declaration of Human Rights, a formal asseveration which has the same importance in the international field as had the American *Declaration of Independence* and the French *Déclaration des Droits de L'Homme* nearly two centuries ago in the national field. The earlier declarations represented the advance-guard of thought on the subject, while the present is the main army: or, if you will, the United Nations declaration generalizes and brings up-to-date the earlier, which were designed for particular countries in different historical conditions.

It is no longer possible for us, as it was for our ancestors in the Age of Reason, to conceive of human rights as existing in the abstract, merely waiting to be deduced from first principles by the human intellect, or as something permanent and unchangeable, independent of time and place. Indeed, it is perhaps theoretically impossible to arrive at any universal declaration, couched in terms of the rights of the individual, which shall stand up to the logical, philosophical, biological and sociological criticism with which it is bound to be assailed.

Nevertheless, such formulations have a value, and a very high value. They focus men's aspirations, their moral beliefs and political ideals, their sense of justice and decency; they relate these beliefs and moral ideals to the painful lessons of past historical experience and the cool conclusions of reason; and then proceed to distil the result in a form which makes an appeal that is both potent and general. What matter if, as with material distillation, the product may sometimes go to people's heads? The great majority of men do not renounce the alcoholic products of distillation on account of the ill effects which they exert in excess; they make use of the equally indubitable good effects of their rational and sociable employment — but make use also of all the other varieties of food and drink required for health and social intercourse.

CONTENTS

INTERNATIONAL STANDARD BOOK NUMBER:
0-8369-2381-2

LIBRARY OF CONGRESS CATALOG CARD NUMBER:
78-156725

PRINTED IN THE UNITED STATES OF AMERICA

Freedom and Culture

Compiled by
UNESCO

Introduction by
Julian Huxley

Essay Index Reprint Series

BOOKS FOR LIBRARIES PRESS
FREEPORT, NEW YORK

to introduce any principle of restriction. Even if restrictions are apparently well-founded — for instance the restriction of freedom of opinion to such opinions as are not contrary to the general welfare — one can be quite certain that they will speedily be used to justify actual repression on a large scale.

On the other hand, we must realize that, in practice, some restriction of Human Rights will necessary occur. Not only must there be adjustment of rights against duties, but of the rights of the individual against the rights — or, if you prefer, the claims — of the community.

As illustration, let us return to the problem of authority in relation to freedom of opinion and of belief, reminding our-selves at the start that the Universal Declaration lays down that these include the right to teach beliefs and to impart information. I have already pointed out certain ways in which these rights are properly curtailed. The existence of a state of war is univer-sally recognized as justifying other and further restrictions. Even Martin Luther, with his revolutionary affirmation of the freedom of individual belief, wrote that 'wherever possible, opposing doc-trines should not be tolerated under one Government', and this was emphasized by the bitterness between the various Protestant sects that rapidly sprouted in the rich soil of the new freedom.

In point of fact, whenever a set of beliefs comes to be held with religious fervour, and at the same time is associated with a social or political system radically different from the existing one, freedom of opinion is likely to go by the board and they to be banned or their proponents prosecuted. This is what happened as between Islam and Christianity during the centuries that the two faiths represented two conflicting centres of power; and it is happening today to Communism in the United States, in Australia, in South Africa and other countries on the western side of the cold war between the U.S.S.R. and the non-communist democracies and of course to western freedoms and ideas on the other side of the iron curtain.

Besides this rough-and-ready practice, there is today in many quarters a feeling that some broad general framework of ideas is desirable and perhaps necessary as an organ of a modern so-ciety, and that, while the fullest freedom of opinion and belief should be allowed and encouraged within this, it might be nec-essary to restrict freedom within the limits of the framework, and to prohibit ideas which theaten its fabric or even stray beyond its boundaries. The feeling is generally an uneasy one, for it is hard to see how it can be reconciled with the feeling for toleration and the belief in human rights, or with the necessity for change in outlook and social structure.

However, there is one fact which the framers of Declarations of Human Rights and the social philosophers have perhaps not taken sufficiently into account, and that is the rise of natural science and the scientific method in the modern era. The scientific method involves suspension of judgment and the willingness to change opinion in the face of new facts. But — and this is often neglected — it also leads to the building up of a permanent and growing body of established fact. It is the only way in which certain essential kinds of truth can be discovered, but the truth is never absolute and never complete. Science is the only way of increasing our knowledge of the phenomenal world: but is does so by disclaiming any finality for its results.

In addition, the rise of evolutionary science has necessitated our viewing all phenomenal existence, including human history, as part of an inevitable process of change, and is beginning to clarify the rôle of opinions and ideas in furthering that process in the human sphere.

I imagine that in this vital field of belief, opinion, information, and education, the conflict between freedom and restriction, between individual opinion and collective authority, will eventually be resolved by the building up of a broad framework of ideas which will be generally acceptable because it is based on tested knowledge in all relevant fields, which is fruitful of practical results because it is consonant with facts, and yet is flexible and tolerant within wide limits because it is founded on the flexible and tolerant methods of science.

One of the great intellectual inventions of man has been the working hypothesis, so fruitfully used in the natural sciences. A scientist conducts his experiments and makes his observations as if his working hypothesis were true, instead of only the most probable explanation that he can suggest at the moment. He may then find that it *is* true: but equally he may find it is *not* true, and he is always willing to scrap it or modify it, if the facts so demand. Here we have a pragmatic half-way house between the paralysis of complete indecision and the rigidity of absolute certitude, which would be very desirable and useful in the social sciences and in human affairs in general, where so often doctrine or dogma take the place of scientific hypothesis or theory, and there is an idolatry of the Absolute.

True freedom, as many philosophers and moralists have pointed out in various ways, consists not just in doing what you like (which implies servitude to your likings and cravings) or in exerting irresponsible preferences, but in discovering what is necessary on the highest and most comprehensive level, and then willingly performing that necessity. As we discover more truth, and make it more available, and if we utilize it more fully in education, freedom of opinion and belief will increasingly result in the acceptance of truth and rejection of error: a framework of ideas will become freely accepted by enquiring minds, and the restrictions on freedom of opinion and belief will become increasingly self-imposed.

However, such a consummation, though it must be believed in and worked for, will not be achieved in our time. Until that time arrives, we must rely on Declarations of Rights, on international Conventions or Covenants which legally bind their signatories to honour certain rights, and on national legislation and regulation which translate rights in terms of law and detailed practice.

Meanwhile we require a profounder and more comprehensive theoretical analysis of the problems involved in Human Rights, and a readiness to adjust our formulations to changing social and political conditions.

In pursuing these objectives, we must keep present in our minds the most comprehensive right of all, the right to individuality, always remembering that individuals do not come into being full-fledged but have to achieve whatever degree of individuality they may attain, by a long process of development. This process of development demands a suitable social environment, and should lead towards the formation of an integrated personality. Its satisfactory realization involves an increase in complexity, but also an increase in organization and unity which offsets the complexity and utilizes it to best advantage. And finally it involves the paradoxical process by which individuals attain their highest development and fulfilment by transcending both themselves and their individual limitations, and also the limitations of time and space and present social organization.

Until these implications of the paramountcy of the individual are fully grasped and their practical consequences embodied in law and custom, social structure and outlook, the affirmation of Human Rights will continue to be necessary to protect the individual against the oppressive tendencies of organized power.

GERMAN ARCINIEGAS

Culture - a human right

CULTURE - A HUMAN RIGHT

1

Like many other cities in America, Lima has its own archaeological museum. Learned Peruvians, French and German excavators, poor peasants from the mountains — all show nowadays a keen interest in recreating the history of civilizations which existed in the Western Hemisphere before the arrival of Christopher Columbus. The centre of interest has shifted. Discoveries now being made in America arouse the same public curiosity as did, in their day, the Assyrian excavations and the finding of Tutankhamen's tomb. Diggings undertaken in sandy stretches of the Peruvian desert are revealing mummies between five and ten centuries old, wrapped in cloaks of the most exquisite texture and colouring. The dry particles composing these arid dunes have preserved the cloth, which looks as glossy as if it had only just left the unknown hands and primitive loom of its native weaver. But neither mummies nor cloth can compare with the museum's eighty thousand pieces of pottery. Until the Europeans arrived, the Indians made clay figures of animals, birds, flowers and men. They achieved technical perfection. The thin layer of terracotta, covered with enamel, has withstood the action of time. The work is the living expression of an age-old spirit.

Clay represented for those earlier peoples poetry, the theatre, and books. It was the natural vehicle for the expression of their genius. In clay the artist depicted with one bold stroke the proud heads of warriors, or the loving, submissive brow of the Indian woman. In his representation of old people, the irony and malice of the ceramist have the same corrosive effect as has the hand of time, when it wrinkles and shrivels up the skin. It is unlikely that sculptors of our own day will be able to put greater meaning into their work. These old artists of Peru had some magic quality in their finger-tips. They combined poetry with realism superbly. In a design showing two doves or the head of a llama they could convey the rhythm of a subtle gracefulness with a delicacy which has never been surpassed in the decorative arts. When representing scenes of daily life, they showed man engaged in all his crudest activities with a frankness — ingenuousness — of expression which no present-day artists have ever ventured to use.

Four centuries ago, this culture came to a standstill. Then began the colonial epoch, introduced by the Spanish sovereigns in the name of Christianity. Little by little, the fruits of a new culture began to take shape. They have not yet reached maturity. For instance, it is impossible to find in Peruvian ceramic art of today works as perfect as the old ones, or which reflect so faithfully the life of a people. Nevertheless, those forgotten nations which entrusted their innermost poetic dreams to the care of so fragile a material as clay continue to live. The humble, unknown potter can never have imagined that the frail vessel on which he stamped a woman's fugitive smile would remain floating above the current of the centuries and be turned into a message from his then isolated and remote native land — a message of wonder to our modern world which he must have been quite unable to envisage.

This provides an excellent lesson. It shows us that there is something about culture which is immortal. Today we can get to know a lost world, simply by looking at pieces of pottery in a Lima museum, just as we can make contact with other worlds in the gilded halls of the Cairo museum, or among the ancient stones of Yucatan, China or Rome. Learned men labour to determine the number of dead civilizations. But are they really dead ? Is it not rather we who are deaf to the voices of the remote past ?

Emerging from their libraries, archaeologists point to some place in Asia, Africa, America, the islands of the Pacific or the Indian Ocean and say 'Underneath those sandy wastes, or among those mountains lies a buried city.' Then, for example, the University of Chicago sends out a party to those dry, deserted regions, once green and well-watered and with wealthy cities like those of the Assyrians, with their gay and noisy festivities, hanging gardens, famous bridges, and soldiers who frightened kingdoms into submission by covering the backs of their camels with dark skins so as to make them resemble hosts of elephants. And the explorers start digging, and discover monumental bulls with human heads and curly beards ... and history is born again.

It is born again in action. Forgotten paths are revealed to modern art. The thread is picked up again. The artist who modelled some fabulous bull begins to inspire the twentieth century painter, sculptor, or mere visitor to the Chicago Museum. How deep these remote influences penetrate, how strong the impression they leave, it is hard to calculate. There have been times when they have proved decisive. The taste for collecting antiques, coins, statuettes, parchments and literary and artistic fragments from the Greek world impelled the fifteenth century Italians forward upon the road leading to the Renaissance. Today, in Indo-Spanish America, the museums of Lima, Mexico, Guatemala, Bolivia and Colombia are magic schools where nations which have remained dumb for the last five hundred or thousand years recover their speech.

The great Mexican painters of our day — Diego Rivera, José Clemente Orozco and José David Siqueiros — strike us as geniuses of great originality because of their idea of covering the walls of the more important public buildings with frescoes illustrating Mexican history. Nevertheless, they have wielded their brushes in obedience more to native tradition than to their own original powers of invention. Similar frescoes cover the walls of public or religious buildings in Teotihuacan or Yucatan. They were painted by artists of the sixth or eighth centuries. Nowadays, this process is being repeated.

2

Today the civilized structure of the world is menaced. At any moment the democratic order which we have been striving to establish on this earth may break like an eggshell. During the past thirty years, one-man governments have arisen in many countries, some of which are among the most cultured in the world. Sometimes these dictatorships have been transitory; sometimes they have tended to take root. Every time one of these dictatorships seizes power in a country, that country's culture seems in danger of annihilation. And yet, amid all the instability characteristic of human undertakings, there is something which hitherto has remained unchanged and unchanging: culture. It can be checked; rising generations can be cut off from it; it is even possible to turn back to a primitive era in search of a starting-point for another, newer culture. But neither by destroying cities, burning books, or massacring peoples has it ever been possible to bring about the total disappearance of a culture.

Culture will defend itself even in a black-out. Its vitality springs, not from any particular man of genius, but from the uninterrupted flow of generations of men across the centuries. It is historical continuity that gives man's brief passage on this earth a resonance transcending the limits of his mortal life. Political systems can change. France passed from government by feudal chieftains to government by absolute monarchs, and thence to the radicalism of the Republic, to the Consulate, to the Empire, and then to another Republic. These events, so far as they have affected her culture, have merely had the interest-value of experiments. Culture, which is an ethereal message of the spirit, floats above the most violent upheavals, or remains hidden in the shadows for generations, patiently awaiting the opportunity of claiming its right to live.

In a certain sense, culture is the only thing we leave behind to testify to our pilgrimage on this earth. And when culture has struck deep roots, has acquired a consciousness of its own, it becomes immortal. Those clay vessels of the ancient Peruvians are, without a shadow of doubt, immortal. Culture can even jump from one civilization to another, spanning intervening epochs, and evading the law of the conquerors, who in the end are themselves conquered by the very peoples they thought they had subdued.

In guarding culture, we are guarding that foretaste of immortality to which alone man by his own works, can aspire. And it is an immortality worthy of the name; for it represents enrichment of spirit, increase in stature.

'Who,' asks Toynbee, 'have been the great benefactors of the living race? Confucius and Lao-Tse; Buddha and the Jewish prophets; Zoroaster, Jesus and Mahomet; and Socrates. None of them was the child of any of the civilizations existing today. Confucius and Lao-Tse belonged to one of the earliest civilizations of the Far East, which disappeared centuries ago; Buddha to one of the earliest civilizations in India, now obliterated; Hosea, Zoroaster, Jesus and Mahomet to the extinct Assyrian civilization; Socrates to the extinct Greek civilization . . .'

We are living today under the divine inspiration left floating throughout the world by marvellous civilizations, before they sank into the depths. The Greeks were able to talk about their 'immortal' gods though they realized the ephemeral, transitory nature of their political empire, of their 'civilization'. And if the Peruvians have left us their pottery as a material record of worlds which existed before Columbus, yet the rhapsodies of the Greeks, which remained floating in the atmosphere, have, by their very immaterial quality, proved the more lasting. A conqueror cannot reduce *these* to potsherds. The soul which disappears steals back again through a chink in the door of memory. There lies the best part of culture.

3

But is there today a universal admiration for culture? Or does some sinister menace attend it? Is the world paying this essence of our being the respect due to it? Let us recall the incident, already well-known, which closed the last chapter in the life of Don Miguel de Unamuno.

Don Miguel was, in Spain, the university — the whole university. He was Salamanca. All the passion for life and knowledge which since the Middle Ages had inspired this city built in stone, lit up by the flame of learning, was depicted in the face of that professor of Greek, who, while teaching Greek, taught Spanish. As Rector of the University, dramatist, poet, essayist, controversialist and talker, he was, for Spaniards, at once a symbol and an incarnation of the written and spoken word. His life was one of struggle. He faced all comers, after the style of Socrates, mortifying them in turn; for he considered his rôle in life to be that of a gadfly preventing the herd of his fellow-citizens from taking a quiet siesta. For this he suffered exile. And then, towards the very end of his life, he returned one afternoon to the university, as one who should feel under an obligation to put things to a final test. From the raised platform on which the old man, firm as a rock, presided over the academic ceremonies, he surveyed a mixed assembly of professors in their robes, uniformed students, military men, bishops and diplomats. When the official speeches came to an end, Unamuno said a few words about Spain — his Spain. He desired she should be varied and united, in her fine old spirit of federal autonomy, with all the different parts of her body in activity. His words were a sudden blaze of faith.

When he had finished, and in the silence which succeeded the applause, an army officer jumped to his feet and hurled these words at the venerable beard of the master: 'Down with intelligence!' It was a dagger-thrust. And old Unamuno, who had been a great walker and had climbed with mighty strides over all the Spanish sierras in his enthusiasm for pure air, went forward now towards the shades, grievously wounded in spirit. A few steps further, and the tomb awaited him.

What happened to Don Miguel is neither new nor peculiar to Spain. Relations between the cultured and the uncultured man, the world over, have not always been cordial. Socrates was the most learned man in Athens because he knew that there were many things he did not know. Naturally, those who thought they knew everything when, in fact, they knew nothing despatched him to the next world. This happened in the most cultured city of the time — in a sense, the most cultured in the whole of history.

Such things result from political incompatibilities, which need not surprise anybody. In exercising government, men look for simple ideas which will work directly on the people, or get themselves ready to enjoy the fruits of power. In either case, they are exasperated by the wise man's doubts and reservations — his moral allocutions, or that superior mental development which provides him with an intellectual coat of mail impervious to the clumsy assaults of an ignorant man of action.

An intellectual, conscious of the dignity of his calling, moves in a climate of free criticism. If his political shafts hit their mark, this is not because party politics play any sort of part in his natural functions. For the genuine man of intellect who works for the cultural advancement of his country, the only possible political party is the country itself. He pursues truth through dialectical criticism. And the most important adversary against whom he has to fight is himself. Doubt is a permanent battlefield where his soul and spirit have a daily rendezvous. And the first thing he must know is how to lose, sacrifice prejudices and discard truths which prove not to be truths. Freedom is essential if he is to carry out these activities, which are the means whereby we approach greater certainly in our ideas.

But, obviously, freedom inconveniences a dictator. With this dialectical, contradiction-creating process, it may happen that the decrees of the Leader (who considers himself infallible) have judgment passed upon them, in the name of reason and good sense.

Let the reader bear this clearly in mind. He who accepts dialectical argument as the means of investigating truth, must respect the freedom of such as are not afraid to formulate the antithetical side.

4

Thus, there are collisions, on the personal plane, between the intellectual and political worlds. They are truly allergic to one another. But there is more besides. Nowadays, 'intelligence' has come to be associated with a certain 'bourgeois' class. Nor is this an entirely arbitrary classification. For when the middle classes rose to power in Europe it was in the company of the intellectuals. These gave them a philosophy, wrote treatises for them on the art of government, gave them their poetry and their music. All this is undeniable. And when the new sovereigns, or the republics, made their appearance and the industrial revolution got under way, the intellectuals were drawn from the ranks of the middle classes. The nobility had little use for letters. Their traditions were such as to make them rather cling to their characteristic illiteracy than allow themselves to be pushed into the libraries. Workmen had small opportunity of sending their children to the university, and when from their ranks or those of the peasantry men appeared who reached the higher branches of learning — or, to put it more concretely, the professions — they were in the habit of breaking with their antecedents and joining the ranks of the new class; that is, turning themselves into 'bourgeois'.

This was the general state of things during the nineteenth century. The doctor, the lawyer, with their top-hats and gold repeaters, together with the learned gentlemen who accompanied them in academic processions, constituted one of the most striking adornments of the middle class. Much of this kind of thing is still preserved in those countries where the cult of the liberal professions remains strong. Where, on the other hand, the university is in more intimate ·contact with common material activ-

ities, serves directly the cause of industry, and encourages academic theses on everyday subjects such as to bring a smile to the
lips of learned folk, those who specialize in philosophical activities associate freely with those who, as it were, will not become
more than workmen with superior technical qualifications. In
this way, not only are class divisions reduced to vanishing point,
but the outlook of the intellectuals is modified, by their being
humanized.

By pointing to intelligence as the distinguishing mark of a
class that is behindhand in the field of social justice, we turn that
class into an easy target for popular resentment. Of recent years,
we have seen workmen's manifestations calling for the university's
blood and attacking the student body. Perhaps no other age has
witnessed to the same extent as ours mass deportations of teachers,
bonfires of books, patrolling of libraries, humiliation of faculties,
censorship of manuscripts — all done in the name of popular
opinion. Sometimes, when the strong man in the State picks out
the most venerable figure in the university to bring it low, he is
playing up to a people which looks on intelligence with suspicion.

But it so happens that when we look on the reverse side of the
medal we discover something equally reprehensible: this time it
is the irresponsible intellectual. He is a cultured man whose intellectual enjoyments and contact with abstract ideas have caused
him to become separated from the vulgar plane occupied by his
fellow men — who thereby cease to be his fellows. The ordinary
worker has not, in order to be able to face the hard, daily grind,
any ingenious philosophy on which to fall back; nor does his
intelligence appear clothed in learned trappings. So, in relation
to him, the irresponsible intellectual takes on an Olympian attitude. Rejoicing in his privileges, he shows himself indifferent to
the decay of liberties which for him have ceased to be of fun-
demental importance. In overvaluing his superior position he can
become arrogant. Increasing in power, he tramples disdainfully
on the personal dignity of those below him. He does not seem
to realize that personal dignity is a feeling which is just as likely
to be found in the heart of the humblest countryman or the
blackest of blackamoors, as in that of the whitest and most respected of citymen. Furthermore, he forgets that it is precisely
in the world of the frustrated and the dispossessed that feelings
are most acute.

One can explain the aggressive attitude of men of little schooling with regard to the intellectuals: they lack education, that cultivation of the spirit which would enable them to appreciate the highest forms of thought. The offensive attitude of the intellectuals with regard to those below them can also be explained: they lack human feeling, that understanding of the heart which would enable them to appreciate the basic qualities of people less educated than themselves. These two sorts of men have not, in fact, been friends. They have not known how to converse together, to shake hands.

Thus, it is a question of two niggardly lives running parallel: of two lives which, coming into contact, have turned the history of our times into a life story of animosity. These two men, the cultured and the uncultured, belonging to opposite sides of the medal, are both equally limited. As representatives of human values, they are diminished beings. Neither can understand life in its historical purposefulness. The one below does not see that by casting mud at ideals which are above the present level of his understanding he is militating against his own potential development, against something towards which he ought naturally to be drawn, were he not led astray by the bitterness engendered by his frustrated existence. While the one above, in his turn, forgets the humble sources which form the root of culture — of his own culture.

5

The word 'culture' is one of the characters that has suffered the most ups-and-downs in all languages, in a universal masquerade of misunderstanding. Those responsible thought that, by taking the word away from its obvious and natural meaning (stemming directly from the root word 'cultivate') and trying to turn it into a grand lady dressed in her Sunday best, they were going to create the most important character in the 'drama of enlightenment'. We are now coming to the moment when it is necessary to consider whether such an aberration must be considered definitive, or whether the time has not arrived for a radical change which should place culture in the simple context of human rights — not in that of a privilege pertaining to an intellectual class. For culture is a forward movement whose object is to cultivate the mind, to form the personality. At the root of all nations lie the common hopes, the imaginative stirrings of the popular mass: on the golden bough we find their poetic image, philosophical expression, and mystical perfume. Everything comes from the same tree. To keep unobstructed the stream of vital sap rising from below to above ground — that is the primary function of culture.

In the sixteenth century culture was synonymous with cult or worship, which is cultivation of the love of God. In an old French chronicle — *La Couronne Margaritique* — we read: 'She ... chose from among them all Agilulfo, Duke of Turin, a warrior, handsome and circumspect, who was nevertheless given up to the false culture of idols.' In our century, culture has been turned into the cultivation of self-esteem: 'we, the representatives of culture,' say the intellectuals in their manifestoes. A humanized culture, if a revision of the concept were undertaken, would consist in the cultivation of something which already figures as a divine ordinance: Love one another ... Maybe we have here a valid inter-connection between what is a commandment to love and at the same time an essential principle of culture. Fundamentally, culture is born of love — is an incarnation of love.

At all events, culture is not a privilege reserved for men of letters. There is such a thing as a literary culture. Books are today one of the most powerful means of spreading and advancing many different cultures. If books were placed under lock and key, the circulation of thought would now suffer a degree of paralysis. But there have been analphabetical cultures: peoples which have reached the highest levels of imaginative expression, which have had a poetry, a religion, a civilized life, and epics, without ever having invented any alphabet. This is evidenced by the clay vessels of the Peruvians, of those Incas whose arts and government Prescott recorded in a book which is conclusive as regards the history of cultures.

When Professor Vittorio Santoli composed for the Italian Encyclopaedia his article on culture, he confused literary culture with culture, defining the latter thus: 'Culture is the *ensemble* of accomplishments and capacities, mental or social, to acquire which wide and varied reading is necessary, though not by itself sufficient.' Enlarging upon his definition, the Professor goes on to explain how the essential thing is to read, to read a great deal; not like the chemist, who only reads books on chemistry; but to read about everything under the sun, to approach the world through the medium of books. More likely — we might add — to go away from the world...

The alphabet has been one of the happiest manifestations of many cultures, while remaining one of the most recent inventions. The world is old, and culture was not born yesterday. There have been cultures, which in many ways we have doubtless not been able to surpass, deriving from illiterate or semi-illiterate peoples. We find the case of the Incas repeated in that of the Mayas, or of the Egyptians, with whom an undeveloped hieroglyphic form of writing was not of any vast importance. Even the Greeks used oral communication in preference to written. Recitals of poems and the theatre were the best vehicles for the formation of intellectual opinion. To the philosopher, the debates in the academy were more important than reading. Moreover, architects, sculptors, painters, musicians and dancers were all 'integrated', culturally speaking; in their works the whole spirit of Greece is reflected; yet they may well have been illiterate. Is the culture of the Middle Ages only to be found in the theological works of churchmen who specialized in literary production? Must we not also turn our eyes towards the cathedrals, lend an ear to the anonymous Romance ballads and seek out the works on which the lamps of the library never shed their light?

In our age, literary expression has acquired supreme importance, owing to a mechanical invention — the printing-press — rather than to the alphabet. And doubts arise as much regarding the culture of those who read a great deal, as regarding the lack of culture of those whose eyes are attracted more readily towards the heart of a fellow creature than towards the printed word. Was Gandhi a cultured man? The extraordinary power he attained over his own frail body; the depths to which his watchful eyes penetrated; the fine quality of his speech; his ability to interpret the longings of a people whose history goes back farther than that of Europeans — are not all these the products of a profound culture? Were they not culture?

When Julian Huxley, Director General of UNESCO, wrote to Gandhi to ask him his opinion about the proposed Declaration of Human Rights which was being prepared by the United Nations, Gandhi replied in the following words, which briefly summarize the philosophy of a culture springing from the soil of India:

'I am a poor reader of literature past or present much as I should like to read some of its gems ... I learnt from my illiterate but wise mother that all rights to be deserved and preserved came from duty well done. Thus, the very right to live accrues to us only when we do the duty of citizenship of the world. From this one fundamental statement, perhaps it is easy enough to define the duties of Man and of Woman and correlate every right to some corresponding duty to be first performed. Every other right can be shown to be a usurpation, hardly worth fighting for ...'

6

'Culture is something which has to grow. You cannot build a tree; all you can do is to plant it, and look after it; and wait for it to mature in its own due time.' These are words of T. S. Eliot. True words and words that should be elevated into a symbol. They should bring to mind the Tree of Life, the Tree of Science, the tree-mast of the sailing ship, the family tree, and even the Tree of Good and Evil — everything in fact, which has a root, a history, a past and a future, so as to make us feel culture as we were meant to do. Everything has to be planted; and we must 'wait for it to mature in its own due time'.

In the history of languages, the first thing to appear as culture is the cultivation of plants, the labour of the soil, agriculture. Let us recall the line of Pope's:

We ought to blame the culture, not the soil.

It would seem as though, before appertaining to the history of literary development, culture were, by natural right, a word belonging to natural history.

If, in referring to a 'tree', Eliot were not speaking symbolically, he would be leaving something unfinished. For, so far as culture is concerned, there is something more than just a tree, subject to decay. What gives culture its particular quality is its power to transmit a heritage, a treasure, from generation to generation — what is called a tradition. Trees, also, take on a movement in history, and can even carry to distant lands news of their country of origin. From wild, 'uncultivated' plants, the most disciplined and 'cultivated' are developed; which no longer give a bitter or tasteless fruit, but a delicious one full of sweet juices.

The culture of mankind is of the same order. In encyclopædias which are more scientific than literary, the word 'culture' is usually defined in its anthropological sense. In that of Columbia, that is the only meaning attached to it; a group of human beings and their art of living; their culture thus including their language, industries, customs and religion. In the *Encyclopædia Britannica,* on the other hand, we have to look up culture under articles devoted to anthropology, archaeology, bacteriology and the history of civilizations.

All this suggests that when we dehumanize culture and cut it off from its branch in order to stick it in a flower-vase, we hasten the day of its death. Culture is rooted in the depths of human existence. It begins on the very day man discovers the means of raising himself above the level of the beast — when he controls fire, invents the arrow and begins to speak. Between these first discoveries and those of the wheel, the metal wing, the waves which carry the voice and even the light and shade of photographs across the oceans, lie centuries of research, generations which have sweated blood, rejoiced and suffered under the chancy pendulum of life. All is part and parcel of this development of human culture.

But when we say 'culture' in the singular, we are using an abstraction; as such it is unsatisfying, giving the term a generic, amorphous sound. We must look at the species in its plural aspect, for then 'cultures' — in the plural — evoke wonderful facts: Egypt and Mexico, Greece and Japan, France and China, the Amazon, Polynesia: in naming them thus, the vital significance of the term becomes apparent. Representatives of every nation take on colour, voice and shape as they move across their own magic screen. I would almost suggest that 'culture' is not a noun but a verb, indicating the action carried out by the peoples as they move forward under the urge to rise, take shape and mould their characters.

The right to culture is therefore an individual one. It is the human right of every people to reveal its soul, to express itself freely. And it is a permanent right. It took many centuries for the Egyptians to acquire an architecture of their own and a hieroglyphic style of writing and to evolve methods of preserving their dead, portraying their great national leaders in stone, and bringing the Nile valley under control in order to turn it into the nation's granary.

The archaelogy of the great cathedrals of Europe is the best witness to the slow development of cultures. We see in these cathedrals how the ages overlap one another. We begin with the Romanesque crypts with their dog-tooth arches, and end with the Gothic spires, which had to wait centuries before the stone sprouted forth in floral decorations, strange and fabulous creatures, and all that the Middle Ages produced from their miracles and magic, their patience and their dreams.

Finally, we may say that the right to culture is, as it were, the ultimate right of all peoples. It must be upheld until they are able to loosen their tongues and untie the knot in which their hidden longings are held bound. It is the most important factor in the development of their internal freedom. It has made possible the creation of languages, symphonies, mural paintings, ornamental capitals, figures in marble and bronze, and books.

7

A culture is born in the following way. It is the year 1300. At the bottom of a valley, on the left bank of the Arno, enclosed within its ancient ramparts, lies Florence. It is a stone-built city. Under the blue sky, in the clear, sparkling air of the south, rise the high, solid square towers whence, in days of battle and siege, stone-blocks, boiling oil, or insults harsher than any stone and more scalding than any oil, can be hurled down upon the enemy. The dirty, narrow streets are crowded with people — weavers, carders, saddlers, locksmiths, carpenters, bricklayers, notaries, friars and soldiers. All rise with the dawn to attend early mass. Mass over, the majority repair to their workshops; whence, at the ringing of the Angelus, they return to their homes. They fear to go out at night, for it is then that in the hands of Florentine night-birds gleams a dagger-blade, as coldly as the light of any star . . . and an evil star at that! In the houses, everything is ready to be thrown out of the windows in case, owing to some carelessness, the thatch catches fire and the house begins to burn, a thing that happens frequently. Sometimes, too, the Arno rises and over-flows its banks, and then chests, truckle-beds, drowned children, dogs, hens, wine-barrels, bales of wool, leather upholstery and bits of cloth go floating down the flooded streets.

The lords, counts of the vicinity, representing a former illit-erate culture of the lusty and blood-thirsty, make up the country nobility. From their proud castles they look disdainfully upon the nest of villeins down in Florence. But the villeins continue to increase in wealth and power. They have become expert in the art of weaving, carding and cleaning wool. They have or-ganized themselves into powerful guilds. From China, Ceylon and India merchants are importing those substances to which Marco Polo refers in his travels, that can be used for dyeing wool and silk. There is no finer cloth, none that has been so improved by a secret art which makes it strong and smooth, than that of Flo-rence. From England, Spain and France, in sailing ships or by trains of pack-mules, come bales of cloth in the rough. The Flo-rentines give them all just that Florentine finish. Traders who cross seas and continents to serve this industry — which already in the Middle Ages has established close links with the most distant parts of the globe — return with pearls from the Persian Gulf, Byzantine images of the Crucified, carpets from Arabia, gold thread for brocade, and cinnamon, cloves, nutmeg and sugar to add flavour to the townspeople's food. In every workshop, the humble hand is turning himself into a thoroughly expert artisan — into an artist.

The guilds of artisans become more colourful. Everything is done to the accompaniment of music and singing. People talk — they talk a great deal among this population of talkers, all in that local idiom in which the sentences seem to be poured forth from a musical box and every word has an authentic ring about it of this city, made for the rollicking jargon of merchants and skilled operatives. The love of argument, of telling stories of other countries, of mortifying by a display of wit, is so prevalent among all classes that it is hard to know where, in any man, the manual worker ends and the intellectual begins. The richer represent-atives of the Woolmerchants' Guild take upon themselves the duty of erecting the marvellous cathedral of Santa Maria dei Fiori and the church of San Miniato, looking towards the hills around

Florence. The same guild orders Lorenzo Ghiberti to make some doors worthy of the Baptistry of San Giovanni Batista. St John the Baptist is the guild's patron saint; and the Baptistry, with its white marble roof and scenes from sacred history done in Byzantine mosaics all over the interior, and even the symbolical fact of its standing where once a pagan temple stood, must necessarily represent something of prime importance for any native of the city. For twenty-seven years Ghiberti works with his chisel at the ten door-panels of bronze, and covers them with gold. When the double doors are in place, all Florence comes to admire this history of the Jewish people, written as it were in pages of gold: the life of Adam, the Flood, Abraham visited by the three angels, Moses receiving the Tables of the Law, David cutting off the head of the giant, and Solomon receiving the Queen of Sheba. To think that they were wool-merchants who conceived the idea of having that amazing story, which fills the first acts of the human drama with resounding flourishes and shining prophecies, written in this fashion! When Michaelangelo beheld the masterpiece, he exclaimed: 'These ought to be the gates of Paradise!'

It is like this with everything else in Florence. These same woolmerchants commission Giotto to build the campanile, which now, in the twentieth century, is still the most beautiful tower in the world. Giotto is only the son of a poor farmer in the neighbourhood, who whiles away his time with a piece of chalk, making drawings on the rocks of the sheep he has been given to tend. Some Florentine, who happens to be walking through the countryside, discovers the rural draughtsman's talent. So Giotto goes to Florence. This ability to discover, through some fleeting sketch, a genius in the making soon becomes one of the most successful pastimes of the Florentines. The simple sincerity of Giotto's portrayal of men and of the saints ushers in the most tremendous revolution in painting. With his Franciscan frescoes of the fourteenth century, he continues to teach and inspire our painters of the twentieth. He inaugurates an epoch. In regard to painting one has to say: pre-Giotto and post-Giotto.

Men of genius, certainly; but they are men who have sprung from the popular womb. Their feet are firmly planted on their native soil. Like Giotto, and about this same time, there arises a poet who is to glorify this New Life. How does Dante speak? 'I speak like an ordinary, common poet, who desires that his mistress should understand his words; for a mistress finds listening to Latin verses a tedious business...' That common speech should form the language of love is the first thing Dante discovers. Subsequently, he extends this discovery to include politics and ethics. It is he who arranges the marriage between the vulgar tongue and poetry. With the hand of a magician, this Florentine who descended into the nether regions draws back the curtain so that the Divine Comedy can begin and the Renaissance be inaugurated.

After Dante comes Petrarch, 'that plebeian man of letters who conversed with princes and kings as man to man...' He not only chooses the popular idiom wherewith to place upon the brow of his lady a garland of immortal verse; he also pulls Latin out of its theological tomb and makes it human again. His cultural mission was to humanize letters, which the metaphysicians had dehumanized.

How wonderful popular history turns out to be! The descendants of wool-merchants, not to mention weavers, become bankers, literary leaders and patrons: such is the line of the Medici. Masters from the Academy frequent the workshops of the book-binders and there continue their discussions about Aristotle and Plato; while the book-binders drop their tools to lend an ear, and even to put in comments of their own from time to time. Anybody may have an original idea. In the shadow of the church where Michaelangelo is working as an architect, and where the stone-cutters are squaring the blocks of smooth stone, problems of aesthetics are discussed. And it is of no particular consequence that suddenly, in the middle of such a discussion, Michaelangelo himself should have his nose punched by somebody; for passion plays its part in such dialogues, which are frequently charged with irony, intensity of feeling, or malice. Inside, the walls of the churches and palaces are illumined by the frescoes of Ghirlandaio or Gozzoli. In the convent of San Marco the paintings of the blessed Fra Angelico have such clear skies that all the shining atmosphere of the valley seems to penetrate and chase away the semi-darkness of the cells.

On the huge wooden chests where the bridal trousseau is kept, painters reproduce scenes of domestic life. Painting becomes an expression of folklore. The customs, hair-styles, wedding processions, coats of armour, fabrics, simple beliefs, miracles, superstitions, civilities, balls, festivities, gardens — in fact, the whole output produced by these anonymous hands — furnish the themes inspiring the noble schools of painting in the fifteenth and sixteenth centuries. The painters have worked in the workshops of the artisans; they belong to the guilds; it is their descendants — artists like themselves — who have set on the wool, silk, leather and iron industries the seal of an age-long culture.

Those who have worked the brocades so that the rich and beautiful ladies of Florence shall be brilliantly dressed for the great weddings, for the arrival of Pope or King, or for attendance at the jousts, see the silks which have left their hands represented by Ghirlandaio in his frescoes in Santa Maria Novella and by Botticelli in his picture of Spring. Thus their designs form a single whole with those of the greatest masters. The same thing happens with the cabinet-makers, architects, goldsmiths, calligraphers, book-binders and armourers. Everything is integrated, bound up with the rest.

In this way Florence makes herself the capital of the Western world. There are a few years during which the paths of the following contemporaries cross one another in the streets of this small city: Michaelangelo, Raphael, Machiavelli, Lorenzo dei Medici, Botticelli, Polizziano, Marsilio Ficino, and Savonarola! Whence comes this vigour? What is it that inspires this collective enterprise? In the first place, it is a current which passes from the cobbler's bench right up to the Academy. From the days when Boccaccio used to read and comment on Dante and Petrarch in the public square, as the City Herald, to the time when Lorenzo the Magnificent and Pulci would go out at night to join with the crowd in singing the Carnival songs, it was always an understood thing that everybody should have access to poetry, music and clever dialogue. Even now, in our twentieth century, there is no more delightful pastime than to converse with the artisans of Florence on any subject; the poetry of Dante, the paintings of Titian...

8

Let us now say something about literary culture. How have letters managed to leap from the anonymous Romance poem, the heroic legend, to heights of renown — to Shakespeare, Goethe and Cervantes?

In the beginning it was not Shakespeare. It was the son of a shoemaker. This shoemaker's son showed, in a few tales, everything of which the English language was capable. He knew something about the poetry of France, and quite probably something about Boccacio the Florentine; but he ended by finding what was most important in a tavern of his native country — in the Tabard Inn, which six centuries ago was situated in one of those London streets leading out into the country, out in the direction of the rural townships. At this inn could be found good stabling, good beds, and an innkeeper who knew how to converse with his guests.

Tonight, at the Tabard, are assembled representative characters of those times: a miller who loses his head when he gets drunk; a knight of the sort who go about in lordly style accompanied by his son and a page; a student who lies down with Aristotle for a pillow; a nun who is prioress of her convent; a friar, and a carpenter ... twenty-nine all told. They are off on a pilgrimage to Canterbury. Some use a refined speech, others the vernacular. All are rapturously relating or listening to racy stories in which love comes by surprise, with violence and in secret; the student's cunning gets the better of traps set for him by the miller; interlarded with bits about ancient Greek warriors, village lasses showing their shapely legs — the whole seasoned with wine and wit, as must ever be the case on pilgrimages.

Of all this Geoffrey de Chaucer takes careful note. Learned writers say that Geoffrey was, like his father, an innkeeper, and, like his grandfather, in the Customs and Excise for the wine trade; that he held appointments at Court and travelled about. All this is as true as that he was born in the Street of the Shoemakers in London and bears the marks of this trade in the very soles of his surname: Chaucer, of pure French derivation. Which is why we may call him 'the shoemaker's son'.

He begins his account in this way: 'Above all, I beg you, of your courtesy, not to be offended that I address you in the

common tongue . . .' Off we go, as pilgrims do, to Canterbury;
and we already know the way pilgrims talk. Here rustics rub
shoulders with princes. Whoever has made a vow, or hankers after
the air of that renowned spot, or likes amusing himself in a
crowd; or whoever feels his heart bid him kneel down before the
shrine of St Thomas of Canterbury, let him start riding or footing
it along those 'rolling English roads'. And he that has eyes to
see, let him see; and he that has ears to hear, let him hear.

As they journey forward, and the dustiness of the road and the
scattering of the various groups puts a brake on conversation,
those who play the pipes raise the morale of some unfortunate
who stumbles and smashes a finger. The nuns ruminate over their
prayers, and the knights — as becomes their arrogance — ponder
some knavery or other. The merchant divides his attention between meditation on the love of God and the tricks he will devise
to swindle his customers. In this way they are all led along by
their own individual thoughts and dreams, until the Angelus
sounds, which is the signal for making towards the inn. The day's
toil ends by providing the horses with a good feed, while the
reeking saddles are hung up on the pegs. And now is the time
for pilgrims, like horses, to take a rest. Gathered round the fire,
their faces glow like copper. The warm ale, in metal jugs, helps
to loosen their tongues. And while the one whose turn it is to
tell a story is speaking, the foot-soldier strokes the silver filigree
on his hunting-horn; the nun, her ivory crucifix; the innkeeper,
his saffron-coloured beard; and the knight, the four rings he wears
on the fingers of each hand . . .

Canterbury Tales — a mosaic of the fourteenth century! Vanity
fair, showcase full of comedy! Here we have the knight who talks
about Greece, for it is in keeping with his profession to feel himself blood-brother to the heroes in Homer. Where have you been,
sir? I? Oh, in Latvia and in Russia . . . And I've trotted around
Granada, Alexandria, Algeciras and Morocco . . . I'm just back
from Asia Minor, and from Turkey *and* Germany . . . And here's
my son, to show I'm not a liar.

The son is a youth of twenty, and as handsome as the devil.
Hast travelled a lot, young man? He doesn't say. Instead, he
volunteers information about more immediate, practical matters:
he's a fine horseman and tilter; he can dance, write and paint and
— as they've all had an opportunity of hearing — how he can

play the flute! And how he can make love and be loved in return; and how he can sleep... What time a nightingale does sleep!

And what of the Reverend Mother Prioress? She is a refined and very sensible nun. She speaks French: not — as Chaucer himself says — the kind spoken in Paris, which is altogether outside her ken; but the kind spoken in Stratford. But you should just see how she doesn't even wet the tips of her fingers in the sauce, nor allow her lips to remain covered with grease or any drops to fall on her dress. And then... what a nicely shaped little nose! And those clear blue eyes, that small mouth and those soft, red lips!

The monk is of a different order. His bald crown shines in the light of the log-fire. But at break of day, mounted on the best horse, he looks a proper rider. He's not the sort of monk who stays in his cell, reading St Augustine like a lady. He was born to be a hunter. He looks well in his huntsman's cap, which is fastened under his prominent chin with a gold clasp. How far removed he is from those pale spectres worn out by prayer and fasting!

The next to speak is the friar, one of those who ask the faithful to offer them, instead of tears and prayers, good silver coin. Chaucer sings his biography: there is not a tavern he doesn't know, not a tavern-keeper or tavern-maid with whom he isn't acquainted. When he prays, his voice is sleepy and monotonous. But when he raises his voice to sing, what a fine baritone!

And then it's the turn of the merchant, the student, the cook, the navigator, the wife of Bath and the parish priest... all join in, and each one tells a story.

Never have so many lies been told as at these stopping-places frequented by pilgrims. One goes to fulfil a vow once in a lifetime. Hence, even the most miserly, those who never yet let drop a farthing, unloosen their purse-strings. When it's time to spend, spend! So they spend on the road, at the inn, and in the Canterbury shops, all crammed with gewgaws. In the same way, they feel a desire to sing, to give free rein to their imagination. They see new faces. They, who have spent all their lives looking at the same old faces of their fellow-villagers as they pass them silently in the street, now meet pilgrims from Ireland, Wales, Scotland and Britanny, each one with his own language, music, tales and yarns.

How do you feel, you men of the twentieth, about taking a

plunge into this life of the fourteenth century? Well, sit down beside these twenty-nine travellers bound for Canterbury. Do not be alarmed if you first find them worn out and covered with dust, those who have come on horseback with raw buttocks, and the foot-sloggers with their feet all swollen up. The evening party will soon sweep aside all the dust and raise a twinkle in the eye. And it is then that, towards midnight, some will take the lids off the houses, lifting up their thin pastry-like roofs; while others will raise the curtain inside the theatre of fantasy. Such is Chaucer's magic art.

And thus great literature is launched. Soon, Shakespeare will follow, and the other literary giants. But let us place at the head of the list, so that we may not forget it, the name of the man who was born in the Street of the Shoemakers.

9

Chaucer, Rabelais, the Archpriest of Hita, Boccaccio... With their highly-coloured description, in a shameless outburst of guf-faws and banquetings, the characters of low comedy, lewd and racy-tongued, make their entry upon the literary scene. No one disapproves of them. Everyone listens to them gladly and profits by what they have to say. Chaucer belongs to the same race as Shelley and Milton; Boccaccio will be quoted equally with St Thomas Aquinas, or St Bonaventure; in the company of the Archpriest we shall find St Theresa of Avila, Fray Luis de Leon and Fray Luis de Granada; Rabelais has Descartes and Pascal for his fellow-countrymen.

Literary culture comprises all that. It is an endless contrasting of characters, ideas, illusions and realities. Nowadays, all the in-numerable riches that can flow from the human imagination appear upon the printed page, just as before they were transcribed in illuminated folios, so that the horizon may be widened for all such as are fortunate enough to be able to read.

That is the great good fortune of cultures with an alphabet. All manner of subtleties of thought have been lost, where nations have remained unlettered. In these days, we can record what is ours and submit it to the judgment of those who come after us. With a book in his hand, the student can travel in time or space;

he can know what is happening in every corner of the world, and what the Athenians in the age of Pericles were like, or the Germans at the time of the Nibelungs. Books enable us to share in the philosophical preoccupations of people whom we cannot see or listen to in person. A chemist or an engineer can be something more than a man limited to the practice of his own profession; through books he can make contact with those working in other spheres of intellectual activity. This magic carpet which our minds possess leads to discoveries, unexpected points of view, rectifications and finds; all of which represents, in a word, cultural capital in circulation.

If the countryman who never, or hardly ever, goes to the city, or the workman or artisan who leaves the workshop to return straight home to his suburb, had not even the possibility of ever being able to find out from books what the world is about, how people live in other countries, that there is something beyond the restricted scene where he tills the soil or carries on his work, they would be slaves under a new slavery: one composed of curtains shutting out any view of the world, and just at a time when, thanks to the marvellous inventions of science, the world is being made to give up its secrets in all directions. Whoever prohibits books, or burns them, or prevents them being written, does so because he has no argument to set against the arguments of others, nor the knowledge necessary to refute them, nor the courage to confront his own ideas with strange and unfamiliar ones, nor the noble humility required to receive the best other people have to show.

So far, the press, the radio and the film have only been able to present a fragmentary view of life. Limited to such means of information, men lack any definite perspective. The press, which plays such an important part nowadays, barely succeeds in bringing into focus a reality lasting twenty-four hours, and breaks it up in almost brutal fashion. It is difficult to follow the simple story of an event taking place in China or Java, that can affect the rest of the world, by just reading about an incident of the previous day, divorced from the causes which have produced it (and which were probably not published because they weren't 'news'), and without being able to perceive the repercussions which it must inevitably entail. The press by itself, without books, would be a monstrous institution. And when we say 'books', we mean *all* books.

Chaucer's tales, the fabulous discourses of Pantagruel or Gargantua, and likewise the lives of the Saints, works of fiction or based on legend though they may be, end up by being of more use than histories themselves for the purpose of giving a true picture of life as it then was. For in reconstructing an epoch, it is not just the date of a battle or the name of a king which counts; but it is even the falsehood about the devil seen by the terrorized maiden; the account given of banquets which never took place except in the dreams of an outrageous glutton, or the mystical swoon of the saint who experiences the Passion of Our Lord through the miracle of the stigmata. Just now, there are accounts of the war, in the form of novels, that give us a truer insight into European life at the time than the memoirs of Churchill himself. It is impossible to estimate, within the mosaic of what is published daily, the relative value of every publication. All we know is that, threading our way through a labyrinth of paper, we go on making for the little lamp that lights our destiny.

It may be that the masterpiece of the present day lies in a collective form of expression. Goethe, Shakespeare and Cervantes had the genius to assemble, in one single work, opposing elements, so as to present in synthesis the picture of a whole succession of emotions, of ideas. The drama, above all, served their purpose, in so far as it was a universal expression of culture. In the drama, the features of the great are brought out equally with the homelier characteristics of lesser souls, with all that these have to offer by way of complement, explanation or fulcrum in all the scenes of the real theatre of everyday life.

When Faust, after cavilling on four occasions, reaches the admirable formula: 'In the beginning was the deed,' he gives us the key to the cultural process. From there one may set out with the certainty of arriving wherever the flight of the intelligence can lead. The act of departure will always continue vibrating, just as the stretch of the bow and the exertion of the bowman continue in the tremor of an arrow shot into the sky.

10

A day comes in the history of literary cultures in Europe when, by a single word definition, the natural destiny of culture is shown: its application to man, its human orientation — its 'humanism' to use the vivid substantive coined.

Yet, by a strange paradox, some of the most qualified exponents of humanism have wanted to dehumanise it. Jacob Burkhardt is a recognized cultural master by reason of the learned grasp which has enabled him to penetrate to the cores of Greek and Italian culture. But when he describes the birth of humanism in Florence, he makes this disconcerting assertion, which defines his attitude towards the problem of culture: 'Humanism,' he says, 'is a new moral element which, spreading from Italy, invades the rest of Europe and becomes, as it were, the climate proper to all men possessing a certain degree of culture. The circumstance in itself is unpopular, for it necessarily leads to a complete gulf between the cultured class and the uncultured class throughout Europe. And why deplore the fact, seeing that we ourselves are bound to confess that this universally recognized gulf still exists and cannot be removed?'

If we consult historical evidence on the subject, including that of Burkhardt himself, it is difficult to see in what this unpopularity of humanism consists. Maybe exactly the contrary occurred. Humanism condemned not what we commonly call the uncultured man, but culture in its spurious form — that of the clerics with their macaronic Latin, that of the ignorant professors whom Erasmus chastises in his 'In Praise of Folly'. In opposition to dehumanised science and metaphysics, the first claim is made for a recognition of man's right to participate in culture. Men and women of flesh and blood occupy once more the front of the stage; so much so that the Renaissance takes on the aspect of a pagan holiday. The Medicis have been called demagogues because they went on the spree and harangued popular audiences. Burkhardt himself admits that in Italy the gulf between the cultured and uncultured man was not a large one: 'So much so,' he says, 'that the poet most rigorously attached to the rules of art, Tasso, is one of the most popular and is read by all and sundry.'

The gulf which Burkhardt describes — and which marked a

current of thought peculiar to the Germany of his time — is a product of post-humanism. This, of course, is no longer humanism. It may very well be the reverse: anti-humanism. Removing the subject from the academic plane, the original argument is settled in superb fashion in a novel: *Don Quixote.*

Was Cervantes a humanist? Many have denied it. They found him too plain and direct to merit the title of a cultured man. Recent criticism has corrected this standpoint. To express what he was in a few words, we quote the following authoritative verdict by Don Federico de Onis: 'Cervantes, carried away by his characteristic eagerness to the point of reading even the scraps of printed matter he came across in the street, read all the books he could find in his own Spanish tongue and in Italian, which he learned in his youth. Even had he not known Latin, which he certainly did, those two tongues enabled him to read the works of Antiquity and those of the Renaissance. Directly or indirectly, therefore, Cervantes, with his marvellous capacity for selecting and assimilating what was essential, acquired the spirit of both ancient and modern culture, with the result that his works are a synthesis of the Renaissance, while at the same time they surpass it. Thus we find in them traces of the *Odyssey* and Virgil, of Boccaccio and Petrarch, of Ariosto and Sannazaro, of Leon Hebreo and Erasmus, of the *Celestina* and Lope de Rueda, of Carcilaso and Luis de Leon...' And Américo Castro has remarked: 'Without Erasmus, Cervantes would not have been what he was.'

Very well: in *Don Quixote* we find this fundamental but unique example of a life of adventure — and a full one, though occupying a brief space of time — during which the 'Caballero', exalted as he is and full of the loftiest ideals, converses the whole time with the most ordinary man of the people. If Sancho Panza had been a stirrup-man — just a regular earthy type, as we say — he would at least have presented a more dignified appearance on his way through the world. Instead, he had to ride on a donkey — forming one with the lowly animal with the large ears. In this way his position in social life, in the intellectual world, and in the order of knight-errantry was determined to a nicety. However, Sancho follows Don Quixote about like a faithful dog, and listens to him... and Don Quixote listens to Sancho, considers his arguments and ends by following him. Cervantes, in his subtlety, often makes us hesitate as to which of the two is the wise one.

In *Don Quixote* Spain possesses her encyclopædia of folklore. Here are to be found the entire collection of proverbs, the witches' recipes that form Don Quixote's medicine, the lives of the servant-girls, muleteers, shepherds, convicts and village personalities. Here, also, the wayside inns, the roads, all the popular life of Spain, now in full cultural swing; for it is the Spain of errantry, ranging over enchanted lands in search of her ideals.

And in the same book, for the confounding of the 'academicians' is that thirst for justice, that insane desire to reform the world which has blossomed in Don Quixote as a result of much reading. Don Quixote succeeds in actualizing his dreams. On the approach of a flock of sheep, he finds it to be, correct in every detail, the army of knights-at-arms which adorned an enchanted age with adventure and the clash of steel. 'Hear'st thou not, Sancho, the neighing of the horses, the blowing of the bugles and the roll of the drums?' 'All I can hear, Master, is the loud bleating of a lot of sheep...'

Here, at least, is to be found all Spain. The crazy man rushes upon the phantoms, and ends up spitting out a lot of teeth; while the incident closes with an immensely tender conversation. 'Thou art quite right, Sancho,' says Don Quixote. And like brothers, and just as if nothing had occurred, they continue together along the same road, moving onward to the same crazy adventures — Don Quixote incited by imagination, Sancho by hope.

This passage is not part of a novel; it is part of the history of Spain, and to a certain extent of humanity. It manages to coincide, even in its details, with events that actually took place. For example, Bernal Diaz del Castillo, referring to one of the battles during the conquest of Mexico in which his companions-at-arms saw the apostle St James himself, on his white horse, fighting for the Spaniards, goes on to say in his History: 'Maybe this was so, and that I, being a sinner, was not worthy to see it... What I did see, and recognize, was Francisco de Morla on a chestnut horse...' Thus, those who saw the apostle, as well as he who saw Francisco de Morla, followed together, hand in hand, the road of heroic achievement.

11

The original conception of humanism has become distorted. So has that of culture. Today, in the midst of the turmoil, we return to these topics because we have the feeling that in these two words 'humanism' and 'culture' lies the seed of our common good. We are impelled by a natural curiosity to probe into their origins. Did the rise of humanism really bring about a new class division? Does *Don Quixote* just represent some extravagant idea on the part of Miguel de Cervantes? Was culture destined to be an imperial instrument in the hands of a coterie of the elect? Are not humanism and culture two natural rights of man, which can be invoked to guard his liberties, defend human dignity and promote an ideal of common justice? And, having outlined the terms of the matter, and coming to grips with the problem of our time, are culture and justice, humanism and justice, words without any blood-relationship between them?

When humanism makes its appearance, Europe is not in a state of peace. The destruction left in their train by the imperial armies is not exactly an edifying spectacle. All realize this: few say anything about it. But a band of philosophers — and more especially one of them — tackles the subject openly. This individual publishes a very bold book, seeing that it is addressed to Charles V. The author is a Spaniard. It is a serious business that this man who shouts the truth should be a Spaniard; for Charles, before being Emperor of Germany, is King of Spain. The man is Luis Vives; his book, *De Concordia et Discordia in Humano Genere*. In it Luis Vives analyses the European culture of his time in the light of humanism.

What does Luis Vives represent in Europe? Above all, he is the great friend of Erasmus. It is Erasmus who encourages him to dedicate his commentary on St Augustine's *City of God* to Henry VIII of England. The king, if rather too human in certain respects, receives the humanist philosophers with open arms. He asks Vives to come to Court as tutor to the Princess Mary. So Vives goes to England. In his chair at Oxford he lights a lamp which even today, after four centuries, remains unextinguished. Erasmus, Thomas More and Luis Vives form a circle of the erudite whose fame can only be paralleled centuries later, if then, by that of the little court Goethe gathered round him. However, these three men of the sixteenth century are not exactly lyrical. They do not seek out the front of the stage. Nor are they burning with romantic illusions. They are simply moralists. All the same, they are listened to, applauded and followed. They have in them an impulse from the heart, directing them towards man and enabling them to probe into the depths of his soul. In this sense, what Vives writes is sublime.

Another aspect: Vives is not a mystic, but a thinker. He carries God in his consciousness, he is a Christian; but his problem is Man. On returning from England and settling down in Bruges, the warlike ardour of the troops of Charles V worries him and causes him sleepless nights. Rome has been sacked - and how! Spain has jumped from the obscure isolation of her petty kingdoms to the resounding supremacy of Empire. Vives addresses four books to Charles V on the causes of war. Dealing with the destiny of culture, he writes: 'In times of discord, culture cannot exist.'

He refers to intellectual culture, basing it upon responsibility of a moral kind. Culture can never be irresponsible. One should examine the origins of pride and see to what pride leads. Pride exists not only among illiterate leaders. It also makes its home among those who lose their balance through conceit, because they happen to know a few things. 'How do those behave whose learning separates them from the vulgar, and who are looked up to as models and superior beings, for their greatness of soul, moderation and modesty? I am ashamed to reply and would prefer to keep silent, lest it should be thought I wish to speak ill of those of my own class. But the thing is too well known to be hidden ... The hates of ignorant folk are unsubstantial; those of learned folk, solid! — as solid as a main wall, without windows through which the light of truth and reconciliation could penetrate.'

These ardent declarations by Luis Vives mark the authentic trend of sixteenth century culture, which is humanistic and Christian. What unrestrained violence leaves behind, after treading underfoot the works of generations, is the lees of melancholy. 'With culture and knowledge despised, and books trampled upon and held to be useless and a cumbersome burden, they end by destroying and burning them. Hence those catastrophes resulting from the disappearance of whole libraries and of the works of celebrated authors, now sorely missed. It is impossible to estimate the damage which art and science have suffered by such losses. That is what happened in the wars with the Goths, the Vandals and the Saracens, and recently, as it appears, during the sack of Rome ...'

It was in these terms that Luis Vives of the Spain of errantry, son of a Valencia tradesman, and the great Erasmus, whose words we all remember, defended the rights of Western culture. Their ideals were of humble origin. Doubtless they themselves had been victims of theological humbug, of social tyranny. And Vives may even have had special reasons for holding persecution in horror if, as seems possible, he was partly Jewish. Individual circumstances of a similar kind enabled them both to become acquainted with the most hidden parts of the soul, and thus the flame in their books burns with a more glowing intensity.

It is not possible to speak of culture if we take points of reference lying very close to one another. Only by relating faraway extremes and by making a long pilgrimage of thought and emotion, climbing from the bottom of the valley to the top of the mountain, can we obtain a broad cultural view. In the case of these two men, we must observe the road they followed in order to disentangle themselves from ingenious metaphysical subtleties and reach the living heart of man; to pass from the degradation of an enslaved mind to the free flight of the spirit, from the arbitrary ways of tyranny to the ways of right and justice. Man's culture consists, then, in patient rectifications and in a sleepless search for higher levels. He goes on imaginary journeys from Hell to Paradise.

12

'If we are to take culture seriously,' says Eliot, 'we shall find that the peoples require not only to *eat*, but to have their own particular way of *cooking*: one of the symptoms of cultural decadence in England is the indifference shown to the art of preparing food.'

Culture expresses itself in customs. It is seen in gestures, manners, the expressions which appear on the lips; in the hands, in the looks of the countryman, artisan, soldier or student; it passes from one lip to another, one hand to another, one eye to another, right up to refined circles, until it covers with a mesh of behaviour every human group, which thus reaches its own style of expression. It would be interesting to follow, in painting for example, the history of the different attitudes of the hand; from the hand which grasps, clutches and closes over convulsively, to the two hands that unite in prayer, or are covered with rings, or seem about to bestow a caress. We may recall the oriental hands of Fujita; those of the Dutch peasants painted by Van Gogh in his Supper of Potatoes; those of El Greco's noblemen in the Burial of the Count of Orgaz; those of the Gioconda, and those of the women in Botticelli's Spring. Every expressive gesture disseminates itself by sympathetic contagion. Thus are the customs of each society formed.

At every new stage, with minute variations, attitudes take on greater refinement, polish and meaning and words more colour; while new conceptions, issuing in felicitous gesture, can be attained even among the lowest ranks of society. Whoever has lived among country-folk knows how, under their rough exterior, there is a native civility — some would say even courtesy — that is expressed in such ways as, for instance, hastening, at a meal, to pass the first and best helping to the woman guest, wife or mother. May not this part of our culture have had its origin among such as these, and subsequently have passed into urban usage?

The same thing happens in the case of words. It is a pity that in the rush of modern life there is no time to 'prepare' words, to await the moment when they suddenly become so charged with meaning that they seem to have some miraculous effect on the development of the language. Formerly, in all languages, each of the smallest parts of a house, a ship, or a coat-of-arms was given a name which was a poetic image. In our mechanical age, words to do with the motor-car and the aeroplane sprout up in the catalogues with the same speed at which steel sheets are pressed into shape in the moulds. There still remains, however, a wide margin in the matter of adjectives and of names that spring up in popular intercourse. The greatest writers in all ages, those who have later become the pride and ornament of literary cultures, if in one thing they made themselves masters it was in this: picking up, as they went along, gems of popular speech.

From hands and words we may pass to countless different

aspects of life. There is no piece of crockery we use daily, no household utensil, that does not contain a history of novel shapes developed, transformations brought about by taste which has been free to function creatively. In their handwriting and in the peculiarities of their capital letters the characters of the different peoples show up plainly, and we have the Gothic, English and Spanish scripts. In clothes, in hats, in cosmetics, in polite intercourse and (as Eliot has remarked) in cooking — in everything we see the cultivating hand of man, leaving an impression of his passage, proclaiming his active, personal presence.

This idea is not a new one. Three centuries before Eliot wrote his essay on a definition of culture, Baltasar Gracian, in the chapter on 'Culture and Adornment' in his *El Discreto,* [1] left us with an extraordinarily abundant source of inspiration on the same subject. There, for example, he says: 'Not only must the mind be adorned, but the will also. Let these two higher faculties operate in a cultural sense; and if knowledge is to be adorned, why should desire be given over to grossness and incivility? Grace, good taste and civility were ever brothers: they season and beautify everything; not just the outer texture of a custom, but rather — and far more — its inner texture, which represents the qualities, the veritable ornaments of the person.'

It would be interesting to draw a parallel between Eliot's acute observation on the subject of culture and the book of Gracian. In both we find the same impulse to seek the integration of culture by removing it from the sphere of individual man to the broader plane of society, finally including under the subject of culture, so as to give it its highest value, religion. Gracian used to say that even in saintship there should be culture. How can a saint possibly be a barbarian? Eliot uses a wonderfully telling word when he urges that religion should be 'incarnated' in cultural integration. To consider human culture solely from the point of view of its literary expression is as limited as to see it only through the medium of a branch of art, like sculpture for example. Integration offers us the only true means of comprehending a development embracing all the different aspects which go to make up personality and its forms of expression. And, obviously, if we seek the final bond — the ultimate aspirations

----

[1] *(The) Man of Discretion.*

that bind men to one another — religion is seen to be of the very essence of culture.

13

One cannot talk about culture nowadays without referring to the German interpretation of the word — a word which suddenly, after being lost sight of among a mass of old documents, found itself on everybody's lips. It had become fashionable. And with the mere change of a letter — the initial K — how the traditional conception was altered! Was it just a matter of passing interest, or a reorientation pointing towards some definite objective? How did the word *Kultur* arise?

It arose during the eighteenth century, that is, in the age of the encyclopædia and of enlightenment inspired by France. It was the age of Voltaire, whose European influence knew no boundaries. Thanks to him, the Russian Court is transformed into a great intellectual centre. Catherine, who presides over it, corresponds with him as she likewise corresponds with D'Alembert and Grimm. Gustavus III of Sweden, Christian VII of Denmark and Stanislas Augustus of Poland bring about the same miracle in their palaces, which are turned into libraries and clubs of intellectuals. In Spain, the ministers of Charles III are friends and correspondents of the Encyclopædists. The Paris 'salons' are a collection of intellectual hives over which Reason, the new Deity, presides. The twin notions of a tremendous ideological development and of an absolute monarchy are reconciled in the formula of enlightened despotism. The State begins to undertake the organization of education. The Jesuits are expelled from Portugal, France and Spain, and great plans are conceived for reforming the universities. From Spain, which by its official support of the Inquisition had impeded the advance of science, ships set sail for America under government auspices, laden with French books and with learned Spaniards, Frenchmen and Germans on board. This ideological explosion ends in France with a revolution, and the guillotining of Louis XVI and his Austrian queen. In Prussia, on the other hand, under the influence of this same Encyclopædist movement, the imperial power of Frederick the Great is consolidated. From the monarchical point of view, he is the great figure of the eighteenth century. No one can be compared with him in the importance of his national creation, or the philosophical style of his court. His imperial characteristics are like an ornate cloak blowing about German thought.

For Frederick, French is at that time the only tongue worthy to express the communications of the intelligence. As for German, its hour will come, as he devoutly believes. It is in French that Frederick writes his historical essays; his book announcing the greatness of Prussia; his Anti-Machiavelli and his poems. It is said that before entering into battle he recites verses of Racine which he knows by heart. D'Alembert and Voltaire discuss with him, by correspondence or word of mouth, all the greatest philosophical problems of the day. The king is an early riser, miserly and business-like; he is a keen flute-player and is fond of good food. He was so impudent in his youth, and quarrelled so violently with his father, that he was deprived of his rank of prince and consigned to prison by order of a court martial. Such experiences have moulded his character. In Prussia he is to play the double rôle of prince of philosophers and commander-in-chief.

Boldly he throws himself into the Seven Years War and brings it to a victorious conclusion. It is a war between, on the one hand, Prussia and England (but nearly always Prussia alone, or rather Frederick alone), and on the other Austria, France, Russia, Saxony, Sweden and Poland ... A mighty enterprise to mould a mighty historical figure! In the course of a series of highly dramatic encounters surrounded by powerful adversaries and in desperate straits, Frederick toys on various occasions with the idea of suicide. It is his last resort and a characteristic solution of that century. But in the end the world has to recognize in the Prussian Army a formidable war machine, thanks to its discipline and powers of resistance.

Against this background, German *Kultur,* in its double sense of philosophical and imperialistic, makes its appearance — at times full of Satanic pride, but illustrious always, through the elaborate polish given it by men of genius.

All this must not be forgotten, because the first German dictionary that refers to *Kultur* is Adelung's second edition of 1793. Thirty-one years earlier, in the Dictionary of the French Academy, 'Culture' had appeared with this figurative meaning: 'Interest in the arts and the mind.'

Dictionaries have their political side, which is that of language. As times change and new parties come to power, definitions are altered. The word *Kultur* enters the dictionary at a time when an intellectual and political school is coming into being, whose members will adopt that six-letter word as the emblem of their great enterprises, culminating in the *Kulturkampf* and Pan-Germanism. The word had been imported from France, where it had had a different history. It began there, as in old Spanish, by having a religious meaning — that of 'cult'. Afterwards it became bound up with the country's rural way of life and the tilling of the fields; thence it was extended to mankind almost imperceptibly; for the Frenchman carries the scenery of his country in his soul.

What is interesting is to look at this first definition of *Kultur* in the German dictionary: 'Ennoblement and refinement of the general mind and physique of the human being or of a people: this word embraces both the act of illuminating, of ennobling the reason by freeing it of prejudices, and that of polishing, ennobling and refining customs.'

The novelty of this German definition in relation to the French one, or to the old principles of Gracian, lies in the accent it places on physical culture. This physical culture already has a martial tread about it. It is the opposite of the gentle manners of the cultured man indicated by the Spanish moralist; but it is not out of keeping with the harsh discipline of the ancient Teutonic Knights. Moltke, who in his youth translates Gibbon's *History* for twenty-five pounds sterling in order to buy himself a horse, and is as good a writer as he is an accomplished soldier, is typical of this period in Prussian history. One of the features of Heidelberg and other great German universities is the passion for duelling with swords. In Imperial Germany the facial scars proclaiming the number of duels fought in student days are worth as much to their owner as a certificate of studies, if not more.

Emile Tonnelet has written a short history of the word *Kultur*. These are, in brief, his conclusions regarding its philosophical development. According to Herder, culture is born in Asia, when the sheep and the dog become domestic animals; it subsequently develops with the cultivation of the soil, the working of metals and the appearance of the sciences and arts; in the final resort, it is the road which will bring men nearer to God. For Kant, culture is the antithesis of barbarism, having begun on the day when men first stopped fighting in order to exchange useful articles with one another. Schiller follows the line laid down by Kant, and describes culture as the means of 'liberation from prejudices'. Goethe develops his theory during his travels in Italy: he finds there that Art is a collective creation, no artist being independent of his people; that even in the works of the most individual creators the habits and ideas of the people are reflected. Finally, Fichte finds that Germany is the living image of culture, and that to her belongs the intellectual leadership of Europe.

Looking at this philosophical development in this way — albeit cinematographically — one is better able to understand the resounding impression made by Bismarck's chancellorship in Prussia. That iron hand which welded together the scattered pieces of empire was the same which in opposition to the Catholic Church, and in order to cement the power of the State, gave practical expression to the Kulturkampf. In this latter word, then, we find expressed at once the feelings of German nationalism, the ideas of eighteenth century liberalism, the will to imperial dominion and the pattern of a military discipline. More than a term, the word is in this case a photograph.

Although Goethe makes the most pertinent observations concerning the spiritual bond existing between Nature and Art, and it seems as if when speaking about culture he is merely bringing to life and humanising the architectural stones of Italy, at bottom there is an affinity between his mind and that of Bismarck. Throughout his life, Goethe showed the aristocratic cast of his temperament. His contempt for democratic concepts casts something of a spell, on account of the lyrical substance always to be found at the core of his writings. The spirit of those tough young barbarians who, centuries ago, made the whole face of Europe rattle like the top of an African drum, was not dead in him, but was adorned with wonderful verse. Thomas Mann, who has penetrated discerningly and independently into Goethe's works, records the fact in these words: 'Goethe was Erasmus and Luther, a mixture of the urbane and the demoniacal, a combination whose fascinating grandeur is unexampled in the history of civilization ... What is nordic in Goethe's name — "Gothic" in him, for it is derived from "Goth" — what is, therefore, barbarous in him, is poetically purified by the flute-like notes of his verse.'

14

Kultur is, in reality, an episode in Prussian history.

Are there superior cultures; or are there only different cultures? Upon the answer which we give to this double question depends the whole problem of respect for culture, for the individual spirit of different peoples, for the freedom of expression which is of the essence of such matters. If so much literature had not accumulated on the subject of superior culture, it would be puerile to present the question in its double form. It can only be answered by referring back to the obvious and natural meaning of the word culture. For then we eliminate the deformations imposed by nationalist imperialism, the vanity of certain peoples, or the momentary triumph of certain political tendencies, and arrive at the original and permanent conception that culture consists in the cultivation of Man; which acts as a refining influence on the personality of every people, shaping its individual style in the course of generations. Every people is bound to have its own particular mode of expressing itself, a variety of images, rhythms and gestures, in which Eastern art can be as rich as Western. The painting of the Japanese Sesshu is of one style; that of Rembrandt is of another style. The glory of the world consists in there being both a Sesshu and a Rembrandt.

Culture has what we might call provincial depth. It is essential to observe that culture is a measurement of depth, not of surface. And it is in the provinces where the spirit of a people is concentrated and where greater emphasis is given to the personality. It is this provincial consciousness that gives Europe its highest value. To be able to talk of a Flemish, Provençal, Scottish or Basque tonality — to be found in language, painting, dancing or dress — is to express vital facts about the culture of a continent. It is a pity that the history of Europe is not written from a provincial point of view. It is hardly possible to imagine how much it would gain in vital qualities. We might say — making use of Eliot's purely culinary argument — that the fact that we find one kind of cookery in Hamburg and another kind in Bordeaux is a proof of culture — or rather, cultures. In Cologne a wonderful cathedral was erected — wonderful as a concentrated expression of the whole mediaeval, mystical impetus of peoples living in the interior, with its arrow of dark grey stone shooting up above the Black Forest and the quiet reaches of the Rhine Valley, seeking the Christian sky. About the same time, in Pisa, which nowadays is so close to Cologne by rail, they were building a tower, a cathedral and a cemetery as white as an egg-shell. Here we find something of the Orient placed beneath the clear vault of the Mediterranean sky. From near the sea, where the sailing vessels heave gently up and down, it seems as though the breeze were coaxing that tower-mast into some poetic port of marble. Cologne and Pisa are thus two contemporary Christian and European worlds; but two worlds nevertheless. We do not find there superiority; only difference. They are different cultures, which can be as different from each other as are, from one extremity of the globe to the other, the Maya culture and the Egyptian culture.

There is a world between Dürer, Holbein, Rembrandt and Franz Hals on the one hand, and Titian, Raphael, Botticelli and Leonardo on the other. Just as there is a Flemish School, there is a Venetian, a Roman, a Florentine and a Sienese one. This multiple Europe with its provinces is but an example of what we see happening over all the rest of the world, only with the differences more clearly accentuated. This intercourse between Nature and the arts and customs which Goethe saw realized in Italian culture, occurring as it does in every part, in every single province of the world, produces the wealth of expression characteristic of mankind. Freedom of expression, freedom of study and research, freedom to penetrate into the life of the people and to present the fruits arising out of one's meditations, these open to man the only road by which his passage through this world can be made other than sterile.

The superiority implied by democracy over aristocratic, oligarchic or absolutist systems lies in offering people of every colour, social origin or race, opportunities of access to institutions working for the advancement of culture through the medium of the sciences, the arts and letters. These opportunities are nowadays a human right on which all intellectual progress depends. It is *the* human enterprise *par excellence*. Humanising culture simply means returning to authentic culture.

The fundamental thing about culture is its intimate association with historical development. There is no superior culture; there are only incipient, adolescent or mature cultures. It is all a question of time. The peoples of Europe were able to stabilize themselves quickly, thanks to their geographical situation, which could be most rapidly and favourably exploited. Europe is a peninsula deeply penetrated by good rivers with fertile plains in between. These are ideal conditions, which have made it possible in less than twenty centuries for local styles to mature. In other parts of the globe developments have been much slower: in some, they have hardly even begun.

Great movements of peoples, like those of Asiatic origin to Europe, or those of European origin to America, have brought about, at crucial moments in the history of humanity, new processes of adaptation, preliminary stages of evolution towards new cultures. Thus, the Huns who advanced into Europe from Asia in the year 373 opened an astonishing chapter in the book of European cultures; just as the movement of Europeans to America from 1492 onwards did in the case of the cultures of the Western Hemisphere. In order to bring out the essential point, let us recall that the Goths arrived in Europe before the Huns — about the year 150; and now Thomas Mann finds in Goethe of the nineteenth century, in living and operative form, Gothic origins of the second century.

Coming back to Eliot's phrase, a tree is not constructed or improvised; you plant it and wait for it to grow. Nowadays there are means that can be used to accelerate the development of culture; but there is a limit to such acceleration: it has to conform to natural laws.

The same thing does not happen in the case of civilization, for which reason a distinction must be drawn between the two words, although not necessarily in the Spenglerian sense. 'Civilization' is an expression of the citizen, of civil life, which springs up in the city. When there is a civil authority, a civil law, a civil code, life has become civilized. It makes no difference that the people should still remain uncultured. It might happen, as has been affirmed, looking at the problem from a European standpoint, that civilization represented the final stage of a culture. But this is not essential.

In French, civilization was a juridical term signifying the passage from proceedings under criminal law to those under civil law. In English, its origin is similar; assimilation of the common law to the civil law. To civilize was to 'make civil'; to leave behind a state of barbarity. The Historical Dictionary of the French Language, which appeared in the sixteenth century, contains some curious examples of contemporary translations from Aristotle's political treatises, or of commentaries on Roman Law, where we find the words 'civilization' and 'civilize' used in this same sense. Similar examples are to be found in English dictionaries.

The word 'civilization' takes on a wider meaning and becomes fashionable when the Napoleonic Code begins to extend itself over the world. In 1835 it figures in the Dictionary of the French Academy. Le Febvre points out that up to 1798 it does not appear in any of the big dictionaries of the eighteenth century, or in the Encyclopaedia. What is clear is that •at the bottom of this new French meaning attached to the word lies the enthusiasm of the adepts of enlightenment, full of faith in the campaigns undertaken against illiteracy and in the diffusion of a series of principles which should help to pull the peoples out of their disgraceful state of backwardness. It is a backwardness which can just as well proceed from backward governments as from a natural state of savagery. Civilization in France takes a different direction from that of culture in Germany. Culture is a concentrator; it leads to nationalism; it is a centripetal force. Civilization is a message to the world; it is an optimistic belief in the power of winged words to bring about in the world redemption through progress.

Philippe Berthelot says in the *Grande Encyclopédie:* 'The growth of civilization is due solely to the progress of knowledge, and this progress depends on the number of truths which the human intelligence discovers and on the range of action they achieve. The sum of human actions, from a general point of view, depends on the sum of human knowledge, and since civilization is conditioned by the accumulation and diffusion of accomplishments, it is obvious that if a people neglects one of these conditions it will be outside the number of those whom we can consider as models of civilization . . .'

16

But what is happening today? Civilization can be fabricated. There is no need to plant it like a tree. Everyone is agreed that the progress of civilization has been rapid, and not always favourable to culture. Civilization itself has been shown to have a marked propensity to suicide. It can devour itself for lack of culture. It is obvious that, in order for culture to prosper, civilization is necessary, that is to say a system of civil life in which the dignity of man is respected and the free working of the means for study and self-expression assured; where there is civil justice and work is not carried on under barbarous laws, so that the intelligence is able to retain its spontaneity and freshness which are the mainspring of its activity. The problems of man and of the spirit, which today confront one another in Asia, Europe and America, are thus situated between the two terms 'culture' and 'civilization'.

A brief comparison between eighteenth century conditions and those of our own time clearly shows the need for establishing the different meanings attached to the word 'civilization' at these two moments in history, and all the more so with that great experiment — the American one — before our eyes. [1]

The civilization of our time is the result of an universal process of imitation. It is passive. It has reached the point of considering an international civil code, with international organizations to watch over its implementation. The diffusion of the alphabet — the most grandiose undertaking conceived during the eighteenth century — has become such a simple affair in our day that with the Laubach method millions of people have been enabled to learn to read and write in a single year, whether in China or in Mexico. It would not be surprising if, as a result of the campaigns against illiteracy now being planned in Latin America, in five years time not a single inhabitant were left who could not read a newspaper or write a letter. The same may be said of the other facilities civilization offers for the purpose of improving the condition of the masses and contributing to the progress of the

---

[1] Some of the points of view appearing in this paragraph have already been expressed by the author in *Chemins du Monde*, Ed. Clermont, Paris, 1947.

nations. Nowadays, civilization is above all a question of quantity, of money. Under the eyes of a single generation the economy of a country like Russia has been transformed and its government enabled to dispose of financial resources for acquiring the instruments of civilization. This can happen all over the world, and particularly in America. Already, throughout the entire length of the Western Hemisphere, there are cities which have greater material conveniences to offer their inhabitants than either Paris or Rome. In the theatres they see the same films and elections are carried out in the same way as on the old Continent. Everywhere you will find radio sets, electric lamps, newspapers, trams, policemen, green and red traffic-lights, just the same as in Europe — and sometimes better, without America having had the good fortune to reach this stage after living through the marvellous experience of the Middle Ages, with their outward obscurity and miraculous inner clarity.

In the present development of civilization a new factor intervenes: communications. All inventions are diffused nowadays with a rapidity undreamt of before. Continents are brought together and, in this sense, the world appears to be uniting. It represents far more one civilization than many civilizations, in contrast with the position in the field of culture, where diversity is the rule. Europe is living, to a far greater extent than is often realized, according to an American type of civilization, imported from the United States. Every day we realize more clearly what a superficial coat of varnish civilization — that eighteenth century beacon — really is and how easy it is to administer. In this way, civilization goes shooting along at top speed, thereby marking yet again the difference between itself and culture.

In America, the progress of civilization has attained to an extraordinary velocity. Every year, tracts of territory which seemed irremediably lost in the heart of the jungle or cut off by deserts are incorporated into civilized life. In the southern part of the Hemisphere more progress has been made during the past twenty years than during the four previous centuries. The battle to provide the humble masses with justice, to give the country-people decent housing and to see that the children have shoes to wear and schools to go to even in the mountains and deserts, and that the landless have land allotted to them, has in many of our republics been invested with the vehemence of a romantic episode. Certainly, civilization can be accelerated; just as it can, under a dictatorship, be retarded.

17

The attainment of a civil existence enabling man to cultivate his spirit! That is what the common sense of the ordinary human being demands at the present time, in a world where the passage of armies and the sordid intrigues of the enemies of liberty have left so many ruins behind.

On one occasion, at the General Conference of UNESCO, it was recommended that the Secretariat be charged with carrying out an investigation into the origins of Fascism and Nazism. These movements were directed towards inculcating in man, from early childhood, principles of diabolical pride that were bound to lead to the use of violence against such as were of different blood or of a different religion, or had different ideas from those of the members of a political party. At the base of the new State which thus came into being an infernal contrivance was set up for suppressing all contradiction, any suggestion of liberty. The experiment produced the results which we have all seen, and yet it continues to have an attraction for many people. For this reason, a solemn declaration of man's ancient faith in his liberties has now become a matter of the greatest urgency. Our struggle and the great question of our time are comprised in those precedents whose study UNESCO has agreed upon. In the preamble to the Constitution of this new international organization it is already stated: 'Peace must be founded upon the intellectual and moral solidarity of mankind.' Not a solidarity imposed by the despotic will of some sectarian force, but one originating in the free thought and genuine moral impulse of man.

The world is today tattooed with ruins. But those that horrify us are not those of cities reduced to a heap of dust, but those of men corroded by the venom of hatred. They are the ruins of human culture. A cathedral can show the results of an effort of only two or three centuries: a man is the product of a hundred generations. He is that sort of cathedral, one to which the centuries lasting from the cave right up to civilization have contributed. We had arrived at a man capable of appreciating the blessings of liberty, which had been the aim and object of such infinite struggle; able to feel bonds of solidarity and neighbourly interest that should bring peoples of different nationality, origin and colour together. An active peace, a workers' peace gave the world marvellous machines, delicate instruments with which to exploit the earth's resources in a manner hitherto undreamt of. With all its faults, with all its injustices, this new world left open the road to hope. Means remained freely available for improving the system and reaching a high level of social justice. If one had to support this assertion, it would not be necessary to turn up files or look up newspapers. It would be enough to remember the fond smiles on the mother's lips and the children's happy faces. What a contrast with the ghost-like samples of humanity left behind by Nazidom! Rich and poor could go and listen to orchestras playing the masterpieces of composers, whether Russian, German, Italian, Brazilian, Spanish, Christian, Jewish, white or black. There were signs of happiness never before seen among those whose condition the anti-democratic system in the world did little to ameliorate. People talked together in their homes, in friendly gatherings, in the university, the café, the saloon and the club, and at political meetings. They talked, they listened and they argued without fear, without anxiety. In each one of the roots of these blessings a drop of poison was injected. Men were obliged to become silent, mean, distrustful. Letters could no longer be written or taken to the post, save under the terror of an accursed vigilance. Culture became dehumanised; civilization gave place to a police which, lurking in the shadows, waited for the opportunity to pounce of a free man, and exact payment, in blood, for any words said against the totalitarian order.

In this way, the dehumanisation of culture was instrumental in hastening a process of perversion which culminated in a crime of *lèse humanité:* the turning of culture into a mill that imperceptibly grinds all liberties into dust.

It would hardly be possible to imagine the travail that all this has brought about in the bowels of the world. In recent years, man has been exposed to a hurricane admirably calculated to cause him to lose his bearings. The wretched agents of the perverse doctrine are now living their own tragedy, realizing that the impulsion they have received rends asunder their true personality. From the depths of the collective soul rises a demand for justice, for balance. It is hope, which also is one of the rights of man — an alleviation of his toil and fatigue.

'The Universal Declaration of Human Rights,' says the Director-General of UNESCO, M. Torres Bodet, 'is the most promising international document to which governments have set their names since 1945 ... It is the first international manifesto enumerating the rights of the individual and setting forth the conditions to be fulfilled by those States that desire to respect the liberty and dignity of the human person. It is the extension of honour in man. And it falls most opportunely at a time when collective forces in every sphere of activity are banded together to destroy the human being, whether by propagating the doctrine of a regime, or by maintaining social conditions favouring minorities that have power and capital in their hands. It is an urgent call to governments to remind them that man exists...'

Yes, indeed: man exists! His is the lasting value. Dictators are here today and tomorrow are gone with the wind. Man is the result of generations of struggle, ideals, work accomplished, hopes which form the basis of his rights to life, liberty and a place in the sun. Every step forward in the conquest of civilization, every advance in culture, have been marked by nameless sacrifices, by nights in which enthusiasm overcame all misfortunes.

Centuries of history have given man his strength. He has been a slave in innumerable dark periods in his life that are well known. But every time he has hoped for the dawn. And the dawn always comes in the end. Man does not so much live as outlive himself. He is the work we inherit, the work we continue, and the work we leave behind unfinished when our hands fail, to be carried on by the nimble hands of our youthful descendants.

For man as such the hour for the complete realization of knowledge, justice and liberty has not yet arrived. Open before him lie ever new vistas to feed his dreams, new incitements to struggle, new reasons for not allowing life to become a sterile sleep. Every little bit of knowledge he possesses is liable to become material for free discussion. The explanation of man, and the argument in favour of his liberty, are based on the evident fact that man does not say the last word.

To respect man, born thus to struggle and to be free in order to achieve his culture, is the elementary duty of a political leader, a philosopher, a poet or a factory manager. Part — at least, the essential part — of the function of governments, literature, learning and the arts should be to secure man's free access to his culture. A government leader is only a mandatory, that is, a servant — a servant of man.

That illiterate woman, Gandhi's mother, provided the formula through the lips of her son. The right to culture exists; but anterior to this right is the duty towards culture. There are things worthy of respect that engender a right only by being themselves respected, that confer authority only by being served and that grant wisdom only by being understood. The rest is nothing but presumption, outrage, ashes and silence.

Montclair, November 1949

JEAN PIAGET

The right
to education in the modern
world

THE RIGHT
TO EDUCATION IN THE MODERN WORLD

PREFACE

Article 26 of the Universal Declaration of Human Rights adopted by the General Assembly of the United Nations reads as follows:

1. Everyone has the right to education. Education shall be free, at least in the elementary and fundamental stages. Elementary education shall be compulsory. Technical and professional education shall be made generally available, and higher education shall be equally accessible to all on the basis of merit.
2. Education shall be directed to the full development of the human personality and to the strengthening of respect for human rights and fundamental freedoms. It shall promote understanding, tolerance and friendship among all nations, racial or religious groups, and shall further the activities of the United Nations for the maintenance of peace.
3. Parents have a prior right to choose the kind of education that shall be given to their children.

The aim of this Article was to lay down the obligations of society towards the individual to be educated, and at the same time to stress certain of the social aims of education. In particular, the Article stresses the necessary association between the development of the human personality and respect for the rights of others. And finally it underlines the rôle of parents. These are the various points with which I propose to deal in the commentary I have been asked to make.

1

Everyone has the right to education

The development of personality results from two groups of factors: those of heredity and biological adaptation on which the development of the nerve system and of the elementary psychic

mechanism depends; and those of social transmission and interaction, which begin their influence whilst the child is still in the
chadle and exercise a more and more important rôle in the formation of his conduct and thought patterns. To speak of the
right to education is first to stress the indispensable rôle of these
social factors in the development of individuality.

Only certain of the lower animals have their lives completely
regulated by instinctive behaviour patterns, i.e. by hereditary
factors inherent in the individual of the species. Where higher
animals are concerned, however, the formation of certain patterns
of conduct, even when they seem quite instinctive and inherent
in their origin, is due to the operation of outside social influences
in the form of imitation and training passed on by parents to
their children. A Chinese psychologist has shown, for example,
that the hunting instinct of kittens separated from the mother
cat is much less marked than when their behaviour is stimulated
by maternal example. But family life is brief where animals are
concerned and the incipient education involved is very limited.
Even with the most gifted of the anthropoid apes, the Chim-
panzee, the family-relation between parent and offspring ceases
after a few weeks, and at the end of the first year the mother is
able to recognize her offspring only exceptionally, in perhaps one
case out of five.

The essential difference between animal and human society
lies in the fact that the main factors of man's social behaviour —
the technical means of production, language and the whole world
of ideas to which it gives expression, morals and rules of conduct
of all kinds — are no longer determined from within by already
fixed hereditary mechanisms awaiting only contact with the outside world to begin their operations. Man's behaviour is acquired
from without and transmitted from generation to generation, i.e.
by education, and it develops exclusively from a variety of differentiated social actions and reactions. Since man learned to speak,
for example, no idiom has become hereditarily fixed, and it is
always by education outside itself, in the family circle, that an
infant first learns what is so aptly called his 'mother tongue'.
Certainly, the potentialities of the human nerve system first
permit the acquirement of language, which is refused to the
anthropoid ape, and man possesses a certain 'symbolic function'
as part of his inherent aptitudes. Human society does not create

these things, but it utilizes them, and without external social transmission (primarily of an educational nature) there could be no collective continuity of language. Such a fact reveals at once the importance of this formative process. It is not self-sufficing, but it is absolutely necessary to that intellectual development known as education.

Now what is true of language, which is the means of expressing collective values, is equally true of those values themselves and of the rules they obey, beginning with the two systems of values and standards which are of prime importance for the ultimate adaptation of the individual to his environment, namely logic and morals.

For a long time it was held that logic was inherent in the individual and belonged essentially to that 'human nature', which was generally regarded as preceding the development of social life. Hence the idea which prevailed in the seventeenth and eighteenth centuries (and which is still widely held even today by the average man) that the 'logical faculties' etc, are 'natural', even essentially 'natural' as opposed to the artificial products of social life. Descartes, for example, regarded 'common sense', i.e. the ability to reason logically, as truly one of the most common of faculties, whilst Rousseau founded his whole educational system on the supposed antithesis between the congenital perfection of the individual and the subsequent demoralization induced by social life. These were the ideas which inspired the doctrines of the traditional school of education: man being adumbrated in the child, and individual development being nothing but the development of already inherent faculties, the rôle of education was confined to that of simple instruction. All that was required was to furnish the mind and to encourage the already existing faculties, and not to form and fashion them. In short, it sufficed to accumulate knowledge in the memory, and the school was not regarded as a centre of real activities and experiments pursued in common where the individual logical intelligence might develop from social action and interaction.

Now logic is not at all innate in a child, and the incontrovertible result of a series of investigations involving not only the verbal thought of the child but also his practical intelligence and the practical operations by which his ability to classify things, and his notions of time, space, arrangement, quantity, movement

and speed are formed, demonstates that certain forms of reasoning considered logically necessary from a certain mental level
on, are quite foreign to anterior intellectual levels.

To give a practical example, any normal child of seven or eight
will realize that if two glasses of different shape, A and B, contain
the same amount of water, and if another glass, C, contains the
same amount of water as glass B, then glass A must contain the
same quantity of water as glass C, even if the two glasses A and C
are even less like each other in shape than the glasses A and B or
the glasses B and C. But with a normal child of four or five there
is no reason whatever why he should realize that the quantities
of water in glasses A and C are equal after he has understood that
the quantities of water in glasses A and B and B and C are equal
respectively. And there is also no cogent reason for him why the
quantity of water should remain the same when it is poured from
one glass into another. [1] And even where children from seven to
ten, or even eleven, are concerned, whilst they appreciate the
reasoning that because A equals B and B equals C, therefore A
must also equal C, where simple quantities of water are concerned,
they begin to doubt the logic as soon as more complex notions
are involved, for instance, weight, [2] and, *a fortiori*, where simple
verbal reasoning is present without the demonstrative manipula-
tion of objects. Formal logic in the current adult sense of the
term (I mean the ability to reason logically as Molière's character
M. Jourdain did when he triumphantly discovered that he had
been talking prose all his life without knowing it, and not the
understanding of such a discipline) is not really present until
the eleventh or twelfth year, and it is the fourteenth or fifteenth
year before it is fully present.

Such incontrovertible discoveries obviously involve profound
modifications in the classic terms of the educational problem, and
consequently in the meaning of the right to education. If even
logic itself is acquired instead of being inherent, then the first
task of education is obviously to form the capacity to reason.
Thus the proposition solemnly affirmed at the beginning of
Article 26: 'Everyone has the right to education', must mean pri-

[1] Piaget and Sgeminska, *La genèse du nombre chez l'enfant*, Delachaux
et Nestlé, Chapter One.
[2] Piaget and Inhelder, *Le développement des quantités chez l'enfant*.
Delachaux et Nestlé, Chapter Two.

marily that: 'During his formative period everyone has the right to an educational environment which will permit him to fashion in their completed form those indispensable instruments of adaptation, the logical faculties.' Now this process is more complex than it would seem, and no special perspicacity is required to realize on observing the general run of normal individuals, i.e. the average man, that really logical beings, masters of their reasoning powers, are as rare as really moral beings, living fully in accordance with their consciences.

What has just been said about the instruments of reasoning applies, it is easy to realize, even more readily — in theory at least — to moral development. It will be generally admitted that although certain innate aptitudes permit man to construct certain moral laws and develop certain moral sentiments, their further development requires the operation of a group of socially determined factors, first through the family and then through society generally. Thus up to a certain point it will be generally admitted that moral education has a formative rôle to play as against purely hereditary tendencies. But here again, and by a parallelism between the moral and the intellectual development of the individual, rendered even more striking in analysis, the question arises as to whether the external contribution we expect from education towards the informing and completion of individual aptitudes, inherited or acquired, can be confined to a simple transmission of ready-made rules and knowledge. Is it, in fact, only a question of imposing certain duties and a certain obligation to obedience in conformity with the intellectual obligation to retain and be able to repeat 'lessons', or does the right to moral education, like the right to the development of reason, suppose a right to the actual construction, or, at least, a right to participate in the construction of the discipline which will guide the conduct of those who themselves collaborate in its construction? Thus moral education involves a problem of self-government parallel to that of the auto-formation of reason within a framework of collective effort. In any case, it should be stressed at once that the right to intellectual and moral education involves more than the mere right to acquire knowledge, and more than the mere obligation to obey; it involves above all the right to fashion certain most precious spiritual instruments, and to do so in a specific social environment which is not exclusively one of submission.

Education is thus not simply a mere forming, but a necessary formative condition of natural development itself. Thus to say that everyone has the right to education is not merely to say, as popular individual psychology supposes, that everyone, capable by his psycho-biological nature of attaining a certain level of development, is entitled in addition to receive from society his initiation into its cultural and moral traditions. On the contrary, and much more profoundly, it is to say that the individual would not be in a position to acquire his essential mental structure without external assistance involving a definite social formative environment, and that at all stages (from the most elementary to the most highly developed) the social or educative factor represents an essential condition of his development. Certainly, before the age of three or four, or perhaps six or seven in some countries, it is the family rather than the school which plays the educative rôle. It might be argued that even admitting the constructive rôle of initial social action and reaction above all, the right to education concerns the child already formed by his family environment and ready to receive school education, and that thus it is not really a question of formation but of mere instruction. But to divide the educational process into two periods in this way, and to say that the first is formative whilst the second confines itself to the transmission of particular knowledge is once again to impoverish the significance of the right to education; not only is the constructive significance of education restricted, but the school is isolated from life. Now the essential problem is to make the school into that formative environment which is already provided to some extent, but not sufficiently, by the family, and which represents the *conditio sine qua non* of a full emotional and intellectual development.

To proclaim the right of everyone to education thus involves a much greater responsibility than merely to teach each child the three R's. It means to guarantee to each child the full development of his intellectual functions, to give him every opportunity of knowledge, and to inculcate the moral values which correspond to the exercise of those functions to the extent of proper adaptation to modern social life. And in consequence it involves above all the obligation, taking into account the special constitution and aptitudes which distinguish each individual, not to destroy or damage any of his potentialities, and not to waste any of them or suppress some of them, so that society may ultimately benefit by them all.

Thus the proclamation of the right of everyone to education involves — if we want it to take on a significance beyond that of mere phrases — the utilization of the psychological and social knowledge we possess of the laws of mental development, and the working out of methods and a technique adjusted to the innumerable discoveries this knowledge has given the educator. Thus our task is to determine by what means the social environment represented by the school can develop the best formative procedure, and whether it should consist of the simple teaching of rules and knowledge, or involve, as we have already indicated, rather more complex relations between the teacher and his pupils and amongst the pupils themselves. We shall deal with this point again when we discuss 'the full development of the human personality'.

Let us confine ourselves for the moment to formulating the principle involved, and establishing the obligations of society towards the child which devolve from it. In principle education is thus not a simple auxiliary process which adds to an individual development regulated by innate factors, or brought about by the family alone. From birth to the end of adolescence education is one single process and it constitutes one of the two fundamental factors necessary to man's moral and intellectual development, so much so that the school bears a quite considerable share of the responsibility for the ultimate success or failure of the individual to realize all his inherent potentialities and to adapt himself to his social environment. In short, the innate development of the individual furnishes merely a number, greater or smaller according to the aptitudes of each individual, of potentialities capable of being developed, destroyed or left in a rudimentary state. They are no more than potentialities, and it is social and educational action and reaction which develop them into effective behaviour patterns or destroy them for ever. The right to education is thus no more and no less than the right of the individual to the normal development of his inherent possibilities and the obligation of society to do everything possible on its part to transform these possibilities into effective and useful realities.

2

'Education shall be free . . .'

The great gap which exists today between the educational system as it is and the educational system as it should be by all the
implications of the right to education, if the principles we have
just set out are accepted, can be bridged only by stages. First of
all we must distinguish between the right to primary education,
which is recognized by all countries though its practical application still meets with as yet insuperable difficulties in vast
areas of the world, and the right to secondary education which
is not yet recognized by all. Secondly we must distinguish between
the right to attend an ordinary school and the right to demand
that it should provide everything which is necessary to 'the full
development of the human personality'.

Let us take first of all the school as it actually exists today and
the right to receive primary education at it. 'Education shall be
free, at least in the elementary and fundamental stages. Elementary education shall be compulsory.'

Elementary, or primary, education is compulsory by law in almost all countries today. But we must not deceive ourselves; there
is a distinct hiatus between the state of the law and its application,
and the number of schools and the number of teachers available
are not sufficient to provide all children of school age with proper
education. In a relatively important group of countries a new
contingent of youthful illiterates is added each year to the already
very considerable army of adult illiterates. Thus one of the first
educational tasks which devolves on UNESCO is to combat illiteracy.
A great campaign in favour of 'primary education' has been
launched in those parts of the world in which modern civilization
is of comparatively recent origin (in certain parts of Africa and
Asia for example). There are also quite a number of countries
whose civilization reaches back a long time, but which have not
been able up to the present to solve the problem of illiteracy
amongst children of school age. Further, in some countries the
question of primary education involves adults as well as children,
and very good work has already been done in a number of countries to combat this particular aspect of illiteracy and to develop
new methods of education specially adapted to this purpose. For

instance, there are the 'Educational Missions' instituted in Mexico at the instigation of the present Director of UNESCO, when he was Minister of Public Instruction there. These Missions travel to the remotest parts of the country, including the mountainous districts, to bring primary education to the inhabitants.

But the problem of compulsory primary education involves a problem of social justice as well, or, in the alternative, educational justice as a facet of social justice. Compulsory primary education is useless unless it is at the same time free, including, of course, its extension to adults who are still illiterate. This is recognized by all countries which have introduced it. However, free primary education should not be merely negative and content itself with the abolition of school fees. Many other problems are also involved, some of them of, so to speak, an extrinsic character, such as free transport for pupils living at a distance from school, [1] the arrangement of school meals, and even the supply of school clothing, etc, and others of vital importance to the educational system itself. In this latter category falls first of all the question of free school materials. [2] All school work involves the use of materials, and the more advanced the educational methods the greater the importance of the materials involved. Now it is quite clear that a pupil will take his work more seriously if the materials with which he works and, above all, the results of his work, belong to him. In the traditional system of education this means only text-books, exercise books and paper, and certain materials essential for drawing lessons and manual subjects. Now, where more advanced methods of teaching are concerned, the rôle of text-books will diminish, whilst such activities as the work of the school printing press, the making of posters, the construction of all sorts of things (graphic and otherwise) will progressively increase the materials involved, and then the performance of the pupils will be all the greater when he knows that the work he produces is to be his own property. The principle of free school materials is not yet sufficiently widespread, despite a general tendency almost everywhere to abolish all costs. The whole question is just as vital for education as free tuition itself: 'The principle of free school mate-

[1] Tenth International Conference for Public Instruction, Recommendation 21, Article 6.

[2] 'Free School Materials', UNESCO and the International Education Office.

rials should be regarded as the natural and necessary corollary to compulsory education.' [1]

Very many countries have already taken steps to solve these problems, but unfortunately the same cannot be said of the principle of free, compulsory, secondary education. Since the Third International Conference for Public Instruction, called by the International Education Office, international study of the problems involved in the 'prolongation of compulsory education' and 'free admission to secondary schools' has revealed a great variety of obstacles to the solution of these fundamental questions of educational justice, i.e. 'the right to education', arising from the social problems implicit in the organization of society and the existence of professional bodies, in short, implicit in the division of society into socially heterogeneous classes.

The dilemma is, in fact, as follows: either free secondary education is made available to all, fixing the higher and lower age limits uniformly and providing families with the means to fulfil their educational obligations, which would raise the question of the various possible types of secondary education and the guidance of pupils in varying vocational directions; or the non-compulsory nature of secondary education is recognised, reserving to certain categories of pupil the preparation for higher education, or simply for secondary diplomas at the end of their studies, and accepting the fact that all other pupil categories will abandon their schooling entirely and go to work. But this second alternative would immediately raise the question of what criteria to set up to determine the selection of those to enjoy secondary education and what procedure to adopt to decide between the divergent possibilities. Both alternatives involve the same problem of educational direction as a preparation for economic life either more or less immediate or more or less remote. And both alternatives involve the two same factors on which the ultimate choice depends: the personal merit of the pupil or the social and economic conditions of his family.

Could one speak in such conditions of a right to secondary? And what meaning has such a right? Paragraph One of Article 26 of the Universal Declaration of Human Rights is quite explicit

[1] Tenth International Conference for Public Instruction, Recommendation 21, Article I.

on the point: even if in certain countries economic considerations compel the limitation of free education for the time being to primary education, 'technical and professional education shall be made generally available' and, above all, 'higher education shall be equally accessible to all on the basis of merit.' In other words, the right to secondary education remains, no matter what the ultimate occupation of the pupil is to be, and this right implies training for all occupations and the preparation necessary for practising the free professions, i.e. acess to higher schools and universities is to be determined by merit and not by any conditions of class or race.

The complexity and gravity of the problems raised by such a declaration are immediately obvious. They may be grouped around three principles, each presenting itself in an antinomic form: (1) from the social and economic standpoint education must be prolonged irrespective of the student's family fortunes, since his merit may well be at variance with his material position; (2) from the standpoint of the teaching of collective values an adequate general level of culture must be reconciled with occupational specialization, whereby the conflict between these two requirements increases with each new advance in science and technics; (3) from the standpoint of the development of personality the student must be assured the widest possible opportunity of physical, intellectual and moral development in accordance with his own aptitudes (an aptitude is by definition that which distinguishes one individual from others on the same intellectual level). But these aptitudes become more and more differentiated with increasing maturity.

One fundamental fact conditions the solution of all three problems. It is the fact that in the most highly civilized societies normal intellectual and moral development is not reached until about the age of fifteen. Not until this age approximately is it possible to discover with any accuracy the aptitudes which differentiate the one individual from the other. All attempts to discover them at an earlier age remain highly problematical and there is always a risk that important potentialities may be overlooked. Thus, purely in the interests of students and of society itself, general secondary education should be assured up to that age, and at the same time occupational questions should be left open. This would give teachers a chance to know the abilities of each student adequately and greatly assist in guiding him into some suitable occupation at the end of his schooling.

This brings us to the problem presented by what has been termed the 'single school'. The expression has let loose floods of wasted ink and torrents of useless verbiage, because in some countries particular parties have seized on the label and thereby provoked the opposition of their political opponents to an idea they might otherwise have found acceptable. So much do party struggles tend to revolve round words rather than round ideas that the same idea has sometimes been defended and at other times condemned by one and the same party at different times or in different countries. Let us therefore leave the expression out of account ald hold fast to the idea, which is one upon which educational opinion is becoming more and more agreed. No matter how great the diversity of types of school catering for children from about eleven or twelve to about fourteen or fifteen years old, which is the age at which classic, scientific or technical training begins, it is essential that the totality of all these schools should make up one system or one institution, so that the possibility of transfer from one section to the other remains open always in the light of the successes and failures met with on the way, and the belated appearance of aptitudes (above all aptitudes which escaped detection at the beginning of secondary education). It is also essential that such transfer from one section to another should not be regarded as exceptional, but as a necessary condition for the suitable determination of educational direction.

Once this principle is admitted its application supposes that there is a solution to the three problems just enunciated. It is here that we come up against the diversity of national educational methods and the hiatus, more or less great, between existing reality and the ideal we are aiming at.

In the first place, and dominating all others, there is the economic question. Secondary education is already free in a number of countries (though, except in rare instances, this does not include boarding-school education), but it is by no means generally so, and even then it does not always include free educational materials. Even in cases where secondary education is free, it is quite clear that the mere negative abolition of secondary-school fees does not solve the financial problem that secondary education raises for the family of the student. The student has to be kept; he is unable to contribute to the maintenance of his family; there is the question of fares if he lives far away from the secondary school he is to attend; and, in particular, there are expenses for his board and lodging if his education requires that he should live in some other town. All these problems arise, of course, and to a still greater extent, where university education is concerned.

The remedy generally applied to relieve these difficulties is the scholarship system, and it has rendered, and still renders, an immense service to very many talented students. However, it is a palliative and not a solution, because it is still not sufficiently widespread and it has not developed into a permanent collective guarantee of secondary education. The scholarship system operates in a great variety of ways. Generally speaking the amount of the grants is determined both by a combination of the merit of the candidate and his family circumstances. Very much has been done with a view to discovering which students are particularly gifted, and sometimes families are urged to take advantage of the scholarship system in cases where they hesitate to do so, as though a scholarship represented some sort of exceptional subsidy or even an act of charity. Thus there is still a long way to go before there is general agreement on the one hand that scholarships are not reserved for specially gifted students, but are a stage on the way to secondary education for all, and on the other that the granting of a scholarship is not a matter of generosity on the part of the educational authorities but a definite responsibility of society towards the individual.

The general situation as it exists today has given rise in many different quarters to a general movement in favour of real equality of access to secondary education and even in favour of 'secondary education for all'. [1] There is no doubt that this represents one of the most urgent problems of educational justice — in fact of social justice itself — which faces us today.

It goes almost without saying that general secondary education does not mean in the least that henceforth the educational system is to have one common direction, e.g. that all students will be guided indiscriminately towards university entrance examinations.

[1] 'Equality of Opportunity in Secondary Education', UNESCO and the International Education Office.

On the contrary, as secondary education becomes general, so it must at the same time become more differentiated, so that the future manual worker, the future farmer and the future business man may find secondary education as useful to him when he undertakes his job as does the future technician or member of the liberal professions, very different though their requirements are. It is here that the last two of the three problems we mentioned earlier arise again: an adequate general level of culture must be reconciled with occupational specialization, and the personality of the student must be assured the widest possible opportunity of development in accordance with his special aptitudes. They are two aspects of the same problem perhaps, but the one concerns the development of collective values whilst the other concerns the individual personality.

From the standpoint of the imparting of collective values it is becoming more and more obvious that the various activities of the individual represent an indissoluble whole. For instance, it is quite impossible to form a real idea of the life of society without realizing the complete interdependance of scientific ideas and scientific techniques. Whether the one is the reflection of the other, or the result of the other, makes no difference to the fact that they are interdependant in a continuous historical process; and the different aspects, even the literary aspects, of human culture are equally homogeneous in varying degrees — in the form of opposition as well as in that of direct dependance. That 'general culture' which it is the task of secondary education to impart to the student cannot limit itself, as is too often supposed, to abstractions (moderns, classics or mixed) without roots in the basis of real social life regarded as a whole, but should embrace all the different aspects of social life, practical and technical, scientific and artistic, in an organic whole, relating it to an historical conception of civilization in the fullest sense of the term and not merely to its political and military aspects (which are consequences rather than causes of the underlying social events). It is by no means certain that the extension of secondary education to all students, no matter what their subsequent work is to be, whether exclusively manual or exclusively professional, will lead to any *impasse* with regard to the respective demands of general culture and occupational specialization. On the contrary, general culture has all to gain by returning to its original real basis and setting out afresh from the fundamental interactions of the different aspects of social life; in short, by rediscovering man as he really is, and always has been, and not by regarding him as scholastic tradition has always sought to present him. At the beginning of secondary education it is quite easy to conceive of certain curricula common to all, together with others which are already specialized.

The third problem we have mentioned is undoubtedly more complicated. To reconcile an adequate general level of culture with specialization, when it is a question of educating an individual and not of teaching a whole generation a certain number of collective values, either common or specialized, is a task which comes up against the essential difficulty that no two individuals are alike. As things stand today, the future career of a student is primarily a matter of family tradition and of economic and class conditions. It is a matter of course that a child born into a family of professional people should adopt a professional career in his turn under pain of losing caste, whilst the son of a peasant remains a peasant — unless he happens to reveal quite exceptional abilities. But if in the future, in accordance with the solemn affirmation of Article 26 of the Universal Declaration of Human Rights, which itself is a reflection of a more and more widespread movement in civilized communities, access to university education is to depend on merit alone, whilst secondary education is to be extended to all students irrespective of their future occupations, then it is clear that the school will be charged with new tasks of a singularly onerous and responsible nature. Its tasks of selection and guidance will have to be carried out not merely with a view to higher education as at present, and it will have to take all occupations into consideration, regarding them all as of equal dignity. In consequence it will have to reveal and develop a great variety of individual aptitudes, and not judge them merely as it does at present from the exclusive angle of subsequent academic success, i.e., with one final aim in view: the University.

Thus the preliminary problem is one of guidance. How is the school to arrive at an adequately objective diagnosis of aptitudes at an age when they are only too often not clearly manifest, and how is it to complement its diagnosis with a prognosis, which may well determine the career and influence even the whole life of a student? Leaving the rôle of the parents out of account for the moment, there are only two ways in which this can be done: by examinations and by an analysis of the whole work performed throughout the school career. Incidentally, each of these two methods can be subdivided into two. The examination method can be an ordinary academic one, or it can be of a psychological nature conducted by a specialist (of course, the teaching personnel may themselves have had the necessary psychological training). In the same way the analytical method may confine itself on the one hand to academic performance in the narrower sense of the term, involving various tests (held weekly, monthly, etc), merely generalizing the examination method in the first sense of the term, or, on the other hand, it may be applied to the general activities of the student, including those which are spontaneous, thus approaching the methods of psychology, into the general intellectual behaviour of the student, and eschewing 'tests'.

Everything there is to say about the value of academic examinations has already been said, and yet that cancer continues to flourish at all stages of the educational system and to bedevil — the word is not too strong — the relations between teacher and student, undermining the joy they should both normally feel in their work, and often destroying their mutual confidence. The two fatal defects of the examination system are first of all that generally speaking it does not produce sufficiently objective results, and secondly that it inevitably tends to become an end in itself. Even entrance examinations are in effect final examinations; the entrance examination for the secondary school becomes an end for primary education, and so on.

The academic examination is not objective, firstly because chance plays a certain rôle in the final results, and secondly, and above all, because it makes demands on the memory rather than on the creative ability of the examinee — as though the latter were condemned once he had left school never to be able to consult his text-books again. Further, anyone can see for himself how wide of the mark examination results often are when compared with the subsequent performance of the examinees in real life. The academic examination becomes an end in itself because it dominates the outlook of the teacher instead of encouraging his natural vocation which is to awaken the conscience and intelligence of his pupils, and because it induces him to concentrate their work on the artificial result of a final examination instead of using it to stimulate their real activities and develop their individual personalities. The only reason for the continued existence of the academic examination system must be sought in social conservatism, and sometimes even in social rivalries which seek to set up a defensive mechanism before the higher reaches of the educational system and consequently make it necessary in the lower reaches as well. When we learn, for instance, that in some countries medical examining bodies demand that the study of Ancient Greek shall be obligatory for would-be medical students, thus setting up a totally artificial barrier which must first be surmounted, we obtain some idea of the motives which are behind the opposition to the replacement of academic examination by a real test of aptitude. Such ideas were, of course, not the prime reason for the development of the examination system, which is more a survival of primitive 'rites of initiation' and represents one of those discordances which arise so often in the history of social rites between the thing itself and its purpose. But to understand the survival of a system, about whose value very few people have any illusions today, we must turn to causes buried deep in the unconscious mind of man.

The adoption of psychological methods of examination is a question of simple justice and constitutes a necessary corollary to the right to secondary education. This is realized in an increasing number of countries and it has given rise to a strong movement in favour of the institution of school psychologists [1] and the training of teachers generally in psychology. [2] Psychology itself has made a valuable contribution to the study of mental development, of differential aptitudes and of the methods of investigation best calculated to determine intellectual levels and aptitudes. These methods may consist of examinations by 'tests' (themselves capable of indefinite variation and correlation) or of more elastic and detailed analytic procedure. [3] They are by no means perfect, and like all scientific methods they are subject to constant revision and transformation. They do not, of course, in any way take the place of an analysis of the actual results obtained by a student in

[1] *School Psychologists,* published by UNESCO and the International Education Office.

[2] *L'Enseignement de la psychologie dans la formation des maîtres.*

[3] B. Inhelder, *Le Diagnostic du raisonnement chez les débiles mentaux,* Delachaux et Niestlé.

the course of his school career (when such an analysis is distinct from academic examinations and deals with the real work of the student and not with memorised knowledge). At the same time they are most certainly superior — and generally speaking very greatly superior — to simple academic examinations, and they are destined to supplant them more and more as entrance tests.

The second means of discovering how things stand is based on the actual work of the student during the course of his school career. To the extent that the lower classes of secondary level (from twelve to fifteen years, for example) are essentially regarded as a phase for establishing the aptitudes of their pupils, and that they are so organized that it is possible for a pupil to pass (say after three months, six months or a year) from one division to another according to need, the most reliable method of diagnosis and prognosis is certainly that which is based on the observation of the pupils and their actual work. However, it is a delicate method and in our view it involves constant collaboration between teachers and school psychologists, whose task it will be to follow the development of pupils both in success and failure. Naturally, this is a procedure the value of which is related to that of the educational methods themselves. If the educational system consists merely in 'giving lessons' and causing them to be repeated in 'repetitions' and 'tests', and applied only in a few pre-determined practical exercises, then the results obtained by pupils will hardly be of any greater significance than those obtained by ordinary academic examinations, ignoring the question of chance. It is only to the extent that the educational methods employed are 'advanced', that is to say to the extent to which they attach increasing importance to the pupils personal initiative and spontaneous activity, that the results obtained will be of any real significance. In this case the methods are very reliable, and represent, so to speak, a sort of continuous psychological examination as against that kind of chance sampling which, in the last resort, all tests represent. But, we must stress once again, it will not obtain fully satisfactory results unless it is accompanied by an intimate association of educational and psychological analysis (whether the ladder is conducted by special school psychologists or by teachers who are themselves sufficiently well trained in the technique of psychology).

Once the proper aptitudes of a pupil have been discovered by this combination of psychological tests and a protracted study of his individual activities, his studies can be guided happily into the channels best suited to his abilities: occupational training of one kind or the other, or preparation for higher education.

3

'Parents have a prior right to choose the kind of education that shall be given to their children'

The educational guidance of children such as we have just described is subject to Paragraph 3 of Article 26: the consent of the parents, a condition that seems to go without saying. Nevertheless it should be pointed out that the whole history of human society has been marked by a progressive diminution of the rights of the family (from the 'clan' to the 'gens' and the patriarchal family, etc) and a corresponding increase in the powers of the State. In education, by analogy, the absolute power of the tribal elders, then of the *pater familias,* and finally of parents in modern times, has been increasingly limited by educational rules, a development which, incidentally, has not generally been to the disadvantage of the child. It is therefore of some interest to analyze the given situation today in which both the State and the family are faced with a system of entirely new educational methods.

First of all, parents are only human. Some of them are excellent, but others are less so, and it is often necessary to protect the children against their desires. There are intelligent and instructed parents, and there are others who are unintelligent and backward, the sort of people, for instance, who are afraid to consult a doctor or who do not follow his instructions when they have done so. It is no use talking to such people of psychological methods or new educational techniques, and the difficulty is to know just how to deal with them. They are often good people who want the best for their children, but their ignorance and conservatism makes them oppose things which would really be of benefit to their children.

Most educational innovators have suffered the same experience. They have found that parents are often the chief obstacle to the introduction of more advanced methods of education. There are two related and easily understood reasons for this. The first is that when parents have confidence in what they consider tried and trusted methods they are not unnaturally disturbed at the idea that their own children should serve as subject for an 'experiment'; that they should be used, so to speak as 'guinea pigs'. As though any change whatever in the traditional methods of education, whether a change of curriculum, or of textbooks, or of masters, were not equally 'an experiment'! The second is a dominant anxiety with all parents at all stages of the educational system, and even at pre-school age, namely that their children should not 'lag behind'. A baby has to walk at a certain age even at the risk of becoming bow legged. A rather older child must be able to count up to twenty at a certain age, although all authorities are agreed that any attempt to force the development of a child can be dangerous, and advise that this preliminary period in a child's life, procious above all others, should be used to lay the best possible foundations for the future. But all the multifarious activities, the encouragement of the child to build and play, which are so necessary if a sound basis is to be laid for future learning, are regarded by many parents as an unnecessary luxury and a waste of time, merely delaying that solemn and long awaited moment when the young neophyte can count up to twenty or begin to read. And much the same situation arises at every subsequent stage of the child's development.

When the question arises of determining in which direction a pupil's studies shall be guided when he reaches the level of secondary education, further clashes of opinion are likely between the advice of the teacher or the school psychologist on the one hand and the wishes of the parents on the other. It is not that parents are always indifferent to the very real efforts made by teachers and school psychologists at what might be called the 'feeling the way' stage to determine the special aptitudes of their children and to give them advice accordingly; but what often happens is that the advice of the school on the point clashes with the already formed wishes of the parents. What is to be done then?

Despite these notorious difficulties, Article 26 still proclaims that 'Parents have a prior right to choose the kind of education that shall be given to their children.' The reason for this is that in all recorded human social life, and despite the many changes which have taken place in the nature of the family, the family still remains an essential part of the social structure. One can always appeal from ill-informed parents, who are, so to speak, themselves ill-educated, to better informed parents, whose parental education has, so to speak, been completed.

In this respect it is a matter of course that if 'everyone has the right to education' then this applies to parents too, and even 'by priority', though perhaps less in the sense of being educated as in the sense of being informed, and even having their minds moulded, with regard to the best education for their children. Two methods have been employed towards this end, and both of them deserve serious encouragement.

First of all parents' associations have been formed and congresses held on family education with a view to interesting parents in the problems of education within the family circle (emotional conflicts both conscious and unconscious which arise in the family) and keeping them informed about educational questions in general. In some countries a series of popularly-written pamphlets on educational and psychological questions have been published.

And secondly, and in particular, a movement for collaboration between the school and the family has been launched wherever new methods of education have been adopted to any extent, and the work of this movement has proved very fruitful and profitable for all parties concerned. The school has everything to gain from knowing the attitude of the parents, and the latter on their part will profit increasingly by being initiated into the problems of the school. A close and permanent relation between teachers and parents leads to much more than a mere exchange of infomation; it brings about mutual assistance and it often results in a real improvement in educational methods. By bringing the school into closer touch with the world outside and with the anxieties of parents concerning the future careers of their children, and at the same time creating an interest amongst parents in the affairs of the school, a real sharing of responsibility is achieved. In some countries joint councils of teachers and parents have proved a real inspiration for new educational methods, thus bringing about that highly desirable synthesis between the family and the school.

4

'Education shall be directed to the full development of the human
personality, and to the strengthening of respect for human rights
and fundamental freedoms'

Article 26 of the Universal Declaration of Human Rights does
not limit itself to proclaiming the right to education; it goes on
to explain in a commentary, which is quite as important as the
proclamation itself, just in what the essential aim of education
consists. Now it is clear that this implies a choice between the
two kinds of function it is possible to attribute to any educational
institution, whether public or private; a choice, or at least a
postulate, of unity. From the standpoint of society a preliminary
question can be raised: is the function of education necessarily
to develop personality, or is it rather, and even essentially, to
mould the individual according to a model established by previous
generations and best suited to conserve the collective values of
society? When in primitive tribes the adolescent has to go through
a ritual ceremony of initiation and receive over a period, which
sometimes lasts for months, and in an atmosphere of tense emotion
and mystic respect, the sacred knowledge which transforms him
from an irresponsible child and ushers him into the adult body
of the tribe, it is quite clear that the principal aim of this form
of education is not the full development of personality but, on
the contrary, the subjection of the individual to social conformism
and the full preservation of tribal tradition. Now we may fairly
ask ourselves whether the submission of the pupil in the traditional school to the mental and moral authority of the teacher,
together with the obligation imposed on him to store up sufficient
knowledge to pass his final examination, does not constitute a
social situation which is functionally approximately analogous
to the primitive tribal rights of initiation and pursues the same
general object: to impose on the rising generation a sum of
common truths, i.e. that social tradition which has ensured the
cohesion of previous generations. To proclaim that the aim of
education is the full development of personality is to say that the
school should diverge from such a classic model and that there
can be a synthesis between the development of the individual
and his induction to his proper place in the framework of social
life.

What is this development of personality? And, above all, what educational methods are necessary to bring it about, seeing that its 'full development' is certainly not the aim of the forms of education we know generally; that it represents something which is contrary to the habitual aims of conformist education; and that it is an ideal which needs to be reconciled with the collective aims of education?

Article 26 gives us no sort of definition of personality, but it does say that its development should be accompanied by a respect for the rights and liberties of other personalities. Such a statement seems almost tautological, but in reality it is fraught with consequences. It implies a whole conception of personality by defining it as the expression of a reciprocal relationship. In fact both from the psychological and the sociological points of view we must distinguish between the individual and the personality. The in-individual is the ego centred in itself, and by that moral and intellectual egoism it is in opposition to those reciprocal relations which are inherent in all fully-developed social life. The personality on the other hand is the individual freely accepting discipline, or contributing to its development, and voluntarily submitting to a system of reciprocal standards which subordinate his own liberty to a respect for that of others. Personality is thus a certain form of intellectual and moral conscience as far removed from the essential anarchy of egoism as it is from absolute subjection to outside forces; it secures its own freedom by subordinating itself to the discipline of reciprocity. To put it in a simpler form, the personality is contrary both to anarchy and to tyranny because it is autonomous, and two autonomies can maintain nothing but a reciprocal relationship. We conclude therefore that to 'be directed to the full development of the human personality and to the strengthening of respect for human rights and fundamental freedoms,' is to fashion individuals capable of intellectual and moral autonomy and respect for the autonomy of others in virtue precisely of that law of reciprocity which legitimises their own.

Now the problem which arises when education is given such an aim amounts to the central question of that whole educational movement which is known as 'advanced': is it possible to form autonomous personalities by means of techniques which imply intellectual and moral constraint in varying degrees? Have we fallen into a contradiction in terms, for does not the formation

of personality presuppose free and spontaneous activity in a social
environment based on collaboration rather than submission? We
must examine this problem in some detail because it is the central
question of all education, whilst the sense and significance of
Article 26 of the Universal Declaration of Human Rights depends
entirely on its solution. The right to education which it proclaims
so explicitly is not merely the right to attend school. Inasmuch as
'education shall be directed to the full development of the human
personality' it is also the right to find in that school everything
necessary for the building up of active intelligence and a living
moral conscience.

a.   Intellectual Education

From the angle of this full development of personality which is
proclaimed to be the aim of education, can it be said that the
methods of the traditional school do, in fact, succeed in building
up, both for the infant and the adolescent, an active and independent intelligence?

The traditional school offers the child a considerable degree
of knowledge and provides him with an opportunity of applying
it to various exercises and problems. Thus it 'furnishes' the mind
and puts it through a course of 'mental gymnastics' which is supposed to strengthen and develop it. Should all the knowledge it
imparts be forgotten later (and we all know how much is left of
the knowledge acquired in school days five, ten or twenty years
later) the school is at least supposed to have provided exercise for
the intelligence of its pupils. What does it matter that later on
a man should have forgotten how to define the *cosinus* or how
to deal with a Fourth Conjugation Latin verb, or be unable to
recall historical dates? The main thing is that he knew it all
once. To this the supporters of the advanced school reply that
if after a while so little remains of all the knowledge the school
imparts, then the extent of the curriculum is less important than
the quality of the work, and that knowledge which is independently
won by free inquiry and voluntary effort is far more likely to
be retained. At the same time and above all, in the latter case
the student would acquire a method of procedure which would
serve him well all his life and tend to stimulate his curiosity rather
than stifle it. At the very least, instead of allowing memory to
take precedence over intelligence, or confining his intelligence to

exercies imposed from without, he would learn to use his brains for himself and to develop his own ideas freely.

It is not a point which can be settled by one simple discussion, and education in general is not a matter of 'authorized opinions'. Teaching is an art like medicine, and like medicine it cannot be practised successfully without special 'gifts', but, again like medicine, it is an art which is based on exact and experimental knowledge of the human beings who are its subject. However, this knowledge is not anatomical and physiological as is the case with medicine, but psychological. It is no less indispensable on that account, and the solution of the problems raised by the advanced school and by the training of the intelligence depends on that knowledge in the most direct fashion. Psychological investigations into the development of rational operations and the acquisition or building up of basic ideas have, in fact, provided us with evidence which appears decisive in favour of advanced educational methods, and implies an educational reform much more radical than even many supporters of the advanced school themselves realize.

For instance, no matter how dependant they are on the nerve mechanisms, whose growth and maturity permit their successive use (the more recently developed parts of the human brain do not come into operation until towards the beginning of adolescence), the operations of logic do not constitute themselves and acquire their integral structure except by exercise which is not purely verbal, but attached above all and essentially to things and experimentation. An operation is an action properly so called, but interiorized and co-ordinated with other actions of the same nature in accordance with the laws of its own structure. On the other hand, such operations are not exclusive to the individual and they necessarily suppose collaboration and exchanges with other individuals. Thus it is not sufficient to let a pupil listen over a matter of years to even the best possible lessons in the way that an adult listens to a lecturer in order to develop a sense of logic, and it is truer to say that any real development of the instruments of reasoning demands an environment of active and experimental collective inquiry and free discussion.

Let us take as a representative example of this type of basic educational problem the teaching of elementary mathematics (in primary and secondary schools). The greatest difficulties are encountered here, and no matter how high the quality of the teaching may be, the traditional methods normally imposed on teachers, always present them with the same old obstacles. It is a notorious fact that in otherwise normally intelligent classes, only a fraction of the pupils do well in mathematics, and this group does not necessarily coincide with the group of pupils most gifted in other subjects. An ability to grasp elementary mathematics had sometimes been regarded as a sign of special aptitude, 'the bump of arithmetic', whose presence or absence is supposed to explain success and failure, and it never occurs to anyone to wonder whether it is perhaps the traditional method of teaching which is responsible for the latter. Now mathematics is nothing but a form of logic, a most natural extension of ordinary logic similar to the logic of all fairly advanced forms of scientific thought. Thus failure in mathematics would seem to signify an inadequacy in the very mechanism of reasoning. Without accepting such a grave judgement on what is undoubtedly the majority of pupils and the great majority of the former pupils of our schools (for what remains of mathematical knowledge amongst the great majority of adults who do not happen to be scientists?) let us ask ourselves instead whether the responsibility lies with the methods of teaching.

It is an astonishing thing that by virtue of a tradition which was not developed either by the educational authorities or the actual teachers themselves, but which nevertheless weighs heavily on the system of teaching as a whole, everyone seems to think that in order to teach mathematics properly it is sufficient for the teacher to be well up in the subject himself without bothering his head about how these new notions develop in the child's mind. Certainly, some attempt is made to be concrete, to teach by direct perception, and even to draw inspiration from the history of mathematics, as though the succession of discoveries from the days of Euclid to our own bore any analogy to the real psychological development of mathematical operations. No one bothers his head about this psychological process.

Now psychological study of the development of spontaneous mathematical intelligence in the child and the adolescent has established a number of facts of importance for education. In the first place, when mathematical problems are put to the child without his realizing that they are, in fact, mathematical (for instance, in the course of practical experiments introducing questions of proportion, of rules in the form of successive inverse operations, of absolute and even relative speeds, etc), [1] the child resolves them by virtue of his general intelligence and not by an special individual aptitude (the latter is not, of course, to be ignored, but it does not play the preponderant rôle ascribed to it). In particular it often happens that children who are poor at calculation give evidence of real understanding and even ingeniousness when the problems are put to them in relation to some subject or activity which interests them. Remaining indifferent and often at a loss in situations which demand the solution of abstract problems (i.e. problems with no relation to any practical requirement), and, above all, being fully persuaded of their inadequacy and therefore giving up in advance, pupils with a reputation for being poor at mathematics often reveal a quite different attitude when the problem relates to a practical situation and involves other interests. They then succeed by their personal intelligence just as though it were a problem requiring only intelligence in general. An important fact results from all this: every normal pupil is capable of sound mathematical reasoning if his own initiative is brought into play and if in this way the inhibitions which only too often give him a sense of inferiority in everything related to mathematics are removed. The whole difference consists in the fact that in most mathematical lessons the pupil is expected to accept an entirely ready-made intellectual discipline which he may or may not understand, whereas when the subject is introduced into his own independent activities he is called upon to find out for himself the relationship and the ideas behind it, and to do his own thinking until the time comes when he is happy to receive guidance and further information.

In the second place, experiments made with regard to the development of mathematical and physical ideas have indicated that one of the most important causes of the lack of interest displayed by many children in such subjects, which should, but do not at present, encourage the free development of intellectual activity, is the insistence on a close relationship between questions of logic and numerical and metrical forms. In a speed problem, for exam-

---

[1] Piaget, *Les Notions du Mouvement et de Vitesse chez L'Enfant*, Presses universitaires de France, Paris.

ple, the pupil must simultaneously determine the distance travelled
and the length of time taken and make his calculation on the
figures which express these quantities. Now until the logical structure of the problem has been thoroughly grasped, numerical
considerations remain meaningless and serve only to conceal the
actual relationships involved. But as the problem revolves around
precisely these numbers a child will try all sorts of calculations,
blindly applying all the operations he knows in the hope of
striking on the solution, with the result that his reasoning powers
are stultified. This is a further example of the pitfalls which
result from the assumption that logic is an inherent faculty instead
of one which is built up in practice. If, on the other hand, we
dissociate these two factors, we shall make surer progress whilst
approaching the real aim of mathematical teaching: the development of the deductive faculties. It is a simple matter, for
example, to present children between the ages of ten and twelve
with even quite complicated problems relating to speed (a combination of the speed of two moving bodies the one of which
changes place with, or in relation to, the other, acceleration on an
inclined plane, etc.) without the aid of any numerical quantities
and by turning their intelligence to simple logical relations ('more
or less', instead of 'how much', i.e. in the way Aristotle reasoned on speed). Freed from the difficulties of calculation the
child will take a delight in working out the logical relations involved and in doing so he will develop elastic and accurate, often
even really subtle, ways of working. Once he has done so it will
be possible to introduce the numerical factor, and it will then
mean something quite different to him than it would have done
if introduced right from the beginning. It might seem that this
method wastes a good deal of time, but in the long run it actually
saves time, and, what is much more important, it greatly encourages the individual activity of the child.

In the third place, psychological study of the logical and mathematical faculties of the child has shown that there can be a real
and spontaneous development independent, not, of course, of
social environment (which is a necessary stimulant of all thought),
but of formal knowledge acquired either in the family circle or
at school. To take an elementary example, up to a certain age a
child will think that an object which changes in form (for instance
a lump of plasticine) also changes in quantity, weight and volume.

Now by an independent operation of logical co-ordination the child travels beyond this (generally unsuspected) initial stage and arrives, around the age of seven or eight, at the conclusion that the quantity remains the same; around the age of nine or ten, that the weight remains the same; and, around eleven or twelve, that the physical volume remains the same. Just as the adults around him are not aware of these logical and mathematical developments in the child's mind, so they are also ignorant of the development by which he begins to form his first notions of elementary geometry [1] (conservation of distances, parallels, angles, perspective, the construction of reference systems in physical orientation, proportions, etc). Now this spontaneous intellectual development is not only considerably greater than is generally supposed, but it also reveals a definite law of intellectual growth, namely that all mathematical ideas begin with qualitative construction before they acquire a metrical character. With regard to space in particular, the child's ideas are at first much less influenced by the obvious metrical relationships involved than is generally imagined. On the contrary, they proceed from that kind of relationship which the mathematicians call 'topological' and they arrive only much later at the stage of Euclidean geometry (a 'fact which is of the greatest interest from the standpoint of modern mathematics). Thus educational methods need considerable adjustment to the results of psychological study of how development really takes place, and if this adjustment is carried out we can hope for a much greater appeal to the child's independent and spontaneous activity.

Fourthly — and this sums up all that has been said previously — mathematics are now taught as though mathematical truths were accessible only by means of abstractions and even of that special language of operative symbols. But mathematics are first of all, and essentially, actions carried out with things, and the operations themselves always remain actions, but co-ordinated amongst themselves and carried out in the mind instead of being carried out in fact. It is certainly essential to proceed to these abstractions, and it is even quite natural to do so in all spheres of adolescent mental development, but an abstraction is nothing

---

[1] Piaget and Inhelder, *La Représentation de L'Espace chez L'Enfant,* and Piaget, Inhelder and Szeminska, *La Géometrie spontanée de L'Enfant,* Presses universitaires de France, Paris.

but a kind of deception, a confusing of the intellect, unless it represents the culmination of a logical succession of previous practical actions. The real cause of the failures of formal education must be sought primarily in the fact that it begins with language (accompanied by illustrations and fictitious or narrated action) instead of beginning with real practical action. The preparation for subsequent mathematical teaching should begin in the home by a series of manipulations involving logical and numerical relationships, the idea of length, area, etc, and this kind of practical activity should be developed and amplified in a systematic fashion throughout the whole course of primary education, gradually developing at the beginning of secondary education into elementary physical and mechanical experiments. In this way mathematical instruction would remain rooted in its natural world of things and provide a much greater fillip to the intelligence than it can when it remains merely verbal and graphic.

To take a single example, every teacher knows the difficulty experienced by secondary-school pupils (and often by university undergraduates too) in understanding the algebraic formula 'minus times minus equal plus'. Now the rule behind that very formula is discovered in practice by children between the age of seven and eight under varied qualitative forms. When a small piece of wire passing through three beads A, B and C is turned over behind a small screen which reveals the movement of the wire but not the beads, the child realizes that the order A, B and C has been turned into C, B and A. He also realizes that two turns will bring the order back to A, B and C, and that three turns will again change the order to C, B and A. In this way he discovers, without knowing it, the rule that two reversals of direction cancel each other out, in other words, that 'minus times minus equals plus'. But when he reaches the age of fifteen or sixteen he will have great difficulty in understanding algebraic operations unless they are presented to him as an extension of early experiments of this sort.

We have dwelt rather long on the question of mathematics because there is no sphere in which 'the full development of the human personality', and the conquest of the logical and rational instruments which ensure its intellectual independence, are more readily obtainable, though as things stand at present they are constantly hampered by the methods of traditional education. There is nothing more difficult for the adult than to find ways and means of appealing to the real and spontaneous activity of the child or the adolescent, but at the same time only this activity, guided and constantly stimulated by the teacher, whilst remaining free in its efforts, its trials, and even its errors, can culminate in intellectual independence. The knowledge of the theorem of Pythagoras will not ensure the free exercise of individual reasoning; the student must re-discover it and demonstrate it for himself. The aim of education is not to secure the repetition or preservation of ready-made truths, for a mechanical repetition of a truth is only a half truth. No, the real aim of education is to induce the student to win truth for himself, even at the risk of losing time and taking all the devious routes implicit in real personal initiative.

And if this is true of mathematical instruction, how necessary it obviously is to make the same appeal to the personal initiative of the student in the teaching of languages, geography, history and natural science, etc, i.e. in all those spheres in which the knowledge of facts is valuable only through the process of discovery which permitted their establishment.

But the full development of personality in its full intellectual aspect cannot be dissociated from the whole body of emotional, social and moral relationships which constitutes school life (we have already referred to that kind of emotional inhibition which often frustrates the reasoning of students as a result of failure in mathematics). At first sight the development of personality would seem to depend primarily on emotional factors, and the reader has perhaps been surprised that in order to illustrate the idea of the free development of personality we began with logic and mathematics; but in reality education represents an indissoluble whole, and it is not possible to develop individual personality in the moral sphere if at the same time the individual is subjected to intellectual constraint which compels him to learn by rote without an opportunity of finding out for himself. If he is intellectually passive he will not be morally free. Conversely, if his moral life consists exclusively in submission to adult authority, and if the only social relationship during his school life is of the type which attaches the individual student to a teacher exercising absolute authority, he will not be intellectually active.

Thus the educational methods referred to as 'advanced', which are alone calculated to develop the intellectual personality, necessarily suppose the existence of a collective environment simultaneously developing the moral personality and representing a systematic source of intellectual exchanges. Real intellectual activity in the form of experiment and spontaneous inquiry cannot, in fact, develop without the free collaboration of individuals, i.e. in the case in point collaboration amongst the students themselves and not merely collaboration between the individual student and the teacher. Intellectual activity requires not only constant mutual stimulation, but also, and in particular, mutual control and the exercise of the critical spirit, and these things alone develop objectivity in the individual and the desire for verification. Logical operations are, in fact, always co-operative operations, and they imply a whole series of intellectually reciprocal relationships, and co-operation which is simultaneously moral and rational. But the traditional school knows no other social relationship than that which exists between the teacher as a sort of absolute monarch, the vessel of moral and intellectual truth, and each individual pupil. Co-operation between the pupils themselves, and even direct communication with each other, are thus eliminated from work in the class and from homework — because of the general 'examination' atmosphere and the 'marks' to be given to each individual pupil. The 'advanced' school, on the other hand, requires the establishment of a working community in which individual work alternates with group work, because collective life has proved to be indispensable to the development of personality even in its most intellectual aspect. In consequence a whole technique of 'team work' has been developed in many countries under many different names. [1] Here is a single example: once whilst I was with Decroly inspecting one of his schools we quite by chance came across a group of secondary students in a room on their own wrestling in common with a problem of analytical geometry. Listening to their talk I remembered that the few ideas I had on the subject — one which, incidentally, terrified me — at their age had also been due to explanations proferred by a fellow student. But the difference was that the assistance given to me had been, so-to-speak, unofficial and even illicit, whereas in this group mu-

[1] *Le Travail par Equipes à L'Ecole,* International Education Office.

tual aid and work in common was the normal and recognized method of progress.

b. Moral Education

The problem of moral education is exactly analagous to the problems we have just been discussing in connection with logic and the teaching of mathematics. Do we want to produce individuals subject to the constraint of tradition and the outlook of previous generations? If we do, then the authority of the teacher and possibly lessons in 'morality', together with a system of combined rewards and punishments to reinforce this morality of obedience, will be sufficient. But do we not rather wish to produce both free consciences and individuals who respect the liberties of others? In that case it is quite clear that neither the authority of the teacher nor the best lessons in morality that he can give will suffice to engender those living relations which are at the same time both independent and reciprocal. Only social life amongst the pupils themselves, i.e. self-government, encouraged as far as possible and forming a parallel to the intellectual work in common, can hope to lead to that double development of personality, master of itself and yet imbued with respect for the personality of others.

Many educational experiments have revealed the practical results of self-government where it is not introduced as an artificial system imposed from above and in consequence a contradiction in itself, but corresponds to the spirit of the school as a whole. At the same time psychological investigation has established the respective influence of authoritative and reciprocal relationships between adults and children and amongst the children themselves. Already far advanced before the last war, these educational and psychological experiments found a valuable sphere of operations in the tragic circumstances which produced the numerous 'children's towns' in the wake of the war itself, and their results have been very encouraging. It is perhaps from these little societies of children brought together by their common sufferings that we have obtained our soundest reasons for hoping that a better future may be ahead of mankind, because they have shown us that a renewal of the human being is possible in an atmosphere of love and liberty, i.e. not one of authority and obedience, but of responsibilities freely assumed.

We have already seen that the two correlative aspects of personality are independence and reciprocity. Unlike the individual who has not yet achieved the stage of personality and who characteristically ignores all rules and centres on himself all the relations which attach him to his physical and social environment, the personality is the individual who see himself in his true perspective in relation to others, i.e. he takes his place in a system of reciprocal relationships involving simultaneously an independent discipline and a fundamental decentralization of his own activity. The two essential problems of moral education are thus to facilitate this decentralization and to establish this discipline. But what means, provided either by the psychological nature of the child or by the relationships already established between the child and the various persons who play a rôle in his environment, are at the disposal of the teacher to enable him to achieve this double aim?

Three kinds of sentiments or emotional tendencies of importance to the moral life are present from the beginning in the mental constitution of the child. First of all there is the need to love, and it plays an essential rôle and develops in a variety of forms from the cradle to adolescence. Secondly there is the feeling of fear of anything which is bigger and stronger than himself, a feeling which plays no small rôle in habits of obedience and conformism exploited in varying degrees by various systems of moral education. And thirdly there is a composite feeling composed simultaneously of love and fear; this is the feeling of respect, whose exceptional importance in the development or exercise of the moral conscience is stressed by all moralists. Some moralists regard respect as a secondary emotional state unique of its kind. Unlike love or fear, it does not attach itself to other individuals, but directly to the values or the moral laws incarnate in these individuals. To respect a person, according to Kant, amounts to a respect for the moral law within him, or, according to Durkheim, for the discipline he represents and exercises. According to other authors, respect, whilst it may subsequently take on higher forms, is first of all, like the two other feelings, a sentiment from the individual and takes its rise from that mixture of love and fear that the infant feels for his parents and for the adult in general (before the advent of conflict and disillusion affects the original attitude).

The relationships between the infant and the various persons of his environment play a fundamental rôle in the development of moral sentiments according to whether the one or the other of the three kinds of emotional tendencies we have just mentioned is uppermost in them. It is, in fact, essential to realize that whilst the child has within himself all the elements necessary for the development of a moral conscience or 'practical reason', just as for the development of the intellectual conscience, or simply 'reason', neither the one nor the other are given, already formed quantities at the beginning of mental development, and they both develop in close connection with their social environment. Thus the relations of the child with the individuals on whom it is dependent are, properly speaking, formative, and they do not confine themselves, as is generally believed, to exercising an influence, more or less profound, but, as it were, accidental, in relation to the development of elementary moral reality.

One of the first types of relationship is that which produces a feeling of obligation and with it the first duties accepted by the child and felt as obligations. What is the origin of that striking, and on reflection surprising, phenomenon we now encounter? The baby, though hardly able to utter a few words, and at an age when all actions are spontaneous and in play, accepts orders and feels himself under an obligation to obey them (whether he actually does so or, in disobeying them, feels a sense of guilt and embarrassment towards the adult). It has been shown [1] that when two conditions are present together the feeling of duty will arise. The first is that the child should receive orders from some one (don't go into the street; don't tell lies, etc). But why does the child accept such orders instead of ignoring them (as he can do so cunningly when someone is telling him stories which bore him)? His acceptance is not brought about merely by the imposition of a stronger will. Fear alone does not compel, but produces obedience which is purely external and, incidentally, of an interested nature (the order is obeyed in order to avoid punishment, etc). The fact that there is an internal acceptance, and therefore a feeling of obligation, remains to be explained. It is at this point that the second condition comes into play and connects up with one of the three things enumerated above in connection with the

[1] P. Bovet, *Les conditions de l'Obligation de Conscience, Année psychologique*, 1912.

spontaneous tendencies of the child. The order is not accepted freely and does not produce a feeling of obligation unless it comes from a person who is respected, i.e. a person who is loved and feared simultaneously, and not merely one or the other of these emotional states. Thus a child will not feel itself obliged to obey an order given by a brother whom it loves but does not fear, or of a stranger, whom it merely fears, whereas the orders of a mother or a father will be accepted as an obligation, and the obligation will still be felt even if the order is, in fact, disobeyed. This first type of relation, which is certainly the initial factor in the formation of moral sentiments, may well remain operative throughout the whole period of infancy and prevail over all others according to the type of moral education adopted.

But although we realize at once the importance of this first form of moral relation we also realize its inadequacy from the point of view with which we are dealing here. This respect of the child for the adult is the source-of obedience and submission and it remains essentially unilateral, because although the adult may respect the child he does not do so in the same way (he does not feel himself in any way obliged by the orders of the child). In so far as it is unilateral this initial form of respect is thus above all a heteronomous factor. As he grows up the child soon discovers that the adult himself is subject to influences outside himself, and sooner or later the law is regarded as superior to the respected person. And further, one day the child realizes the multiplicity of orders, some of them contradictory, which he receives, and he is thus compelled to make a choice and establish priorities. But without a source of morality apart from unilateral respect alone, the latter will remain what it was in the first place, an instrument of submission to ready-made orders and to rules whose origin remains external to the subject which accepts them.

At the other extreme of those relations between individuals which form moral values is the feeling of mutual respect. [1] Arising between equals and containing no element of authority, mutual respect is still composed of love and fear, but the latter is merely the fear of losing the respect of the other. Thus it replaces the external heteronomous pressure characteristic of unilateral respect by the independence necessary to its own existence and recog-

[1]   Piaget, *Le Jugement Moral chez L'Enfant,* Alcan.

nizable by the fact that the individuals who feel themselves obliged by it themselves take part in setting up the rules which oblige them. Thus mutual respect is also a source of obligations, but it engenders a new type of obligation which, properly speaking, does not impose ready-made rules but only the method by which they are made. Now that method is nothing but reciprocity, not in the sense of an exact balance of good and evil, but as a mutual co-ordination of opinions and actions.

Now what are the effects of these two forms of respect, unilateral and mutual, from the double standpoint of the decentralization of the ego and the constitution of an independent discipline which we have postulated as necessary for the education of moral personality? We shall recognize them without difficulty in exact parallel to what we have already discovered earlier on concerning the education of the intellectual personality. In fact, education founded on authority and merely unilateral respect has the same disadvantages from the moral as from the intellectual viewpoint. Instead of leading the individual to develop the rules and discipline he is to recognize, or to co-operate in that development, it imposes a system of ready-made and immediately categoric imperatives. Now just as there exists a sort of contradiction in adhering to an exterior intellectual truth without having first re-discovered and verified it, we can ask ourselves in the same way whether there is not a certain moral inconsistency in recognizing an obligation without having discovered its validity independently.

There is a great deal of psychological evidence on the point arrived at by greatly differing methods; studies of the behaviour of children at first subjected to authoritarian methods, or placed in self-governing communities, then changed from one to the other and having to adapt themselves to new conditions; [1] investigations into the development of moral judgement in children; the analysis of emotional conflicts between parents and children, and of the unconscious persistence of parental authority, etc. Now the results of these various investigations are seen to conform: discipline imposed from without either stifles the moral personality or thwarts rather than favours its development. It produces a sort of compromise between an external layer of duties or conformist behaviour and an ego still centred on itself because no

---

[1] Cf. the work of the Lewin school (Lippit, etc).

free and constructive activity has permitted it to experience a reciprocal relationship with others. In other words, just as the schoolboy can repeat his lesson without understanding it, substituting mere verbalism for rational activity, so the obedient child may well be an individual merely outwardly conformist and quite unable to understand either the real significance of the rules he obeys or the possibility of adapting them to changed circumstances or forming new ones altogether. When studying the way in which children of various ages react to the lie and morally judge the various types of lie submitted to their consideration, I have been very much impressed by the close resemblance between their reactions, in moral terms in this respect, and certain of their intellectual failures to understand. For instance, for a child of seven or eight it is much 'naughtier' to lie to an adult than to a playmate (because the prohibition comes in the first place from adults), and the gravity of the lie is measured by its objective or material falsity and not by the intention to lie. To say that one has seen a dog as large as a horse is 'a much bigger lie' than to say, falsely, that one has obtained a good mark at school, because the latter lie, unlike the former, might have been true and because, above all, the parents might believe it. The rule of truth, accepted as obligatory before it is understood, i.e. before it is experienced in the course of reciprocal social life, produces a state of affairs reminiscent of the conception of 'objective responsibility' in primitive juristic forms, whereas once he has reconsidered it in the light of social experience and reciprocal relationships the child becomes capable of moral judgements of great subtlety.

The educational significance of mutual respect and of methods based on the spontaneous social organization of children amongst themselves is precisely that they permit children to work out a form of discipline whose necessity they discover in practice, instead of having a discipline imposed on them ready made before they can understand its necessity. It is in this way that advanced methods of education render the same invaluable service to moral education as they do to the education of the intelligence, namely to lead the child to fashion for himself the instruments which transform him from within, i.e. which really transform him and bring about more than surface changes.

The best proof that all this is not mere deduction or mere theoretical psychology lies in the growing body of valuable experience obtained from the practice of educational self-government. Even before the war there had been a sufficient number of experiments to permit certain valuable conclusions. However, it must be admitted that most of the pre-war experiments were inspired by the ideas of leading educators rather than by existing conditions, a circumstance which suggested to the general public that they were theoretical rather than practical, or at least that they were exceptional and carried out in particularly favourable circumstances, for instance at private boarding schools untroubled by financial difficulties and without any very definite obligations with regard to their curricula.

But in the years between 1930 and 1935 I was able to inspect an institution which was not in the least of this type, and which nevertheless made a deep impression on me. It was an institution for young delinquents, a reformatory school in Poland. The headmaster was a man of vision, and he had the courage to place confidence in the children and adolescents in his charge even to the extent of entrusting them with the maintenance of discipline. The most difficult characters were given the most clearly defined responsibilities. I was struck in particular by two aspects of this experiment. One was the way in which newcomers were re-educated by the whole social group, and the other was the way in which the inmates had organized their own disciplinary tribunal, whose running was entirely in their own hands. It is easy to imagine the deep impression made on newcomers when they discovered that discipline was imposed not by adults but by their fellow inmates. A child or an adolescent caught in an offence and brought before a tribunal would naturally expect exceptional severity and protracted punishment. Instead he would find himself brought up before young people like himself, but already on the way to betterment and regeneration (many of whom had passed in the same way before the tribunal). They formed an organized social group, and its ranks would open themselves immediately to him and he would be entrusted at once with work, obligations and responsibilities. Of course, this does not mean that once the youthful delinquent found he had to deal with his own kind and not with warders he was immediately transformed and cured of all his faults. But it was here that the genius of the director as an educator came into play. Once a delinquent was taken into the community his subsequent offences were judged by this tribunal whose members were his own comrades appointed exclusively by his own comrades. The deliberations of this astonishing tribunal and its judgements were all recorded. Thanks to one of my assistants I was able to study its minutes. It would be difficult to imagine anything more fascinating for the psychologist. Unfortunately the document was no doubt destroyed in one of the many battles which raged around Warsaw. The humanity, the understanding and the subtlety of judgement of these adolescents, themselves former delinquents, were both moving and encouraging.

Be it remembered in this respect that one of the most difficult aspects of moral education, and one in which the greatest discrepancy of all exists between the methods of autonomy and reciprocity which fashion personality, and authoritative methods is precisely the problem of punishment. There are punishments which are degrading for those who administer them and whose principle is felt by the child to be fundamentally unjust even before he has become accustomed to identify habits and customs with morally valid laws. On the other hand, there are ways of gaining confidence instead of imposing punishment, of using the methods of reciprocity instead of authoritative methods, and the former are much more favourable to the development of personality than any forms of constraint and any outwardly imposed discipline.

Now this experiment, which I had the privilege of studying between the wars, was certainly exceptional, but since the war it has been repeated on a much bigger scale with children who had lost their parents or had been orphaned by the war, with children who had lived through such dreadful experiences that they had lost all sense of right and wrong. It has also been repeated in the most divergent educational environments, by Soviet teachers, by Italian priests, by the upholders of one school of thought and the other. Nevertheless the results have been the same everywhere because the sociological laws of children in the mass and the psychological laws of the development of personality are relatively constant, unlike the variety of relationships which differentiate the development of the child in differing adult environments.

All things considered therefore, whether it is a question of the education of the reasoning powers and the intellectual faculties or the education of moral conscience, if 'the right to education' is 'to aim at the full development of personality and seek to consolidate general respect for human rights and man's basic liberties', we must realize that such an ideal cannot be attained by any of the ordinary educational methods in operation today. Neither the independence of personality, which supposes its full development, nor that reciprocity which permits respect for the rights and liberties of others, can develop in an authoritarian atmosphere of intellectual and moral constraint. On the contrary, both these desirable ends categorically demand living experience and liberty of inquiry, without which the acquisition of all human values must remain a vain illusion.

5

Education 'shall promote understanding, tolerance and friendship among all nations, racial or religious groups, and shall further the activities of the United Nations for the maintenance of peace'

The problem of international education which is raised in the passage quoted above, is one of the most difficult with which educators are called upon to deal. Unlike the problem of intellectual and moral education, in which we may consider the level attained by the adult as superior to that of the child and as an example which can be held before the child, it is impossible to regard the present international situation as a model of perfection. The search for an adequate technique in international education must begin, at the very least, with a consideration of the difficulties which characterize the spirit of man in general, and an attempt to resolve the problem of the relationship between social groups, and, in particular, the question of international relations.

These difficulties do not prevent some people from imagining that special instruction given in all schools concerning existing international institutions and their work for the maintenance of peace is calculated to encourage a spirit of understanding between the peoples and thus effectively serve the cause of peace. There would be no objection to such attempts (for everything possible should be done to further such an aim even at the risk of employing ineffective measures or measures too little dissociated from the defective methods of traditional education) if there were no danger that they might produce results contrary to those intended. Nothing would be more unfortunate than to give children the impression that the gap between the existing state of affairs and the ideal aimed at is too great before they are in a position to understand the real reasons for that great gap. But who really does understand the reasons?

We certainly do not mean to suggest by this that all verbal instruction is useless either in the sphere of international education or any other. It can be useful, but only when it has been prepared by previous activity and is given in conjunction with a general moral and social attitude. If, as it has been said, a lesson must be an answer, it is even more essential in the sphere of international education than in any other that the answer should be preceded by spontaneous questions arising precisely out of this activity and this attitude.

A practical example will assist us to understand what is required. What is the best way to make a pupil into a good citizen (of his own country, leaving out the question of the world)? Is it to give him in so many lessons during the school year a systematic course in 'civic education', describing stage by stage the various parts of the country's civic structure? That procedure is likely to leave him relatively indifferent despite the eloquence or good will of his teachers? Or would it not be much better to give such instruction arising out of his own experience in educational self-government from which he already has a practical idea of the nature of an executive committee, a deliberative assembly and a court, so that he can work up real interest in the workings of analogous institutions in the world outside, something he would be quite unable to do without such previous experience of his own? We even claim that if it were necessary to sacrifice 'civic instruction' altogether to the practice of self-government in the schools the latter would produce better citizens than the most perfect 'lessons', and that if such lessons are given without social experience to support them they are likely to be of very little use. Incidentally I am talking here not as a teacher but as a former pupil whose memory on the point is still very much alive.

Having said this, let us now ask ourselves in what respect the problem of international education differs from the problems of moral or even intellectual education which we have previously discussed. The problems are approximately similar, though they exist on different levels. However that difference is so important that even adults have not succeeded in finding a practical solution to the problem of the relations between peoples, i.e. they have not succeeded in mutually educating themselves internationally. The problems involved are comparable, because whether it is a question of intelligence, of moral development or of international understanding, the difficulty in each case is the same: to de-centralize the individual and persuade him to abandon his spontaneous subjective and egocentric attitude in order to lead him to reciprocity and (which is practically the same thing) objectivity. The trouble is that whereas it is relatively easy to adjust the points of view of two individuals in a purely intellectual matter (for example to co-ordinate the perspectives of two separate observers) or even in a moral conflict, it seems almost impossible to secure reciprocity and objectivity when national loyalty and international affairs are involved.

Two preliminary observations are necessary here. The first is that social reality in general, and contemporary international reality in particular, are amongst the things we understand least. We find it much more easy to discuss planetary movement or physical and chemical phenomena than the social and international events which clamour constantly for our attention. The truth is that contemporary social reality is something relatively new compared with humanity's past. Every important event taking place in any of our countries immediately assumes a universal character and has repercussions all over the world. Collective phenomena have changed their scope, and the ambient in which they now take place is one of universal interdependence. In spite of the artificial attempts which have been made at economic and spiritual autarchy there is in fact no longer any such thing as a really national economy any more than there is such a thing as a domestic policy isolated from the outside world, or even intellectual and moral influences limited to an exclusive group. Now, banal as this sounds, it nevertheless corresponds to a state of affairs which we do not find easy to grasp and to which we are, in fact, not yet accustomed. Certainly, we realize the causes of this state of affairs readily enough; they are to be found in the technical and economic innovations which have arisen since the beginning of the century. But two world wars were necessary before we realized the interdependence of nations. At the same time they revealed the difficulty of re-establishing world unity and world equilibrium once they had been disturbed, and they demonstrated the close relationship existing between national conflicts and domestic conflicts.

We are not psychologically adapted to our social environment — that is the fundamental fact from which we must proceed in our efforts to lay the foundations of international education. And that 'we' does not refer only to the great mass of human beings lost in a universe of complex and interdependent relations; it also includes our statesmen. As Paul Valèry has shown so strikingly in his *Regards sur le Monde Actuel,* international politics are very much like a game of chance to a contemporary statesman. Even where there is continuity of general policy, as soon as he works out a general plan and a policy going beyond those practical questions which involve the immediate security of the nation he finds himself hesitating and often even contradicting himself in practical details because the upshot of his actions are unpredictable.

We do not understand the modern world either morally or intellectually. We have not yet found the intellectual procedure which would permit us to co-ordinate social phenomena, or worked out the moral attitude which would permit us to master them with good will and understanding. We are in much the same position as the old Eskimo who was asked by an anthropologist why his tribe piously preserved certain rites whose meaning he was unable to explain. 'We preserve our old customs in order that the world can go on,' he replied. For the primitive mind the universe is a great machine of unstable equilibrium in which everything depends on everything else (social customs and physical laws are not clearly distinguishable from each other). If one single piece of the whole machinery is removed, even when the purpose of the piece is unknown, the whole machine may break down. The social universe to us is what the whole universe is to the primitive mind. We perceive a relative harmony in it all, a world mechanism which works smoothly on with friction, but we do not know how it is constructed, and in our doubt we preserve as much of it as we can, often at the very risk of hampering its smooth running.

The first task of the educator in face of the international problem is to seek to adapt his pupils to the given situation without attempting to conceal its complexity. It amounts to forming a new spiritual instrument in the child's mind — not a new habit or even a new belief — a new method, a new tool, which will help him to understand and to act. In speaking of an intellectual instrument we can turn to science, which represents one of the most wonderful adaptations of the spirit of man and the victory of mind over matter. How can we explain the great success of science? It was not achieved merely by the accumulation of knowledge and experience, but much more by the fashioning of an intellectual tool of co-ordination thanks to which the mind of man succeeded in relating one fact to another. Now that is what we must do from the social standpoint. It is not merely a question of giving the child new knowledge concerning international realities and international institutions. Such knowledge will serve no purpose unless an attitude *sui generis* is created at the same time, an instrument of co-ordination which is simultaneously intellectual and moral, valid at all levels and adapted to dealing with international problems themselves.

Further, and this is our second observation, the primary obstacle in the path of intellectual co-ordination and moral reciprocity is nothing but that most spontaneous and most deeply rooted attitude of all individual — and even collective — conscience: egoism, both intellectual and emotional, which is met with in each individual mind to the extent to which it is still primitive and not yet decentralized by social intercourse; and what may be called sociocentrism both intellectual and moral which is met with in its turn in every collective body, once again to the extent that the requisite decentralization has not been achieved. It is an attitude so naturally and deeply rooted in every form of conscience that it is impossible to uproot at once by a kind of total conversion of spontaneous tendencies, and it will reappear, stage by stage, at each new victory of co-ordination. This indispensable emancipation from the ego, including the collective ego, requires a considerable moral and intellectual effort, an unflagging will and sometimes even real heroism.

Science, to which we have just referred, is there to show us just how deeply rooted the egocentric atttitude is and how difficult it is to uproot, not only from the mind but also from the heart. The mind of man has succeeded in adapting itself to the outside world and in predicting and explaining physical phenomena only by emancipating itself more and more from its initial egoism, but that emancipation demanded centuries of struggle.

The history of astronomy illustrates this with particular clarity. The first men regarded the sun, the moon and the stars just as young children still regard them today: as familiar lamps about as high up as the clouds and the mountain tops, having no course of their own and following us about as we walk. Every child thinks at one time or the other that the moon is following his steps, and in some primitive societies man believed that the course of the stars was determined by the movements of men; even in Ancient China the Son of Heaven was thought to regulate the succession of the seasons by his movements. The Chaldeans and the Babylonians made notable progress in releasing man's mind from its original egoism in this respect, and they discovered that the stars have regular courses of their own independent of us. But this victory of man in his march towards objectivity left a second form of egoism still in existence. The earth was first conceived of as a great plateau, then as a hemisphere and finally as a sphere, which retained its apparent position in the scheme of things. Most Greek philosophers still regarded the stars as revolving round the earth, which was believed to be the centre of the universe. Such a belief, as embodied in the system of Aristotle, cannot, of course, be compared with the idea of the child that he is being followed by the moon as he walks, but it nevertheless proceeds from the same sort of egoistic illusion, which burdened the development of man's ideas until Copernicus and Newton discovered the real relation of the earth to the solar system in general. The revolution in man's ideas brought about by Copernicus may be regarded as the most brilliant symbol of the victory of objective co-ordination over man's natural egoism. But defeated egoism was not finally destroyed, and it returned to the attack in another and more subtle form. To co-ordinate his world system Newton postulated a time and space absolutely identical at any point in the universe to those of our clocks and our terrestial measurements. The world had to wait another two hundred years before Einstein demonstrated the relativity of time and space in relation to speed, and constructed a much finer instrument of co-ordination than that of classical mechanics, until one day his theories will be superseded in their turn.

We see from this evolution that although at each new stage the human mind succeeded in freeing itself from a particular form of egoism, which appeared primitive and naïve once it had been exposed, it was only to fall victim each time to some new and more subtle form which, hampered the march to complete objectivity in its turn. From the social point of view the situation is *a fortiori* the same, and the decentralization of the ego and the collective ego and their symbols and domains presents even greater difficulties. Each time we free ourselves from this ego, or these egos, in favour of some collective cause which seems to us entirely altruistic and generous, it is only to fall victim to some new and insidious form of egoism, all the more tenacious because it is unconscious. Thus who can claim to have mastered social and international problems, when national, class and racial egoism, and many other forms of egoism more or less powerful, confuse our minds and induce a whole range of errors from the simple illusion of perspective to the lie due to collective constraints?

It should thus be perfectly clear by now that international education cannot be confined to the mere adding of another lesson on top of all the others, a lesson merely about international institutions as they are today, or even about the ideal they represent and work for. First of all, education as a whole must be made international. This applies not only to history, geography and living languages, spheres in which the interdependence of nations is obvious even to the most obtuse, but also literature and science, in which sphere traditional education often neglects to stress the common effort of humanity, and the rôle of technique and social conflicts. Only if such a spirit is introduced into the work of education as a whole can we hope in particular to create that spirit of understanding and tolerance between all racial and religious groups which Article 26 of the Declaration of Human Rights demands. How, in fact, can anyone study the history of civilization, of literature and science from an international angle without becoming an enemy of all forms of intolerance?

But above all it is only through a system of advanced educational methods, laying the main stress on common inquiry (team work) and the social lives of the pupils themselves (self-government in the schools) that the study of national and international viewpoints and the difficulty of co-ordinating them can take on any real significance for the pupils, and this is true from two angles.

In the first place, international relations are the arena, though on a different level, in which the same conflicts are fought out and the same misunderstandings made as in social life as a whole. The views held in one country about the peoples of other countries, the astonishing myopia which allows whole peoples to wax morally indignant in all sincerity at the very attitude in others which quite signally marks their own behaviour, the inability to place oneself in the other man's shoes, etc, all these are common phenomena at all levels of man's life, and to understand their importance on the international level it is necessary to have recognized them already in one's own experience.

In the second place, once a social life is organized amongst the pupils themselves it is possible to extend it to the international sphere, with international exchanges of students and even joint group studies of specifically international problems. International student correspondence; associations for the assistance of students in other countries; international travel by student groups; student exchanges, even whole class exchanges, during holidays; and many other innovations started between the two wars all advanced educational methods which have proved their worth. And where international education is concerned one could also conceive of secondary study groups formed to investigate and discuss this or that aspect of international relations in common. The usefulness of such groups would be very great provided that they were allowed full freedom, and in particular full freedom of criticism. One could imagine, for example, a group of secondary students seeking to establish the multiplicity of views on the same event by a comparison of newspaper articles, broadcasts and so on, and investigating the difficulties of reaching historical truth — all without the aid of a teacher and in an atmosphere of the free exchange of ideas. It is not impossible that when schoolchildren learn to think, to read the newspapers and listen to broadcasts in such a discerning and critical spirit, the peoples of all countries will hesitate to let themselves be led like schoolchildren — that is to say like schoolchildren of the old dispensation who have not yet benefited from the educational revolution implicit in Article 26 of the Universal Declaration of Human Rights.

LYMAN BRYSON

Freedom of information

FREEDOM OF INFORMATION

The Universal Declaration of Human Rights, adopted December 10th, 1948, by the General Assembly of the United Nations, in Paris.

From the Preamble: '... *the advent of a world in which human beings shall enjoy freedom of speech and belief and freedom from fear and want has been proclaimed as the highest aspiration of the common people ...*'

Article Nineteen: '*Everyone has the right to freedom of opinion and expression; this right includes freedom to hold opinions without interference and to seek, receive and impart information and ideas through any media and regardless of frontiers.*'

1

These specific affirmations on the right to information are not ambiguous and there are, in the same great document, many other implicit references to the right of every man, everywhere, to be informed. There appears to be, at first glance, a wide agreement on these principles. There may be men in the world who deny that freedom of information is a universal right and that civilization is established to realize it as one of the conditions of a good life but they do not appear as spokesmen for any culture or institution or government. Where then is the problem? The right to information would seem to be as well acknowledged as the right to life and safety. There is a problem, nevertheless. We fall short of realizing freedom of information because of two major factors; one is economic, the other political. A large proportion of the peoples of the world are still too poor in material resources to make more than meagre use of machinery for spreading information; the governments of the world are divided on the meaning of the world 'freedom', and follow different policies in controlling the dissemination of facts. Time may remedy both these difficulties but not without immense efforts in human energy and good will. Our purpose in this essay is to indicate, very briefly, the extent of the obstacles and to analyze the elements of the problem in the conflict of ideas.

These words are written by one who believes that objective truth is a value to be sought after, even though there can be little chance of ever completely attaining it, but I admit, at the same time, my own inescapable bias. I believe in the ideas of freedom in the western spiritual tradition, not infallibly lived up to but never forgotten and never lacking stubborn apostles. At the same time, and indeed as part of that same ideal, I am bound to do my best to state the arguments fairly and to do justice to another man's truth even though I believe it to be a deadly error.

The ideas that are now in conflict can be summarily stated as, one, to trust men with a large measure of self-direction in finding their way through arguments on all matters, including basic principles; the other, to protect men from danger by filtering out what authority believes to be evil.

We need to recall the venerable antiquity of both these attitudes towards the function of truth in social development. It is not new in the world for leaders to say that they want their communities to seek truth for themselves and find it wherever it may be, buried among lies and ignorance and honest mistakes. And it sounds even more familiar when we hear, like an echo of history, the leader who says that his community is in a special situation, looking toward a great new goal and needing protection from clever enemies. Both these doctrines are called doctrines of 'freedom'.

Richard McKeon says in the UNESCO Symposium, *Human Rights* [1] (p. 39) 'There is, among the philosophies of the world, a "utopian" or ideal tradition of analysis in which "freedom" is conceived to be a power based on knowledge of the truth; and in that tradition, which on this point is shared by philosophers as different as Augustine and Marx, to express or follow what is false is not to be free. There is also a "circumstantial" or material tradition of analysis in which freedom depends on the power of choice and the power to follow either of alternative modes of action . . . '

[1] Allan Wingate, publisher, London and New York, 1949.

The first of these two concepts of freedom has always been believed in by large numbers of men and women everywhere. It is in one sense a natural and primitive idea. It is now a rule of political action in a large part of the world and has eloquent spokesmen in most international conferences. Not all of them come from the east end of Europe. The second idea, although often breached in practise among the western democracies of Europe and America, has been their general rule. The difference between these two ideas is real. It is less dangerous to the future to keep the difference clear in our minds than it would be to accept glosses on the terms that would rob them of their crucial meanings. The western democracies, which have not recently gone through political revolutions, are tempted to say that the changes in the use of the defining terms in, for example, Soviet Russia at the present time, is the perversion that always comes with revolution, as was noted by Thucydides. Men have always, it seems, insisted that the names of old values can properly be applied to new things. But to believers in Communism, of course, these new meanings have the force of revelation.

Moreover, in recognizing that the differences between these two ideas are real, we note also that each doctrine may, like all things human, fall in practice into evil. The believers in each one see the evil in the other and blink their own dangers. The world as a whole, looking for some viable doctrine of right that can be enforced by world public opinion, may well ask each camp to acknowledge both the good and the evil in the other. The kind of freedom believed in and largely practiced in the western democracies involves every man necessarily in experience with lies and error and seductive half-truths. In one possible extreme development it leads to anarchy; government becomes impossible because spiritual unity has been destroyed. The other doctrine, argued for explicitly in international meetings by delegates of Russia and Poland and Bulgaria and others, involves every man necessarily in restrictions on his natural impulse to enquire and risks dulling his intelligence. Both systems run the danger of partial or complete monopoly of information, in the one case by men who want money, in the other by men who want power.

2

We imply, in approaching the problem in this way, that all human ideals of freedom are products of culture not formerly revealed absolutes, and that all men have learned to desire and seek out freedom in culturally determined ways. It is always of philosophic interest to discuss abstractions but men have not, in the past, got much out of discussions of freedom that were not positive and realistic. UNESCO does well to be more concerned ultimately with the effects of rights in the lives of real men and women than in any question of who can win an argument.

There is one point to be made here, however, that has great importance. Those who want to interpret the term freedom as the chance to go only one 'right' way often appear to make the mistake of thinking that argument is not an essential factor in intellectual life. It is true that healthy men love action and that nearly all normal men find thinking much harder work than action and much more disturbing than danger. The oldest ideal of freedom in the west, the ideal of Athens in the great days, was to test truth in both argument and action. Now there are leaders in some States who appear to think that action is enough, that men can keep intellectually and morally alive in putting principles into practice even if they are forbidden to discuss them.

Experience would seem to show that a healthy intellectual life, and by the same token a healthy spiritual life, cannot be enjoyed by men who put all their energies into the attempt to accomplish even the greatest aims if they never examine critically the nature and sanctions of their purpose. Men, and groups of men, have rôles to play in history, but man is not human unless he also looks thoughtfully at the spectacle and dares to question the themes. This is a reservation that must be made by anyone who believes that freedom should be used to mean conscious choice among real alternatives and not, in the Augustinian or Marxian sense, the opportunity of being compelled to follow a 'truth', even though he may also know that concepts of freedom are learned in one's educational environment.

There is a temporal element as well as a cultural element in all our generalizations about freedom: it is not only that we have learned in our own time and place to hold certain privileges more precious than others; we are also influenced by the current political situation. This is probably a truism; we all take it for granted. But perhaps we do not use it often enough as a corrective on our current opinions. For example, in either Russia or the United States, at the present time, the average citizen is specially conscious of the question of civil rights in the other country because there is a constant competitive contrast drawn between these two countries as part of the international debate on rival political systems. In the United States, it would be much easier at any time to rouse some degree of public indignation over an alleged suppression of human dignity in Russia than it would be to get the same result by alleging that similar events had taken place in some other country, say in Pakistan or Mexico or South Africa.

This is not because we in America judge Russia by a more exacting standard than we apply to other countries. It is rather that we are much more interested at the moment in any possible sins committed by a country with which we are carrying on an ideological dispute than we are in similar actions alleged against a friend. It can be believed in theory that the same principle would work in the minds of Russians, for the same reasons. This is not the same, be it noted, as to acknowledge our ancient human habit of peering around the beam in our own eye to spot the mote in our neighbour's. It is to shrug off any accusations against our friends and show a hopeful interest in any against our ideological antagonists.

3

These admissions, of inescapable cultural bias and current political interest, are both used in the obfuscatory practices of debaters on these great subjects to create the impression that the differences between the two contending ideas can be reconciled, that they are merely semantic, that there is in fact no problem.

There are arguments sustaining the democratic position, however, that seem to their proponents to rise above mere ideology. They dispute directly the concept of freedom as the externally guarded privilege of being right. This totalitarian doctrine, derived in its modern form out of Hegel, perhaps, by way of Marx, that men are 'really' free only when they are acting by some rule that is best for them implies, however it may be glossed over, that someone other than the man himself is to decide what is best. The alternative is that he shall act by choice. Simple logic and a clear use of terms seems to our minds to indicate that if there is no choice there is no freedom. Hence a system of 'true' freedom, by which choice is denied, is the substitution of other values for freedom. These values may be great; they are not the same.

Liberty, in the western democratic view, is meaningless unless one is free to make mistakes; freedom of information is meaningless unless one can know and believe what those in power call false, or wicked, or destructive. The truth or justice of the judgments by those in power are irrelevant. When those who believe in suppressions will meet this issue straight, and argue that other values attained by suppression of deviation are greater than the value of freedom of choice, a better debate can be set up and all men can see better where they stand. This does not often happen. Believers in the absolute administration of truth have notably failed to accept this as the issue, continuing to assert their faith in 'real' freedom which always means 'freedom' without choice.

It is not our purpose to rewrite feebly what has been greatly said, but to examine the modern face of old conflicts and find our necessary strength to carry on an old fight. Those who trust democracy, in the western liberal sense, are led to think that the believers in suppression, for no matter what high purpose, do not dare say to men that they cannot be trusted with choice because their friends in power know what is best for them. They disguise the fact in the new uses of terms. Marx said, 'philosophy has been a reflection on the world, whereas the task is to change it,' and this can be used as a seductive reassurance to the normal man's tendency to feel cosy in his muscles and uneasy in his mind. It may lead him to think that thinking is no longer useful and that anyone who still thinks is dispensable. Marx was answered in advance, on behalf of the western idea of democracy, by the Thucydidean Pericles. 'The great impediment to action is, in our opinion, not discussion, but the want of that knowledge which is gained by discussion preparatory to action.' (Jowett translation.) Discussion is the weighing of known choices. As Hocking puts it: [1] 'The task is always to change the world, but to what end? A free reflection

---

[1] *Freedom of the Press,* by William Ernest Hocking, Chicago, 1947, P. 133.

on the ends of change must be a working partner in all change that is intelligent rather than blind.' The one who has faith in democracy believes that a man blinded for his own good has lost something more valuable to him and to the common future than anything he can in blindness achieve.

We are not done with the deluding sophistications men use against each other and themselves. It is repeated, in much of the modern discussion of this subject, in the symposium of UNESCO, as well as in the discussions in conferences, that a right implies a responsibility. This is unquestionably true. Its insistent reassertion may be, of course, only a natural reaction to the tone in which so much of the older literature on freedom was written. The Europeans and Americans of the eighteenth century who were arguing for the rights of men had heard too much of responsibilities and duties; they were willing to have those taken for granted. They felt an imperative practical need to assert the importance of rights. It is no new discovery to know that freedom is limited at the point where another man is injured or where an accepted duty is neglected. It should not be necessary to reiterate that the problems arise when these limits have to be actually drawn, when in fact any damage to another, caused by my use of my own freedom, has to be estimated. My rights as against you are certainly limited by my responsibilities towards you, but at what points? There can be no easy answer to this question in the day-by-day administration and adjudication of human relations; every case proves the rule.

There is, however, a danger that discussion of this valid principle may be used as a cloak for diminishing the rights of a man, rights to information, to free speech,.or to some other right that has a part in the development of his own individuality. The danger lies in the fact that it nearly always appears, sooner or later, that my right is limited by a responsibility which is defined for me by the group. In modern times as well as past, this means that my responsibility is defined ultimately by the State. My rights cannot have any practical reality except as the government under which I live gives them scope and provides me with institutional chances. A good government exists to help me realize them. But when the notions of government are muddied by ideology or by the ambitions of men in power, the government may withhold my chances to enjoy my rights by insisting on my responsibilities.

In some measure this is required by public order, but, as in so many adjustments between individual demands and social demands, the individual right must generally give way.

We who believe in democracy, western style, argue that the adjustment between right and responsibility must be a just balance. Against the definition, by agents of the State, of both the individual's rights and his responsibilities, we would put a definition, by the individual, of the State's rights and responsibilities toward him. This is as much as to say that the statement 'rights imply responsibilities' applies to the State as it does to the citizen and each member of that relation has a moral right to judge the behavior of the other. To deny this is to take sides with extremists among those who define freedom as the privilege of following an official truth, whether willingly or perforce.

No trick of organization, or modern invention, can take the place of vigilance. We have to guard against having rights destroyed by the tricks of words that change them into duties. These tricks are not, as they are often made to seem, only appropriate reminders of the price in responsibility that must be paid for the enjoyment of freedom. They are used when someone who is in a reciprocal relation with us, involving both rights and duties, takes on himself the whole power of drawing the line between such rights and duties. He then can make rights useless and bury them under a pious phrase.

The same kind of scrutiny should be applied to the present fashion of insisting on the social nature of the right to know. In fact, the ancient right to speak has been transformed into the new right to know, much as if they were not the two sides of the same coin. The reason for this shift, in so far as it is honest and not another attempt to sophisticate rights into duties and thus destroy them, is that we are now much more concerned with the social aspects of our lives than with the individual. The brave men of the eighteenth century were trying to break group bonds that were too tight and turned their attention to the individual side of the interacting reality. Now, in a time of large scale operations both political and industrial, the pendulum has swung and we are looking again at the group aspect of the same thing. The right to speak is individual or particular but it is important for two reasons; it develops individual worth and it gives the group full benefit of individual wisdom. Similarly, the right to be informed is important for reciprocal reasons: it provides all members of the group with available wisdom and it gives reality to the individual's self expression.

The logic is clear, I think, but men do not generally want to think about these matters of principle without insisting on varying emphases, according to the temper of the times. In the western states, as we are loosely grouping them here, these modern conditions have not overcome the conviction that the process of 'truth seeking' is valuable as experience, helping in the development of both our moral and our intellectual powers. Proponents of freedom by choice among real alternatives are not convinced that men would be better off if they could be born into a world where error was impossible. They continue to think of the interplay between the individual mind and the thoughts and facts which human intercourse can offer as a process in which the esurient healthy intellect makes its own version of truth out of information available. This, they believe, is a sign of the slow democratizing of the life of the mind. They have come to expect in every human being an active effort to find truth for himself, making use of both authority and investigation.

Freedom of information as a human right implies that truth has a human dimension. Even in modern circumstances it may be possible to have a simple kind of freedom of speech, by which men can discuss freely within the limits of contrived ignorance of any other systems. This is, in fact, a condition nearly approached in some spiritually encysted countries. But such freedom fails to realize the ideal of freedom by choice because men who lack information are not inspired to truly creative speech nor to the clashes of opinion that test truth.

There are some believers in free speech, perhaps, who look forward to a time when a single canon of truth will prevail and when, they hope, freedom will be no longer useful. They live in a society founded of free choice as conspiring guests. They have probably been numerous in all societies at all times. Between them and those who think the quest is endless there can be cooperation in practical affairs, however, since a system of freedom by real choice is bound to allow all kinds of dissent in doctrine, as long as government can practically function and no private persecutions ensue. It is always salutary to remind ourselves that it is suppression of 'error' that is primitive and natural. Only time and the experience of freedom can produce men who trust the truth to make its own way.

4

We have set out in this discussion to understand as well as we can, within the limitations of our own democratic prejudices, what looks like logic from the two opposing points of view. It has to be taken for granted that there will always be some kind of control, some kind of judgment exercised by human beings in deciding how facilities are to be used. To doubt that men ever work for the public good is as unrealistic as to believe that they never have merely personal motives. We are mixtures of good and evil, and the institutions in which we enmesh ourselves are opportunities for our noblest impulses as well as frames to keep us righteous. In an attempt to be realistic about the problem of information, we need to take into account the patriotism and the professional pride that will lead men and women in every country to use the great instruments of public information for public enlightenment. We can go further, we can believe that there are in every country and in every culture leaders who honestly seek welfare for the citizens of other countries as well as for their compatriots. These are the real citizens of the world and the world civilization we hope for will encourage and reward them.

At the same time, we have to reach our immediate goals of greater freedom by things as they are now and with all kinds of men. The situation cannot be fully understood without an additional analysis on the basis of selfish motives. Men do seek self-aggrandisement, or power, or whatever we decide to call the target of natural aggressiveness; a good society provides channels for these energies in order to bring as little harm and as much good as possible to society as a whole. From this point of view there are two motives, not mutually exclusive, that will direct those who control the facilities of communication: power and profit. We can call the two motives and the two systems that give them different forms of expression, the political style and the business style. The two great systems of control that are used in the countries representing the extremes of difference in the theories of freedom are thus succinctly labelled.

In the United States of America, information is controlled by a business system; in Russia the control is political. Other countries follow one or the other of these two styles, or mixed styles of government and business working in collaboration. In America, private business manages newspapers, books, magazines, the cinema and broadcasting enterprises, while Russia has succeeded in political control of all channels of communication. The form of control is inevitably determined in large measure by the theory of freedom held in the State. In Great Britain, where the western ideal of freedom has been eloquently stated and faithfully believed in, there is freedom of political choice even in a partly socialized economy. In Communist countries, the governmental machinery is the appropriate tool by which men are kept in the paths of right thinking. In such a country, the results and efficiency of the system are criticized; in the western democracies the system itself may also be attacked. The communication systems and technical machinery are appropriately controlled in each case.

We see in all international debates a systematic attack on the business method of control which is generously abetted by spokesmen of various political ideas in all kinds of countries including America. It is based on two points. It is said that a system of communications supported by the revenues of private industry and managed, more or less in the public good, by the managers of private capital, will tend toward monopoly and will use monopoly for selfish purposes even to the extent, if necessary, of degrading the people. There is enough truth in this accusation to compel us to examine it closely but we must examine both systems in respect of the same points.

First, monopoly. It is true that control of communications facilities on behalf of private investors tends toward monopoly. All communications controls tend towards monopoly. Mass media can be used only in dealing with undifferentiated masses of people. Besides, all business tends towards monopoly, which is another way of saying that men overcome their competitors if they can. But political control, for the same reasons, tends equally towards monopoly. In the political control systems we have been discussing, monopoly, or complete, single-centered control, is theoretically necessary. No scheme of control can keep the whole citizenry of any country in the single official way of truth unless it has complete mastery of all the tools of communication and uses them for its own exclusive purposes. Anything else would be a concession to alternative ideas, which is, in the terms of this theory, a surrender to lies and evil propaganda.

Both systems then tend towards single-centered control and the questions remaining are these: which system is likely to succeed more completely in getting absolute mastery of all the information that reaches the people and what happens during the struggle? All of our experience would indicate, I believe, that a political system will come nearest to success in getting final mastery. All monopolies break up in time but political totalitarianisms can go very far in shutting out all dissident voices from the ears and minds of their people. They can even enfeeble the natural instinct of men to guess that there may be two sides to every story. This is indeed what they are theoretically justified in doing because this assures men of freedom to follow the truth and protects them against any possible chance of doing otherwise.

A business system, on the other hand, allows men to seek power through profit rather than through political office. In such a system, as far as recorded experience goes, there is always a recurrent competitive struggle. Monopoly is never finally achieved and the competitive struggle itself is fought out in part by offering competing ideas for public approval. This system fits naturally in the ways of those who believe that freedom must involve alternative choices and that the struggles among ideas are part of the human experience of learning the truth.

All this is a more complete way of saying that information may be used as ammunition in the fight for political power or it may be used as merchandise. It would not be contended by any observant idealist that either way is wholly satisfactory. Information ought to be used for human growth and greatness. It will be so used in the future if some great ideal of freedom can be approached in practice. As is said by René Maheu in the UNESCO symposium, we have to humanize the mechanism by which mass opinion and mass behavior are now exploited. [1]

In the process, however, we have to make a practical bet on one system or the other, business or politics, or on some judicious mixture in which, by the theory of real alternatives, each will check the other. Such systems are being tried in some countries

---

[1] (UNESCO Symposium, *Human Rights*, p. 218.)

in the control of broadcasting. Canada is a good example. Frequency modulation development may make it possible to have many more radio frequencies in the United States allotted educational and governmental agencies and that may modify the system there. These are guesses at the future. In the meantime, the choice of theory and practice has to be made. Shall it be one voice, politically controlled, speaking one message which could be wrong? Or many voices in whose clamour the truth may never get spoken? In which can we more confidently put our faith?

Whatever is decided will apply in varying ways to all the media of mass communication. As we shall see later, the forms of communication such as broadcasting and motion pictures which are most mechanized can reach the largest numbers of people and can also be most easily controlled. The other media, like print for example, tend towards the same condition with the same possibilities and the same disadvantages. But no mechanical answer can solve the problems here raised; no invention will relieve man of responsibility for his own fate.

An English friend of mine was walking one murky night through a street in Dublin and saw a man, all alone, leaning up against a wall and beating a bass drum. There was no one else in sight anywhere and the drummer was not singing, nor talking, nor was he showing any sign of looking for an audience. My friend walked on and in the outer rim of the light he came on a policeman. 'Do you see what that man in doing back there?' he asked the officer.

'Yes, sir,' the policeman answered. 'He is beating a drum.'

'But what could he be doing that for?'

The policeman showed no suprise. He looked at the man's energetic motions for a moment and then ended the whole matter. 'Well, I suppose he's just having himself a political meeting.'

One who has lived in a western democracy finds a tale like that both amusing and touching because he can see, in the gallant futility of a political meeting that is held for oneself, an aspect of freedom. He would not want to live in a world in which such an incident has become impossible. The vagaries of men are part of the richness and loveliness of their humanity and we cannot postpone all our laughter to the coming Utopia.

5

In spite of the importance of political differences, we cannot overlook the fact that technological developments have drastically limited the realization and even the nature of many human rights. The right to be informed must have had a different realit} when there were no mass media of communication. News and enlightenment can not be spread now, copiously and swiftly, in vast tracts of the world where there are no broadcast receiving sets, no cheap print, no cinema. Temple gossip and tea house buzz are ancient disseminators of the peoples' wisdom but they cannot carry all a free man needs to know to act as a citizen in the modern world. Political interference with the free flow of information inside any country is a much more palpable denial of the right when the technical means for public enlightenment are available.

There appears to be no support in the opinions of governments or cultural leaders for the idea that any part of the world would be better off if no attempt were made to increase facilities for learning. The spokesmen for every nation ask for encouragement and help in building up the material means of enlightenment, and it is not unreasonable for the leaders in some poverty-bound countries to postpone discussions of control until there is something over which control can be exercised and by which political purposes can be fulfilled.

The great differences among countries in their equipment for informing their own people can be graphically shown in terms of ownership of radio receiving sets. Broadcasting is one of the most recent devices in spreading information but it is at present the least costly in terms of its effectiveness. A world planner might more quickly provide a means of reaching all the world's population by way of broadcasting than by any other medium. There are reasons, both technical and economic, for expecting that broadcasting may be the first device of actual world wide communication.

Look at the material facts. In the United States there is a receiving set for every two persons. There are a number of comparatively rich or industrially developed countries that have enough sets to provide, on the average, one set per family. The United Kingdom has about one for every four persons, as has

Australia. Sweden has one for every three, France for every five, Czechoslovakia for every six. In Italy there is one set for every eighteen persons. In Brazil the proportion is one to twenty-four. In Spain it is one to eighteen. In Russia it is believed to be about one to twenty-five persons. In all these countries there are enough sets to reach most of the populations in listening groups or with loud speakers in public places.

In the Asian half of the world conditions are much less favorable to quick communication inside a country or across borders. Accurate figures are not at hand but it is certain that there are thousands of persons in India or China for every receiving set now in use. In these places the first task of an enlightened government is to build up these facilities, or others that will accomplish the same purpose, letting the problem of control be considered when it must.

The Commission on Technical Needs in Press, Film and Radio, which reported to UNESCO in 1948, showed how unequally the machinery for spreading ideas is divided among the nations. That UNESCO Commission report, which is as admirable in its general examination of these problems as it is in the scope and comprehensiveness of its assembled facts, indicates that some governments do not seem to be willing to do much now to remedy the situation, putting other practical needs first. The comparative information published may help to remedy that backward policy in the few places where it persists.

There need not be as many radios as there are in America for any country to be well informed through that channel, because it is so easy to get together groups of friends, or even crowds in public places and to bring the voice of one loud speaker to a hundred ears. But there will have to be disseminating equipment, personnel and programme. As facilities of this kind or any other, such as newspapers, cheap books, or motion pictures, are built up, the material productiveness of the population will rise concurrently since information has its economic significance and an informed population will be more productive in any economic system. Where the surplus is to come from, by which information can be spread and the productivity raised to a point where even more information can be paid for, is a problem every country has to solve for itself with whatever help it can get from private bankers of other countries or international funds. Growth of this kind can be expected. As a practical programme of useful reform it can be encouraged everywhere without commitment to any economic or government ideology. The United Nations, UNESCO, the funds and foundations of the world are bound to help.

Sooner or later, in every country, a level of equipment is reached at which it is possible to make significant quantities of general information accessible to the whole population. Then the question of control must have its answer. Since the international problem of freedom of information cannot be separated from the ideas and practices of the nations in their own domestic systems, the same deep fissure continues then to divide the world. Those who believed in the kind of freedom that allows choice and error as part of each man's learning experience, will not oppose the free flow of ideas the world around, and will get ideas from other countries as well as equipment and funds. Those who are committed to the principle that there is a kind of truth, possessed by those in power and too valuable to be risked in open argument, will put up shutters at their national borders, preferring logically to export ideas and ask nothing in return, no matter how successfully they can build up their facilities.

However, referring again to McKeon's two lines of philosophical development, we must not think of this difference as something generated by recent events, or recent political doctrines. The new elements in the situation, as we have said, are technical not political and their importance may have been exaggerated.

6

Radio broadcasting exemplifies, better perhaps than any other modern channel of communication, the effects of technological change. In the first place, any system of radio requires a large initial investment; the machinery of dissemination is costly. In a comparatively rich country like the United States it is possible to have 2.000 different stations as there now are, and also a vast network of telephone lines by which networks can be hooked up for simultaneous programmes. Every citizen who has a message cannot expect to be allowed to send out his words to the world. A broadcaster must be someone who has capital funds for towers and dynamos. If he does happen to have the money, and can get a licence, he must also, in a private enterprise system, succeed in business competition with other licence holders; that necessarily restricts the content of his broadcasting within the limits of the interests and responses of public audiences. If he is a private citizen with a message, he can get at best a very small share of the programme time of any private station for his use, no matter how important his cause. The spokesmen of major organizations and national interests are there ahead of him to use up the margin of time left over from the popular entertainment that pays the costs of the operation.

In a publicly owned system, the great initial investment can be made by the government. The restriction imposed by costliness still is there, however, since the government has its own purposes and must insist on their fulfillment instead of the private demands that would be far too numerous for practical consideration.

The next important characteristic of broadcasting as an advanced example of modern communication is that the operator of the station, if not a government agent, has to have a government license. Even in countries where radio is not a function of state education, we can observe that technical, not policy reasons, make the licensing inevitable because air time is limited and frequencies must be officially divided up among the applicants in order to avoid mechanical interference. If licences are thus required for technical reasons, the agency of government which grants them cannot avoid passing judgment on the performances and promises of contending applicants for private operation of the available facilities.

The largest system in which privately owned stations dominate the air is in the United States. Only a few of the 2000 licensed stations in the United States are owned by educational or governmental agencies. There are a number of countries, like Canada and Australia, for example, where state operated and privately operated stations compete more equally. The British single company, owned by the government, the BBC, is unique and probably peculiar to British political practices. Elsewhere, often for economic as much as for political reasons, broadcasting is a government function. Thus, it can be said that in all systems the State plays a decisive part in distributing facilities for broadcasting. Wherever private enterprise has a chance, the facilities are available only to large aggregations of capital which, under government scrutiny, devote some part of their programmes to public benefit.

Another aspect of the economic structure of broadcasting, typical of machine-borne communication, is that the share of the cost directly carried by each member of the audience is very small. In the industrial countries almost anyone can afford to own a receiving set. The indirect cost is paid in general taxes or in special levies in governmental systems; by the general consuming public by way of advertising in private business systems. In no case is the cost to the user proportioned to his quantitatively measured use.

Still another characteristic of broadcasting that makes it a good example of the development of technological transmission of information is that it cannot be completely confined within the borders of any one state. The same qualities in a modern channel of communication that make it capable of reaching great numbers of persons make it capable of penetrating all kinds of iron curtains in both directions, inward and outward, and make it the natural tool of unwelcome interference by one nation in the internal life of another. We have gone far beyond the German philosopher's unkindly stricture on music, that it was the 'immoral art because it could force itself on an unwilling consumer.'

Inevitably machine-carried communication has become a subject of treaty quarrels, an anxiety to statesmen, a weapon of cold wars, and a channel by which a culture leaks through its outer seams. These things all may be evil or dangerous but the same qualities, quite naturally, make broadcasting the typical channel of communication by which a world civilization can be bound together if we ever have enough good will and intelligence to make one. Other media may follow, and still others to be discovered may be better for the purpose, but we know at least that a possible tool is at hand.

There is a principle in this fact of considerable importance for our theme. All tools are ethically neutral, all machines are both innocent and without souls. They can transmit messages of hate and fear or of friendliness and hope. But the new technologies have not made us better men, with greater things to say; they have only given us the means with which to say them.

These considerations bring us to another point which is also especially appropriate in relation to broadcasting. The new medium, established but not yet fully developed and still a topic of controversy, best shows a process. There are many thoughtful persons in all western countries who take freedom of the press for granted but are not so sure that broadcasters should have the same liberty. They resort to arguments based on the scarcity of facilities in radio as compared with print and other side-issues which do not go to the point. The old truth remains, no freedom according to the principles advanced here can be real if it does not allow the possibility of mistakes.

Free men learn from their mistakes and know the truth better by contrasting it with falsehood. So with institutions and professions. The great newspapers, even the great schools and universities and the other great professional agencies, grew to greatness in freedom, not in leading strings. And even now, after so much has been achieved, where there are great free institutions there are also failures and some of them are ignoble. Great institutions have been built by the developed sense of responsibility and public duty which strengthens the native virtues of good men who manage these institutions but their professional self-respect grows only where men can show their own courage and conscience. It is true that mere freedom is not enough; but it is also true that only in freedom can we build the institutions and educate the men and women who can serve our greatest purposes. The lesson is plain. In the new as in the old media of information, in broadcasting and television and cinema, as long ago in print, we have to allow freedom in order that real responsibility may be learned.

7

It is in this area of material means for spreading information that a direct challenge to the western concept of freedom of information and the concurrent freedom of speech is offered by doctrines and even by the Constitution of the Soviet Union. In has been repeated in proposals made by delegates of that country in international conferences, as in the Economic and Social Council of the United Nations, in August, 1947. The challenge has not been adequately met by the nations whose spokesmen argue for a greater flow of fact and opinion across international lines and greater development of privately owned machinery for disseminating information.

The Soviet argument begins with a denial that private ownership can be trusted. 'Of course, the complete guarantee of freedom of the press for the people is the communal ownership of means of information. This is the only way to ensure access of the broader masses of the people to methods of information and their effective control by democratic and peace loving organizations.' [1]

The telling point against western ideas is made in the corollary. If communal, that is to say government, ownership of the means of dissemination is necessary and is established, then the government, it is argued, can provide the means of spreading information to all recognized groups and persons. '... it must be admitted that merely to proclaim the principle of freedom of the press does not in itself give this freedom to the people, unless large sections of the population and their organizations have at their disposal the material resources without which freedom of the press cannot be made a practical reality.' [2]

To make clear the truth that lies in this assertion we can consider it in contrast with an extreme statement of the western idea. It may be that the position that was taken by John Stuart Mill in 1859 would now be rejected by most British or American or French statesmen as too extreme for practicality. It is still the democratic ideal. Remembering that democracy is not and never has been in the west the mere triumph of majority opinion but rather a doctrine of temperate rule by the majority with freedom for all dissenters to win converts if they can, we follow Mill in his analysis to the final point: 'Let us suppose, therefore, that the government is entirely at one with the people, and never thinks of exerting any power of coercion unless in agreement with what it conceives to be their voice. But I deny the right of the people to exercise such coercion, either by themselves or by their government. The power itself is illegitimate. The best government has no more title to it than the worst. It is as noxious, or more noxious, when exerted in accordance with public opinion than when in opposition to it. If all mankind minus one, were of one opinion, and only one person were of the contrary opinion, mankind would be no more justified in silencing that one person, than he, if he had the power, would be justified in silencing

---

[1] United Nations Doc. E/AC. 7/301 August 1947. Eng. Trans. from Russian original.
[2] Ibid.

mankind.' Voltaire might have said that or Emerson, with his 'Whoso would be a man, must be a nonconformist.' It has been said and practiced in many countries in modern times. It is the extreme, not the *reductio ad adsurdum* of the older liberal tradition. But it has a weakness and the Russian criticism discovers it.

In Mill's example, the one man who disagrees with the world can disagree silently in any political situation. In an ideal democratic state he can speak his mind, subject to derision or obloquy from his neighbours. He can go thus far on most subjects in the actual conditions of today in most western democracies. He can, for example, in the United States, run for office in many municipalities on a Communist party ticket; he can publish a Communist newspaper. He can argue for any kind of unpopular political, economic, religious, or social doctrine. He will be in trouble, of course; even John Stuart Mill does not ask that we reward those who threaten our ideals. But if he can avoid conspiracy- and incitement to physical revolution, he will not be liquidated. Dissent is not treason and opposition is not a crime. This is something but it is an imperfect realization of Mill's ideal; it falls about as far short as most actualities do of being perfect.

The point here is that even if the actual situation were much better, if it were quite up to Mill's demands, there would still be a tragic lack in it, as the Russians have made plain. That one man against the world may speak. Who will hear him? No one man, however right, not even a dozen men or a hundred, can pit their mere voices against the huge costs of modern communication. It takes not only a conviction and courage to be heard; the brave voice, right or wrong, has to be backed by ownership of presses and wires and microphones and cameras and cash for personnel. Otherwise the dim pipe of private truth is effectless.

The spokesmen for the Soviet state would provide, then, that all men be given access to the 'means' of spreading information. The western democracies have not met this challenge in either theory or practice. But to make good Mill's ideal in the modern situation, with mass audiences and mass media, would be literally impossible since it would be necessary to set aside a very large part of the available air and picture time for opinions expressed on private initiative, and these would have to be paid for by public funds.

This raises two points that cast some doubt on the completeness

of the Soviet answer to their own important question. The first is
indicated by the Russian position as given in a number of explicit
statements that 'freedom of the press is the right of all citizens,
with the exception of persons engaged in any form of Fascist
propaganda or in propagating aggression.'

All governments exercise common police powers in maintaining
the State. The crucial point here is that maintaining the State is
not the same thing as to maintain in power the incumbent group
of men. Making another appeal to experience, the western spokesmen say that exclusive and complete ownership by government of
all means of informing the public may very well assure the use
of those means for the purposes of the majority in so far as the
government represents it, but truth lies also in dissent and in
minority opinion. Such a principle as is enunciated by the Soviet
proposals provides, at best, exactly the kind of tyranny that Mill
thought most dangerous, the tyranny of a dominant and intol-
erant majority. At its worst, according to the experience and
beliefs of the western democracies, this principle puts lethal
weapons into the hands of any men who may be determined to
stay in power, whether or not the majority of the people still
want them, and they learn easily how to make the principle of
suppressing enemies of the State an excuse for calling all criticism
treason.

The other question is not a matter of experience but of modern
conditions. It arises out of the facts of mass dissemination. Most
students of government would agree that modern States, with
their large populations and vast spreads of territory, are unified
by mass information and communication carried by the technical
inventions of recent years and that, moreover, it would be very
difficult to hold such great territories in unity without wireless
and press and pictures. Ancient empires were always falling away
at the edges in spite of the roads and the relays of messengers to
which ancient statesmen gave so much attention. These slow communications were the old equivalent of our harnessed electricity.
They were not swift enough nor dependable enough to do their
work and a large territory meant constant physical warfare. Now
Russia and the United States and, in lessening degrees, other
modern States, hold millions together by flashes and signals, by
single voices and single messages spread everywhere, up to the
borders of the State. National unity, a common spirit and a general

devotion to a common cause, can be created by these new channels of public information since one voice can touch millions and all at the same time.

Those who look forward hopefully to a world civilization, whether or not it is ever under a single world government, count on these technological devices to serve as aids, ethically neutral in themselves, but capable of bearing wisdom and good will if men can have wisdom and good will to share with one another. This is a high ideal, so subtle and difficult in its implications for our present uncomfortable world that we cannot here do more than say that freedom of information is desired as a step in that direction.

The second question that must be asked of those who say that freedom is limited also by lack of means remains to be answered. It is more complicated than merely to ask how unity can be achieved if difference is encouraged. That can be answered. The new way of putting the question in an industrial society is this: How can dissenters be heard by mass audiences? To say that microphones and papers ought to be open to everybody is thoughtless. A mass audience is created by the fact that millions listen to one voice, carried perhaps by microphone and many loud speakers. The mass cannot hear more than one voice at a time and the hours that can be devoted to listening must be brief in a working day. If many voices are heard there must be many different audiences, out of touch with each other, hearing dissent and criticism and opposition and originality perhaps but not all hearing the same thing.

It is necessary to belabour this point because so many honest citizens who think of freedom in classical terms do not realize the full implications of their own often repeated saying that modern communications are wonderful and capable of great good because one message can get to millions. They fail to see that if one message reaches millions not many messages can issue. If everyone listens to one commentator or one teacher, not many other teachers or commentators can be heard.

Not monopoly in ownership, nor greed for either money or power, not private ambition or public totalitarianism, has created this simple, enormously significant fact. No one can change it. Technical advances in radio, still using that as our example, are very likely to make it possible within a few years to multiply

the number of broadcasting stations. In the United States, for
example, it will be possible with frequency modulation machinery
to broadcast from five or six thousand points simultaneously instead of from only 2000 as at present. Many more divergent ideas
and tastes and opinions can then get on the air. But it will also
divide up the mass audience in the same degree that it multiplies
the messages. This is true in the same way of any other medium
of mass communication.

There is no doubt an ideal balance between uniformity and
difference in any field of action or belief. We have to face the
fact, whose logic is depressing to many who are eager to reform
industrial society, that mass audiences will get little variety
whether the choice is made by government as in Russia, or by a
few dominant private companies in the communications industries
as in America, because if they get variety they will cease to be
masses and can only be congeries of smaller groups. The ideal of
John Stuart Mill would have proved impossible in modern technological conditions even if we had tried to put it into effect.
And the ideal suggested by the Soviet Constitution, of free speech
and free distribution of information by private citizens protected
by the government, is impossible of full realization for the same
reasons if for no other.

8

The difference between a nation that allows freedom inside its
own borders to many different kinds of opinion, even including
those that oppose the government, and one that commands cooperation in opinion as well as in action, remains a difference in
faith. This can be seen if we continue to make the necessary effort
to understand the attitude of each nation as described by its
national leaders in their own terms. We have been trying to compare honorably ideal with ideal, or practice with practice, instead
of falling into the futile comparisons of one ideal with the imperfect realization of others. There may still be places on earth
where dissident opinions in politics, or religion, or any straying
from orthodoxy whatever, are suppressed by naked force without
benefit of ideology. They can scarcely be discussed since they
claim no moral reason and we are considering only the difficulties

that are caused by divergence in ideas assumed to be honest. When different great cultural groups put their faith in different expectations, the observer who is anxious for the future of mankind can try to understand the differences without being blinded by his own faith. Both parties must abide the sequel.

The communist States in the east of Europe, and their more or less self-conscious adherents elsewhere, put their faith in a single formula of what they believe to be true, somewhat variable in application but absolute in essence, imposed by government on all citizens. For a doctrine to be absolute, it need not be invariable. When the possibility of objective truth is systematically denied and facts are systematically rearranged, or made subservient to a general ideal rule, the spokesmen for the official truth have a continuous task in interpreting orthodoxy for the people. History and science, the records of the past and the observations of the present, are made to serve the truth rather than to testify. In some degree the same process takes place in all cultures because men are influenced by hypotheses and interests as well as by evidence.

The differences now to be seen between countries with the two different ideas of freedom that we have been describing are primarily in the extent to which different versions of doctrine can be openly presented and the extent to which discussion can dig down to fundamentals. The believers in single truth systems welcome talk about means but not about ends. The democratic States put their faith in the result of open conflict among private and public agencies as well as personal voices, wherein truth is a value to be more and more nearly realized but never made formal and never imposed.

The essential character of the first system, the communist or any other totalitarian method of changing the world for the better, is that whoever is in power always knows best. The pursuit of truth has come practically to an end because the truth has been found. It is treason then to appeal from current beliefs to the creative possibilities of one's own country's future. There is neatness and clarity for thinkers in this; they have an infallible touchstone and all the strongest motives of safety, self-advancement and spiritual comfort lead them to follow the line.

The essential character of the second system, in the countries that call themselves democracies by the western pattern, is that no man need ever accept from men in power a declaration of truth. Men are taught to believe that there are truths, tentative perhaps, but still worthy of use, to which power has no special access, and that there are indeed other truths which only one's own conscience can test. This affirms the search for truth as in itself a value that all men are better for sharing and opens to all men not only the experience of creating a State to fit an ideal but also the experience of helping to change even the ideal itself.

In one case, by the totalitarian ideal, the government, which means necessarily certain men in temporary power, tries to create new citizens in a fixed image. In the western democracies the image is not fixed and all members of the State are incessantly at work on it. One is faith in an official truth and in the power of government to impose it. The other is faith in the continuing inventiveness of men.

Those of us who are spritually as well as politically committed to the second faith have to be aware, of course, that the inventiveness of free men leads them to lies, to suppressions when they have the means, and to colouring the truth for special purposes. Those who put faith in official and imposed truth believe that men can be bettered and that a skilfully constructed environment eventually will teach them all to act without the harsher motives such as the love of material gain. There is a touching optimism in this faith, whenever it comes to life in a soul long wearied of the greed and cruelty of men as they often are. The man as he is is forgiven for the sake of the man he could have been or for the men that are to come hereafter. Trouble begins with the inevitable discovery that men resist being made over and that something sterner than faith in their possibilities is needed to change them. This, in the experience of the believer in enforced goodness, is like the shock to the believer in freedom when he discovers what some men will do when set free. But the believer in democracy may have even more faith in men as they may be. What he lacks is faith in established truths or in government by formula. Above all, he has less faith in men in power.

9

Men cannot live alone; they exist and find their opportunities for expression only in institutions, in the available social habits of their time and place. This also is old truth and we did not need modern conditions to make us aware of it. What we do have in these times is better methods of psychological and sociological analysis; we can see repetitive patterns of human behavior in some events that our intellectual ancestors called sacred customs, or unique truths got by revelation. As a consequence of developed insights, we can see now that men build institutions into objective realities to which they give loyal obedience and pious respect, whereas the institutions are in fact only patterns in the mind which have no voices except the voices of the men who control them, and no purposes except as men interpret them, and no authority except what our consciences ascribe.

Government, or 'the State', is real only in this medieval sense. We have no need here to argue the point philosophically, if indeed there is still juice left in the debate; our pertinent point is that actually a government, like any other institution, can affect our lives only when living men, men like ourselves, are allowed to speak for it, to interpret its decrees, to reveal its 'truth'. The government is never an abstraction except in our arguments; in its impact on our lives it is a group of men acting on us in a chain of attributed authority.

On the other hand, we note another illusion; the government is never 'us'. Liberal defenders of collectivist and socialistic tendencies, on whom we are passing no judgment of good or ill, have often used the argument that accretions of power to government in democratic states cannot possibly diminsh the freedom of the citizen because the officials are either elected, or are appointed by their elected superiors, and must be thought of as only 'us'. Anyone who has ever served a week in a government post knows that there is no identification of self with citizen in such a psychological setting and no one who has done more than play with political abstractions can deceive himself with the notion that office holding is only the mechanism by which we govern ourselves. Government is neither a self-propelled and omniscient abstraction, nor is it a disguise for the citizens in general and in particular; it is a group of living men. In any system men are subject to human error and to the corruptions of power.

It is necessary to say a word about corruption, since we are trying to examine the salient aspects of these two ways of 'freedom'. I am not speaking of corruption in the trivial sense of dishonesty or lust. If one system gives greater scope than another or greater temptation to such minor sins, the inefficiency will doubtless show up in the consumption levels and in the safety of citizens and remedies will be found.

The corruption that is more significant is deeper and more dangerous; it is corruption of the strong and the good, not of the weak, and by reason of their goodness, not because they are self indulgent. Power damages great men most because the great men and the good are the ones who are tempted to forget that they are men. They take on the greatness and infallibility imputed to the institution in whose name they speak. They cease to see any difference between their own individual destiny and the fate of the people and believe, with whole sincerity, that they must remain in power and must be obeyed or the people will not be saved. There are many reasons why they will be encouraged in this terrible delusion by the people themselves. All men would like to believe that their leaders are good and great; they do not need much organized suggestion to raise Caesar to a god. And, curiously perhaps, it can be done rather more easily now than in ancient times because mass media can be used for mass suggestion and mass suggestibility offers eager victims.

There is nothing in this to indicate a belief that the apotheosis of the human idol is any more or less justified in one system than in another, nor that power is more terrible to its holder in one form rather than another. It is always and irresistibly terrible. Those who believe in protecting minority voices and substantial oppositions find in these institutions of correction and restraint a possible balance to the ubiquitous institutions by which power can become entrenched.

10

Spokesmen of some countries continue to say that they must keep information from freely crossing international lines because they have to prevent foreign 'lies' from endangering their creative experiments in culture building. We have said that this claim of special reason for state control is not new, nor based on new conditions. It has been made with equal passion and honesty by all kinds of states and institutions and men in all of recorded history.

To consider some past examples we can recall the fate of a State that refused to use that device of suppression to guard the truth. It may well be that Athens lost her independence by allowing political factions a degree of freedom that slipped too often into anarchy. But Sparta, whose stiff order was, at a safe distance, theoretically seductive even to Plato, also went down. Bigger phalanxes have a way of crushing both kinds of resistance, the one inspired by doctrine and the one inspired by free, informed conviction. The glory of a culture, like the glory of a life, lies in its quality not in its duration. The difference between the significance of Athens in history as compared with Sparta is in the uses made by her great men of the freedom given. Who reads a Spartan book? All kinds of social systems, it would seem, can be destroyed; some do more than others to justify their temporal existence.

All suppressions likewise claim that they are protecting the 'only' way; not the best but the 'only' salvation. This laconic formula of escape from the real question will justify any inquisition in saving heretics from the great sin of infecting believers, any liquidation of dissent to save the people from those who would thwart their will, or any misrepresentation of facts because their disclosure would hurt a party.

There are such things as objective facts. Despite the monumental metaphysics of brass which have been erected in some cultures to cover them over they remain. Men can get at them only by heroic submission of will and hope to the disciplined reason, as has been notably achieved in modern science but not there only. They do not provide an answer to many of the most important questions, but they exist. To ignore them, to give up the search because of one objective fact which is obvious even to the doctrinaires, that men are easily distracted by interests and fears, is to abandon the future on behalf of the dubious now. It is to betray the most rewarding and noblest of human traits, the urge to ask always one more question.

A plausible case can nearly always be made out for a 'present crisis' that lasts as long as one group in power in any political system needs the threat of crisis to justify the suppression of critical opposition. Some defenders of the closed cultures, the States which do not permit the importation of ideas, use this kind of argument, promising a future time of freedom when the import of foreign ideas can be allowed because all citizens will then be immune.

The crisis has lasted in these countries, one is bound to observe, for a generation of men and it is interesting to note that some of the more logical defenders of Communism, like for example John Lewis in the UNESCO Symposium (page 70), do not rely on the crisis as an excuse for suppressing what are called, in any country, 'anti-democratic classes'. Mr Lewis says: 'That being so, we do not, on the one hand, regard the liberal suppression of anti-democratic movements as a departure from principle due to pressure of circumstances, so that eventually the ban will be lifted and principle restored. Nor do we, on the other hand, regard communist suppression of anti-democratic classes and privileged groups as inconsistent with democracy though perhaps excusable in an emergency. On the contrary, it is allowable in principle where justified by the circumstances.' This seems, to one of another persuasion, to be a declaration by the Communist theorist that control of opinion is a matter of principle, not of expediency, no matter how securely established the government and the system may some day become.

It seems unlikely that any solution of the difference between two points of view will be found by going down that path. The logic of suppression is good on such premises. We are brought back again, not to a principle of political action but to the more basic principle, the concept of the nature of truth. We can pass over the irony that lies in the modern situation, that so many men who claim that their politics are founded on science have conspicuously rejected the essential principle of modern science which is that all truths are held as practical rules of action, tentatively believed in, not defended by any authority and subject to any man's question.

Modern science in all matters that are susceptible of scientific description moves more and more to a Platonic theory of truth as approachable but never quite arrived at which makes it impossible for any man or group, no matter what political power they may happen to hold, to fix, in the name of scientific truth, any limits to enquiry. Superficial students of the ways of science are often misled by the fact that scientific workers must, for psychological reasons, use some general ideas as master hypotheses. The Marxian interpretation of history is for scientific purposes, such a master hypothesis. But the scientist who believes in the usefulness of an effort to be 'objective' uses this logical apparatus as an aid in framing his questions, not as a test of his results. Those who have been disciplined to think in this manner not only believe in the search for truth as a valuable element in each man's own experience, but believe also that the most useful and productive descriptions of nature will come from the constant effort at objectivity. We might even reduce it to so simple a proposition as this: even the Marxian principle that conclusions of truth are basically derived from the material aspects of social organization is itself a tentative truth to be continually re-examined in the light of further knowledge of man and society, and a culture which suppresses such questioning denies science in principle.

The persistent argument returns, of course, that the social experiment must be protected. The believer in the western idea of freedom, the freedom of difference and choice instead of the freedom to live by one official truth, can only appeal to history. Other attempts to fix history in an ideal mould have ended in a balance between tyranny and stagnation. The conspicuous examples, such as Japan from 1603 to 1868, Iyeyasu to Perry, Sparta in its greatest days, Spain under Philip II, Russia under the Czarist government whose bonds on the human spirit the Communist revolution itself destroyed, were all increasingly unsuccessful. Humanity refuses to be fixed. Is it a fair question for the one whose faith is in the greatest possible degree of free difference and choice to ask the believer in official isolations what he thinks of these isolations in the past? Which one of these past possessors of the 'only' salvation deserved to stop forever the clock of change on the claim that the truth was then finally known? If none of them can by our hindsight be accorded the right, what supports a claim that the circumstances now are different?

In searching out the reasons that determine a choice between free flow of information across boundaries and the voluntary isolation of cultures, we can go beyond the political aspects of the question which have led us to make historical comparisons. We can get some light also from anthropological studies. Horizontal comparisons of institutions and cultures suggest that men behave in roughly similar ways in roughly similar conditions and students of human patterns have discerned two kinds of progress. As Marett puts it *(Faith, Hope and Charity in Primitive Religions,* page 131) '... one as movement along a line, the other as movement in a circle. It would seem that either kind of energy is equally pleasing to mankind to long as the energy is in like degree unimpeded.' It is the primitive man, the one whose future is not likely to change much, who is, in fact, denying himself a place in history who '... envisages his earthly not less than his post-terrestrial paradise as an endless round of the same activities raised to the nth point of smooth accomplishment.' This helps us to account for the continuing enthusiasm of many, perhaps almost all of the members of closed system cultures where no new ideas can get in; they are spending their energies in the round of bettering the present system. It accounts also for docility. But it ought to cause some disquiet in leaders who see that this has always been a trait of the static primitive peoples who believe they have found the best and only way of life. It was not from such people that the states in the east of Europe could ever have borrowed the technologies they are now devoting to the service of the common man.

11

These arguments may be more or less useful to persuade men that the free passing of information, across international borders as well as inside the State, is an ideal worth trying to make actual. There remains a point in one's theory of education, providing further proof that one's beliefs in these matters are part of one's philosophy of education which is also, of course, a derivation from one's theory of truth. If truth be fixed, and also accessible to the present holders of power in any State, and thus a good which the men in power are justified in imposing on the people by direct teaching and by barriers against ideological invasions, then education is a simple task. The growing powers of the young need only to be developed in a straight line. Their minds are to be trained as tools of the greater State and their personalities cannot be, in any measure whatever, taken as ends in themselves. The

Kantian morality is utterly rejected and all men are instruments of the 'social purpose', interpreted necessarily by the men in power. No other mechanism of induction into the culture is then conceivable.

If, on the other hand, all men in power are believed to be only men, whose wills and minds are not made perfect by being obscured behind a screen of 'realistic' abstractions, and the truth is something to be sought by every man for himself, and every man is to be provided with all possible facts and opinions and other intellectual material in order that he may do the best he can within his native limitations in that search, then there must be another way of educating the young and education cannot stop at the threshold of maturity.

It has long been understood in the technologically advanced cultures that some kinds of change will continue to be inevitable after modern methods of production and distribution have been established. Occupations and social ways change or disappear; new ones are created by new machines or new processes. Besides, the swift interchange of ideas that modern mass media make possible, if permitted to do so by the political system, brings to men and women at succeeding stages of their development, through adulthood into advanced age, the latest scientific and moral wisdom. They are not bound to live by the lore of their grandfathers; they can change with the times. They are, by this theory of education, very little handicapped by being older and escape being old fashioned by using the learning power which persists, as we know, from many psychological experiments, in spite of years. Older persons can learn whatever they really need to know; that was established by Thorndike and collaborators twenty years ago. And modern civilization is so complex and so swiftly changing that education must necessarily go on along with living.

By this theory of education, to which industrially mature countries have been brought by necessity as well as by generous logic, to shut a mature citizen away from information of any kind is to deny him that material by the use of which he constantly studies, re-examines and reforms his own ideals of citizenship. If what comes to him is not varied and stimulating and truly challenging to his judgment as well as to his loyalties, it cannot educate him. It can only fill him up.

12

We look to the future. The appropriate Commissions in international bodies are taking a further step in making a world civilization as they change the Declaration of Human Rights into a covenant. Then, if any government offers agreement to the principles of freedom as mere lip service it can be challenged on its violation of an international legal contract. There is enough in the substance of the Declaration, even now, to cause questions to be asked in such international bodies as the General Assembly of the United Nations. But we still lack a common understanding of the meaning of words. There is, in fact, a good deal of debate in the meetings of the Assembly. It cannot be much more than an exchange of recriminations and this is not caused necessarily by bad faith on the part of any of the debaters. They are literally correct in accusing each other of violations of human rights, especially the right to information, according to their own interpretations of the meaning of the word 'freedom'.

If it is a violation of my freedom to permit me to know what views have been held on important questions or are held now by misled men, then my freedom is violated every day in America many times over. I live in a confusion of attacks on my freedom — if that is what the world should mean — and my government is delinquent.

We are led back to the practical need of solving somehow the conflict of ideas. There may be more than three possible solutions; I can find no more. Either we put the world all under one ideal of freedom; or, as a second possibility, we divide it; or, thirdly, we bring different ideas into some kind of adjustment.

All systems of ideas, religious, political or social, are generally managed by men who take it for granted that they deserve to dominate the world and will eventually do so. The passion with which this messianic trait in all great ideas is displayed may differ in time or place; it is always there. The real difference among systems is the degree to which they are committed to the use of force or violence to fulfil their destiny. Force in evangelism brings out force in resistance and cold force is the intermediate stage between rational persuasion and violence. Institutions and States have used force and stopped short of violence; the annals of international disputes are full of incidents in which all kinds of sanctions were used short of war. Our point is to note that any system that will resort first to force and then to war will call up an answer of the same sort and adjustment is almost impossible.

It has generally happened in western history, however, that ideological differences that led to violence seemed after a period of time to be less important than men had felt them to be, and it is certainly true that attempts to make one world, in which only one truth would be possible, have failed.

The invasion of Europe by Islam is a good case in point. When it appeared that it was not possible for Islam to kill off all unbelievers or to frighten them into conversion, the tide of invasion ebbed back to Asia again and Islamic civilization left in Europe only its better part, some of its learning and its ideals of human equality. The same general facts can be seen in the adjustment in Europe of Protestant and Roman Catholic Christianity. It appeared, after the failures of the Spanish power in the seventeenth century, that Europe could not be made either all Catholic or all Protestant and as an American theologian, Reinhold Niebuhr, has pointed out, religious wars cease when a sectarian domination appears to be impossible.

We cannot say that there will never be a single faith in all the world in every human mind, made up of fitted orthodoxies, religious, social, economic and political. That may happen; it has not happened up to now and there is nothing in the record to lead us to expect it, even if perchance we are among those who hope for it. It is the solution that might logically be desired by those who believe in any single standard of truth and almost inescapably by those who define freedom as the right to believe only one true doctrine. Others can honestly resist it and at the same time feel safe against it. They can even live at peace with any in their own society that hold freedom of choice among ideas as only a temporary expedient, a truce that gives them the chance to prepare for domination.

13

It might well be possible, we realize, that all the arguments for the free flow of information might be good when judged from the standpoint of one single country's welfare and still not meet the demand that UNESCO, by its charter, is justified in making on all principles of action. Will it help the world towards peace?

It is possible to believe that peace was more assured when men knew less of one another. At least, wars were on a smaller scale when men lived more parochial lives. They were as cruel but less capable in destruction. Men of great spiritual insight, like Tagore, for example, have gravely questioned the easy thesis that acquaint- ance among nations makes for tranquillity. And it is possible that distribution of all the world's population into separate small groups might keep great wars from getting started. It would also keep modern technologies from working and would in the past have kept nearly everything that we call modern from coming into being. One could perhaps argue that this would be better than our jangled modern life. But who has seriously proposed going back to savagery, since modern ethnology destroyed the dreams of Rousseau and Chateaubriand? We have one world, whether we want it or not, and modern communication by short wave and pictures and print is reaching into the remotest corners. The question is not whether or not we shall live together, but how? Given contiguity, congestion even, how can we be spiritually and physically safe with each other?

Nothing good can get very far, or last very long, in so dangerous and self-destroying a world unless there is peace. It would not be appropriate here, even if we had the wisdom needed, to say why wars begin. But by the piecemeal examination which the humility of our ignorance demands, we can look at some of the things that can happen in a world like ours to bring on our kind of war. Peoples are generally pacific until they are frightened and angered into fighting. When leaders of all the nations say their people want peace they are telling the probable truth. But the people of no country want peace after they have been threatened or scared into hatred, into a desperate energy of what they honestly believe to be self-defense. And if there should be anywhere in the world a set of leaders intent on having a war, or risking one, or trying to manipulate the world situation in such a way that war would have to come — if such men should exist now or soon, as they have existed in the past, they could do their work much more easily if they could completely control the flow of information into the minds of their citizens.

In a world like ours there is always some awareness among the people of the existence of other cultures than their own and other populations far away. But if we lack actual information we have in our minds only vague stereotypes of strangers. The vaguer the stereotype the easier it is to fill it with hatred and menace. Near neighbours have fought, too often, but in most cases they fought because they had learned to hate each other in long years of mutual hostility. When peoples on opposite sides of the earth learn to hate each other, beyond the mild suspicions that we all seem to have of strangers, they have to be fed the notions, generally false, that make an enemy out of a blank human page. This is possible in any country; it is dangerously easy in a country that shuts its borders against all gestures, even friendly ones, from outside.

Philosophers as well as statesmen and educators have been puzzled, for a long time by the problem of adjusting their practices to their concept of truth. What McKeon calls the Augustinian or Marxian answer has not been satisfactory to all the men who have believed in the reality and accessibility of absolute truth, and some men who are philosophically and religiously untouched by modern relativism can still find a way to live with and work with those whose ultimate sanctions are not the same as their own. They are practically compelled to do so because they believe in democracy as a rule of life and they are living in a world where differences in concepts of the truth are very deep among men who live, nevertheless, together.

Jacques Maritain has confronted the problem with courage and generosity as a spokesman for UNESCO at the meeting in Mexico City two years ago and again in his essay in the UNESCO symposium. His statement has already been cited by M. Bodet, the Director General, on this subject. Maritain says, ' . . . because the goal of UNESCO (page 10) is a practical goal, agreement between minds can be reached spontaneously, not on the basis of common speculative ideals, but on common practical ideas, not on the affirmation of one and the same conception of the world, of man and knowledge, but upon the affirmation of a single body of beliefs for guidance in action.'

This is the affirmation of the principle of spiritual democracy. It puts us far from the attitude of those who say they cannot trust any man who works for sanctions or ideals they cannot accept. It unites men in beneficent action without suspicion or any question of motives, and it makes a war of ideologies seem like a tragic waste of time in a world where so much waits to be done. It demands of all participants in the common human effort an energetic willingness to trust in humanity itself, to accept and live by an attitude towards ideas like the old English common law attitude toward all accused men, that they are innocent until proved guilty. It gives us a basis that may be short of friendship or brotherhood, but is at least without fear or threat, on which a warmer and stronger kind of world companionship can afterwards be built.

MAURICE BEDEL

The rights
of the creative artist

THE RIGHTS
OF THE CREATIVE ARTIST

Preface

Is there any greater, more liberal or nobler truth than that proclaimed in the Universal Declaration of Human Rights which asserts the right of all men to the enjoyment of the benefits of civilization and knowledge? And is not knowledge itself one of the pillars of our civilization and the one best calculated to resist the assaults of time and changes in man's ethical concepts?

It is to knowledge then that UNESCO turns, carrying out its beneficial work both through and in the interests of knowledge.

By the terms of its constitution UNESCO exists to further international understanding; it gives its support to agencies providing popular information and it furthers such international agreements as will, in its opinion, facilitate the free circulation of ideas by picture and word.

One of its first tasks therefore has been to protect the rights of writers and artists, and to insist that they shall be recognized and respected so that the freedom of expression and the material independence of writers and artists, without which there can be no true science, art or literature, may be assured.

The object of the present study is to underline the importance of the author and artist in society and to discuss the various ways by which they can be assisted to obtain the position which is their due, secure in the enjoyment of their rights and the dignity of their mission.

What is a creative artist? What are his rights? And what is the work to be protected? These are questions which we must answer before we can go on to discuss the practical ways and means in which protection can be granted.

I

The creative artist

What is a creative artist?

Homer went from village to village on the island of Chios, and around him, squatting in the dust amidst scratching chickens and friendly dogs, men gathered to listen to his melodious recital of how Diomedes stole the horses of the Thracian king or his description of the obsequies of Hector. He sang the simple stories that those before him had recited, but illuminated by his own poetic genius they appeared transformed and beautified for all time. In the 2800 years which have passed since it was first composed the *Iliad* has lost nothing of its noble beauty. Its text, preserved entire, holds a place of honour in the libraries of the world for the delight of all civilized men.

Homer was a creative artist.

In. other climes, and at another time, the Indian poet Valmiki set down the story of Rama's life in the *Ramayana,* and there is not an educated Indian who has not wandered with joy in the vast forest of its 50000 lines.

Valmiki was a creative artist.

Julius Caesar, seeking to emulate the fame of Alexander, went from land to land subjecting the barbarian peoples to the law of Rome. Returning to Rome he fought against the Senate and countered the intrigues of his enemies, and in his rare moments of leisure he wrote a brilliant study of the Latin tongue in which he showed himself an excellent grammarian, and that famous *Diary of the War in Gaul* which gave future historians a splendid example of lucidity and elegance of language.

Julius Caesar was a creative artist.

Michelangelo Buonarotti sculpted his *Night* and *Day, Twilight* and *Dawn* on the Medici tombs with same same sublimity with which he painted *The Last Judgement* in the Sistine Chapel, with the same lyric feeling which informed his design for the dome of St Peter's in Rome and inspired his immortal sonnets.

Michelangelo was a creative artist.

All those who give life and reality to a work of art which expresses their own personality, whether by words, music, colour, the engraver's burin, the sculptor's chisel or the architect's plan, are creative artists.

All creative artists are *authors* in the wider sense. It is a felicitous word. It derives from the Sanscrit root *ojas,* meaning strength,
and it passed through the Latin word *augeri,* to grow, before
developing its modern meaning. Strength and growth — how better
can we describe the source from which artistic and literary creation
springs! The creative artist wrestles with the inertia of words,
line and colour, which would remain dormant for ever did he
not seize them and drag them from their slumbers, and having
seized them he arranges them, gives them form and causes them
to grow.

It is a process which gives rise to strange speculation.

If Beethoven had never been born the *Pastoral Symphony* would
have remained for ever locked away in what the Chinese call the
Palace of Nowhere. If Shakespeare had never seen the light of day
we should never have listened to the famous balcony scene.
Without the happy chance which produced Goethe from the union
of an Imperial Councillor with the daughter of the Burgomaster
of Frankfort we should never have witnessed Faust and Margarete
in the prison scene. How many masterpieces still slumber in the
shades of nowhere for lack of an artist to bring them to life!

The creative artist, an artisan of strength and growth in the
things of the mind, is a man of destiny. Without him the world
would have remained a place from which art, poetry and philosophy were banned; sterile earth knowing only practical necessities, with boredom the one inseparable companion of the spirit.

Thus we must seek to define the creative artist, to reveal the
full extent of his gifts to mankind and his help in our never-
ending search for truth and beauty.

We should never allow ourselves to forget the man who toils
day after day, and often far into the night, concentrating tena-
ciously on the white sheets of paper before him that from his
effort and his ecstacy may spring that poetry, that prose and that
music destined to enchant mankind throughout the ages. Let us
think of a man like Swift who suffered the severest blows of fate
and. yet worked on at his *Gulliver's Travels* destined to be the
never-failing delight of us all. He was a creative artist. Like Balzac,
who undermined his health and went to an early grave at the
age of fifty from an excess of coffee drinking, voluntary confinement
from labouring at his work and lack of sleep, but left behind
a true monument in his *Comédie Humaine.* He, too, was a creative

artist. Like Franz Schubert, who in his short life of thirty-one years composed over 600 songs, dissipating his failing health to give us *The Erl King, The Trout* and *The Wanderer* to soothe our melancholy hours even to this day. He, too, was a creative artist.

When we speak of the rights of the creative artist we should never lose sight of those who have given the expression its loftiest significance. That is why we set such store here by the person of the creative artist himself, as a man, with his strength and his weaknesses, with his fleeting moments of happiness and his long periods of misfortune, with his struggles against sickness and poverty and, only too often, against the obtuseness of his contemporaries. That is why we are anxious to define the nature of the creative artist from the history of art and letters.

What is a creative artist?

Phideas supervising the execution of his plans for the building of the Parthenon was a creative artist; Rembrandt painting his famous *Lesson in Anatomy*; Mozart composing his *Marriage of Figaro*; Albrecht Dürer engraving his *Horseman of Death*; Walt Whitman furiously scribbling his *Leaves of Grass*.

And we should also not forget those artists who worked before the dawn of history, carving on horn, bone and ivory, modelling in clay, painting those pictures of bison, horses and elephants on the walls of their caves which still astonish us by their artistry today.

No matter how far back we go in the story of man's creative genius and inventiveness we shall find such flowers blossoming from his artistic sense harnessed to the service of beauty. At all times there has been that flowering without which the heart and soul of man would dry up and shrivel away. It represents one of the sources of life, one of the mainsprings of man's spiritual existence.

We have said that the creative artist is one who makes things to grow. Let us enumerate the treasures by which he has enriched the cultural patrimony of man's estate.

If Socrates is right that the highest pleasure a man can experience in life is knowledge, then how much we owe to all those who first handed on the fruits of their knowledge to us in manuscripts and later in hundreds of thousands of printed books! Let us recall the names of some of them in order that they may shine in glory inscribed beneath the Universal Declaration of Human Rights, whose trenchant axiom: 'Everyone has the right to the protection of the moral and material interests resulting from any scientific, literary or artistic production of which he is the author' serves us here as our text.

Let us seek their names in the memory of our emotions, in the hidden recesses of our mind, in those sanctuaries which are our refuge in times of doubt. and despair, which are our haven in moments of serenity and recollection. If we limit their numbers it is only to seize the most brilliant at once, just as when we cast a rapid glance into the night sky we see first only the brightest stars.

Hippocrates, Aristotle, Copernicus, Francis Bacon, Galileo, Descartes, Leibniz, Newton, Lavoisier, Volta, Darwin, Pasteur and Einstein are the giants of science.

Plato, Euripides, Lucretius, Tacitus, Dante, Erasmus, Cervantes, Montaigne, Shakespeare, Goethe, Kant, Chateaubriand and Tolstoy stand for letters.

The architects of the Pyramids, Ictinos the architect of the Parthenon, Phideas the architect of the Temple of Tanjour, Michelangelo, Raphael, Dürer, Velasquez, Rembrandt, Goya, Delacroix, Rodin and Picasso represent the arts.

Monteverdi, Handel, Bach, Haydn, Mozart, Beethoven, Chopin, Brahms, Berlioz, Wagner, Rimsky-Korsakov, Debussy and Stravinsky are the masters of music.

These are the men whom Baudelaire called 'Beacons'. We have recalled their names only to enhance in the light of their tremendous prestige the inestimable value they have added to the vocation of creative artist.

But we should not suppose that creative art is dependent on means of expression fixed for ever by tradition. In the twentieth century we have witnessed the birth and universal development of an art which is related to both painting and the theatre, and whose advent has produced new talents and revealed new forms of creative art — the film. This new art has produced, if not its geniuses, at least men whose work has become justly famous.

And the art of photography has already produced its masters. During the course of this study we shall see that here, too, despite appearances, we are dealing with a creative art form.

From a consideration of these men, who, amongst so many

others, have lent undying glory to the ordinary, everyday term
'creative artist' let us now turn to the laws and customs of traditional morality to establish the rights which every creative artist
should be granted and be able to exercise in respect of his work
both in his own person and through his heirs after his death.

2

The legal position

The horticulturist who by care and patience coupled with his
knowledge of the laws of hybridism succeeds in producing a new
rose has certain rights in his creation. That particular rose did
not exist until his imagination conceived it and his skill gave it
form and colour. He names it, and the property rights in that
name are his. He may be said to have composed a flower, given
it a name and produced it. He then multiplies it by graftings or
cuttings, and having, so to speak, made so and so many copies
he sells them to rose enthusiasts. No one even dreams of denying
his right to his own creation, to the name he has given it, to the
special qualities of colour and appearance which are typical
of it.

Such is the right of the creative artist to his work, the right of
the musician to his score, the right of the painter to his picture,
the right of the author to his book.

Let us now consider the meaning we propose to give to the
word 'right'.

The wisdom of the ages grants each man the right to protect
his own property. That implies something which is in accordance
with reason and, in consequence, with law. It is man's sense of
right, a sense natural to him in all ages, the sense which impelled
the first social groupings of mankind, the first beginnings of
human society, to frame their primitive laws. Even in the animal
kingdom we know with what vigour a dog will fight for the bone
he believes to be his, and with what care the squirrel will guard
the nuts he has hidden in the hollow of a tree. Animal laws are
laws of instinct; man's laws are those of reason. As human society
began to develop and man, overcoming his initial disinclination,
began to mix with other men, so the idea of property arose, and
it developed side by side with the increasing number of things

produced by manual dexterity and creative genius. There is little doubt that when man first began to speak it was to establish his claim to the possession of the fruit he had picked or the game he had trapped. Even before he could speak he disputed with others the possession of what he had gathered or caught. A sort of law of possession developed before any other laws. It conformed to man's feeling that what he held was his; that he could do what he liked with it: keep it himself or give it to others. At the same time, though very slowly, man's consciousness of his own individuality also developed, encouraged by the anterior development of a sense of possession and, subsequently, a property sense. The more a man possessed the more clearly he realized his own identity as distinct from the exterior world of other men.

When man became the *homo faber,* the artisan, of prehistoric times, the idea of the origin of property was added to that of its possession. A man realized that the product of his hands was the result of a whole series of deliberately conceived movements carried out by him as an individual.

The fashioning of the first flint tool introduced the idea of its origin and authorship into the laws and customs of primitive society, and, in consequence, the right of its author to the product of his inventiveness.

In the name of UNESCO we should pay homage to those primitive men who first fashioned from inert matter the tools which were the precursors of our modern mechanized civilization. Let us salute these early men with their clumsy fists, their spatulate thumbs and their big-jointed fingers who first gave to stone the requisite form to permit its use as a tool. Let us thank them for impressing their will on to matter which up to then had been inert, formless and useless. And let us affirm their right to the work that sprang in this way from their imagination and their will.

In this sense the rights of creation are as old as human society. They made their appearance when the first rough-hewn tool was produced. They developed with the making of needles from bone, harpoon tips from ivory and arrow heads from flint, and with the painting of those astounding cave frescoes which still arouse our admiration. But such was the innocence of our primitive ancestors that we doubt very much whether they ever made use of their rights.

It was certainly the development of language which first led men to demand the recognition of their rights as creators. The development of language gave free rein to the thoughts of men. The idea of right, still not clearly formulated, was one of the elements of self-knowledge. From this developed the concepts which are expressed today in such words as: 'My right ... By right ... Have the right ...' They express the right of the individual to dispose of his own as he thinks fit, to use the prerogative of free will.

The principle of right, with which we shall deal later on in its manifold aspects and applications, thus dates back to the very beginning of human society, and in consequence it appears almost as natural law.

When we consider the illustrious names we mentioned previously as belonging to some of the more brilliant amongst the many to whom we owe the spread of art, science and letters we shall find it strange that the right of the creative artist to his work was ever called into question. To deny Leibniz the right to publish his *Théodicée* or his *Monadology* when and where he pleased, or Montesquieu his *Spirit of Laws,* or Goethe his *Faust,* is seen at once to be absurd. Today it seems natural to us that the author of a work of literature or the composer of a piece of music should have just the same rights in his work as the horticulturist has in the new type of rose he produces. But, for example, the vast upheaval of the French Revolution was necessary before the rights of French authors were recognized by law. The Law of July 19th and 24th 1793 first protected their rights; up to that time the position had been vague and, uncertain, leaving much room for trickery.

But in the nineteenth century the institution of Copyright on the one hand and the signing of the Berne Convention on the other introduced order and probity into the sphere of international literary and artistic rights to the great benefit of writers and artists.

From that point on it was possible to talk of rights in relation to legally defined concepts. All countries have recognized such rights whether for their own nationals or for writers, musicians and artists of other countries, and they have received solemn confirmation in international conventions. A creative artist can now rest assured that his work, born of his emotion and his talent, will be respected and protected against all encroachments on its form or its integrity.

Apart from the rights he enjoys in his own work, the creative artist has a further right, attached to his own person, which protects him against all practices damaging to his reputation and permits him to defend the inviolability of his creation. This is a moral right, and we shall discuss it further in the course of this study.

Already we can see the care with which the legislator guards the work of those whose purely artistic activities contribute to the vitality, to the very life of the nations to which they belong.

It redounds to the credit of the nineteenth century that it was the first to embody the rights of the creative artist in the law.

3

The work of art

We have spoken of the creative artist; we have spoken of his rights: let us now speak of his work.

Artistic creation, like scientific discovery and literary invention, has its origin in that delicate machinery of human understanding to which we owe those masterpieces which give the history of mankind its lofty spiritual value. What reason should we have for our pride in belonging to the human race if architecture, music, science, painting, sculpture and letters had not confirmed the pre-eminence of man and justified his election by destiny to a place which no other creature living on the face of the earth, in the air, or in the waters around the earth has ever succeeded in reaching?

The history of mankind, short as it is in the ages of the earth, is marked by the creations of man's mind, by works whose existence lend an undeniable meaning to the spiritual, moral and aesthetic mission of *homo sapiens.* How better can we prove it than by enumerating some of the masterpieces which grace the history of our kind?

The library of King Assurbanipal, Euclid's geometry, Aristotle's *Physics,* the works of Archimedes, the *De Revolutionibus Orbium Celestis* of Copernicus, Descartes' *Discours de la Méthode,* Newton's *Principia,* Linnaeus' *Systema Naturae,* Pasteur's work on lactic fermentation, Darwin's *On the origin of Species,* Claude Bernard's *Introduction to the Study of Experimental Medicine,* Becquerel's work on radiation and Einstein's theory of relativity are sufficient in the scientific sphere.

Homer's *Iliad,* the *Ta-Hio* of Confucius, Plato's *Republic,* the *De Natura Rerum* of Lucretius, the *Novum Organum* of Francis Bacon, *Don Quixote* of Cervantes, Shakespeare's *Hamlet,* Kant's *Critique of Pure Reason,* Goethe's *Faust,* Chateaubriand's *Mémoires d'outre-tombe,* the plays of Ibsen, and the novels of Dostoevsky are the gems of literature.

The *Orpheus* of Monteverdi, Haydn's *Scotch Symphony,* Mozart's *Marriage of Figaro,* Beethoven's Ninth Symphony, Brahm's First Symphony, Chopin's *Grande Fantaisie, The Damnation of Faust* by Berlioz, *Tristan and Isolde* by Wagner, the Requiem of Verdi, Mussorgsky's *Boris Godounov,* Debussy's *Prélude à L'Après-midi d'un Faune,* Manuel de Falla's *Fire Dance* and Honegger's *Symphony of Psalms* represent music.

The Seven Wonders of the World, *The crouching Scribe,* the Parthenon frieze, *l'Ange Souriant* at Rheims Cathedral, Botticelli's *Spring,* Michaelangelo's frescoes in the Sistine Chapel, *The Merchant Gisze* by Holbein, Rembrandt's *Bathsheba,* Vermeer's *Woman with a Turban,* El Greco's *Burial of Count d'Orgaz, The Portrait of Philip III* by Velasquez, Whistler's *Portrait of Thomas Carlyle* and Rodin's *St John the Baptist* may serve for literature.

Such masterpieces as these enforce our admiration and awe. Often they command an almost religious devotion, and we observe men of the highest intelligence making a positive cult of them. There are men of science, thoroughly rationalist in temperament, who are overwhelmed by Bach's Mass in B Minor; hard-headed business men who go into ecstasies over a twelfth century ivory: they fondle it, turn it over reverently in their hands and obviously extract a pleasure from it which is far greater than what we usually term the pleasures of life. Others are as though transfixed when they see the Parthenon for the first time; they hold their breath; they have tears in their eyes, and its beauty makes them tremble. On the other hand there are artists who are enthused by reading a biological work on the laws of heredity, and musicians who are thrilled by the science of wave mechanics onces they have read a clear description of its workings.

Thus the works of the creative artists are at hand throughout our everyday lives, or are there for us at those moments when their friendly assistance is most needed. They lift us above the pedestrian boredom of our days; they help us to suffer with patience the ills proper to our natural state; they give us new hope when we are in despair; they raise us up when we are about to sink; they encourage us in our enterprises; they are balm to our wounds; they allay our fears; and they are a charm against the malice of our destiny. In short, their claims to our regard and affection are legion.

Their never-failing and abundant benefits are the supreme justification of those rights their creation confers upon their authors.

4

The history of literary and artistic rights

We propose to deal first with what is known in France as the *droit d'auteur*, and then to go on to the international significance given to the rights involved by the Berne Convention and the American Copyright Laws.

The term 'author's rights' is the one usually employed now and it is tending to replace the expression 'literary and artistic property' because it establishes and stresses the special value attached to the person of the author himself, the word 'author' being used to embrace the creative artist generally.

The *droit d'auteur* is the exclusive right given by the law to the author of any artistic or literary work to derive profit from it where, when and how he pleases. We feel at once that it is conceived and established in a spirit of respect towards the person of the creative artist, and that his person is protected and honoured in his work. In addition to the law which defines and guarantees the material interests of the creative artist comes his moral right to ensure that there shall be no encroachment on the integrity of his work, and that his reputation and honour shall in no way suffer by the possible exploitation of his work against his will. The same right is transferred to his heirs under conditions which we shall discuss later.

Let us welcome immediately a tendency which is becoming more and more marked amongst the nations of the world to merge the pecuniary rights of the artist in his work with his moral rights. It is thus that the word 'property' attains its noblest sense; it is thus that the full extent of the Declaration of Human Rights becomes apparent when it proclaims that: 'Everyone has the right to the protection of the moral and material interests resulling from any scientific, literary or artistic production of which he is the author.'

Thus the rights of the creative artist appear to belong to two distinct spheres, the material and the moral, which now tend to merge. Moral and practical interests are being placed on the same level and treated with equal consideration. It is good to see that the Universal Declaration of Human Rights makes a special point of this equality. The spirit of man is recognized as a formal entity; this breath, this intangible something which no one has ever seen with his eyes or touched with his hands; this airy nothing from which all creative thought proceeds, which has given birth to all the spiritual achievements of mankind, including the exploration of the universe and the tentative attempts to explain life itself; this ethereal source of man's imagination and reflection now finds itself confirmed by law, accepted as an entity which none may mutilate, distort or exploit with impunity. No man may now steal the fruits of another's soul. Popular morality has always condemned the robbing of a neighbour's orchard, and if Hercules is nevertheless admired for having stolen the apples of the Hesperides it is only because it was an enterprise of exceptional difficulty involving the killing of the fearsome dragon Ladon which guarded them. But mankind had to wait a long time before the fruits of the human spirit were also protected by law.

Imagine the fate of a manuscript even of the importance of the *De Natura Rerum* of Lucretius. Its text, embodying an immense accumulation of knowledge and wisdom, written word by word and composed verse by verse from the individual genius of its author, was preserved only on fragile sheets of papyrus, or perhaps the bark of the maple or lime, and then abandoned to its fate. It could be plagiarized; its ideas could be stolen; it could even be made to say what its author never said. And it enjoyed no formal protection whatever. It was very fortunate that Cicero, a friend of Lucretius, obtained possession of the text after the death of the young poet, for he had copies made and taught his age to appreciate its beauty.

For centuries the only protection enjoyed by written works came from the respect in which civilized men held them. They were not legally protected in any way, though they represented perhaps the most precious assets accumulated by man. With nothing more in favour of their survival than the high regard of comparatively few men they had to face the stern test of time. And what terrible risks they ran merely on account of the fragility of the materials on which they were recorded prior to the invention of printing! We should not forget that the writings of Plato, Hesiod and Demosthenes were inscribed on a kind of papyrus; that the *Eclogues* of Virgil, the orations of Cicero and the satires of Juvenal were recorded on the bark of the lime. *Liber,* the Latin word for book, means the inner bark of a tree, which was the material in current use for recording texts. The great library at Alexandria, so famous in the ancient world, was really only a collection of papyrus scrolls, and the fire destroyed them with ease.

In addition to the danger of destruction by fire and the other elements, the writings of the ancients were exposed to the malignity of the envious and the treachery of the forger. There is more than one reference in Juvenal and Martial to the wrongs suffered by great writers, whose ideas were pillaged and plagiarized to adorn the work of mediocrities.

Listen to the bitter plaint of Martial:

> *Fama refert nostros te, Fidentine, libellos*
> *Non aliter populo quam recitare tuos.*
> *Si mea vis dici, gratis tibi carmina mittam.*
> *Si dici tua vis, haec eme, ne mea sint.*

And again:

> *Indice non opus est nostris, nec vindice libris;*
> *Stat contra, dicitque tibi tua pagina: fur es.*

Fur es! Thou art a thief!

And there are the verses ascribed by Titus Claudius Donatus to the author of the *Aeneid,* in which Virgil sighs ruefully:

Hos ego versiculos feci, tulit alter honores;
Sic vos non vobis nidificatis aves...

It was I who composed these fugitive verses,
    Whilst another took the honour and profit.
Thus, O birds of the air, you built your nests,
    But for others.

How well these ancient complaints and reproaches serve as a
justification of our modern laws protecting literary property! How
well they express the indignation of the author at attempts to
plagiarize his work, to steal the child of his thought! *Fur es!* Thou
art a thief! But it was nothing but a cry of helpless indignation.
There was no law to protect the victim or punish the offender.
Without the patrons of Athens and the Maecenases and Popes
of Rome, without the potentates of the east and the sovereigns
of Christendom, the creative artists of the ancient world would
have been helpless; materially they could not have existed; morally
they would have been exposed to every iniquity. Pericles saw
to it that Anaxagoras, Socrates and Protagoras should want for
nothing and that the cares of everyday life should not hamper
their great labours. And it was Pericles, too, who gave Phideas his
patronage and encouraged the builders of the Parthenon, the
Propylaea and the Temple of Eleusis. Maecenas, the Minister of
Augustus, used his wealth to encourage the splendid talent of
Horace and Lucius Varius, the man who saved the manuscript
of the *Aeneid,* which the dying Virgil was about to destroy. The
Emperor Charlemagne liberally opened his privy purse to support
his men of letters. And it was thanks to the good offices of
Pope Leo X the magnificent gifts of Raphael, Michelangelo,
Ariosto and Machiavelli were able to develop freely, whilst Louis
XIV gave Molière freedom to ridicule the morals of his day and
even to mock the courtiers of his own palace at Versailles. The
list of patrons of the arts and letters is a long one, and all of them
deserve our thanks and gratitude for contributing so magnificently
to the birth and development of the masterpieces which did so
much to encourage a love of beauty amongst men before there
were laws to protect the rights of the world's creative artists.

Certainly, many of the world's masterpieces were created in
misery. The history of art and literature is crowded with starving

poets and painters whose ability went unrecognized during their miserable lives, and although in his *Ploutos* Aristophanes makes Poverty claim that she inspires great and beautiful things, the truth is that although inspiration needs neither bread, nor a hearth nor a roof over its head, talent needs security if it is to develop to the full.

It is this security which our modern laws of copyright seek to give to writers, musicians and artists. Towards the end of the eighteenth century, after the splendid flowering of art and letters which had spread over the whole of Europe for more than a hundred years, it became clear that the creative artist could no longer rely solely on the patronage and protection of the Prince.

The invention of printing, for instance, had turned the work of the author into a commercial affair, and it had often suffered at the hands of several printers each exploiting the same book with the result that none of them were in a position to print and sell an edition large enough to show a satisfactory profit. Thanks to the intervention of kings and princes some sort of order was established by granting to a particular printer the exclusive right to print this or that book, with the result that writers began to find themselves sought after by printers desirous of obtaining the exclusive right to publish their work. We can say, in fact, that during the course of the seventeenth century the art of writing began to develop into the profession of letters. Certainly, no one had yet begun to talk about the rights of authors, but authors and the printer-publishers of the day began to agree together concerning the financial conditions of publication, though this generally reduced itself as far as the authors were concerned to the outright sale of a manuscript for a sum of money which we should now regard as a very inadequate return. The paucity of such remuneration played into the hands of the Prince who, by granting pensions, was able to keep poets, playwrights and historians in his service as courtiers devoting their talents to the celebration of his virtues. Creative artists thus became royal poets and royal historians. The poets devoted their muse to immortalizing the victories of their patron and acclaiming the birth of his children. Poetry and even history prostituted themselves with little resentment, even playfully: an ode to a virtuous king one day, a battle epic the next. At least the poet was spared the pangs of hunger. It was not particularly dignified, but at the same time it was also not altogether base. However, with the development of liberty of thought and freedom of expression that sort of thing could not go on indefinitely.

It was in Great Britain, always in the vanguard of the battle for human liberties, that the movement began which liberated the creative artist and assured him financial independence. On April 10th, 1710, an Act of Parliament, bearing the assent of Queen Anne and the long and hopeful title 'An Act for the Encouragement of Learning by Vesting the Copies of Printed Books in the Authors or Purchasers of such Copies during Times therein mentioned', was promulgated. For the first time in legal history the author appeared as a juridical entity accompanied by a reference to his rights in copies of his work. This fruitful innovation was inspired by a desire to encourage learning, and the same praiseworthy motive led from the year 1783 onwards to the adoption of Copyright laws by the majority of the States of the young republic of America. It is with some emotion that we now read in the laws relating to the rights of the author adopted by the States of Massachusetts, New Hampshire and Rhode Island that thenceforth there was to be no property more securely reserved to the enjoyment of its owner than that which derived from his intellectual labours. The laws passed by some of the American States even paid moving tribute to the creative artist himself. The one adopted by North Carolina for instance declared: 'Whereas nothing is more strictly a man's own than the fruit of his study.' In 1783 New Jersey law proclaimed that knowledge embellished human nature, rendered honour to the nation and worked for the general good of humanity, and added that it was in full conformity with the principles of justice that writers should derive profit from the sale of their works. In 1785 the States of Virginia, Maryland and Connecticut adopted legislation couched in the same elevated tone. And finally, in 1790, the Government of the United States promulgated the first Federal Copyright Law.

In July 1793, speaking to the Convention in favour of a bill protecting the rights of the author and dealing with literary and artistic property, the French Deputy Le Chapelier, declared that such property was the most sacred, the most inviolable and the most personal of all property.

Thus the truth that the creative artist is the sole owner of the fruits of his own labours gradually became accepted by the gen-

eral public and embodied in the law and usages of the time, and
it included not only a recognition of his moral and material
rights but also the propriety of making all encroachments on the
one or the other subject to the jurisdiction of the courts.

The right of the author to his work had ceased to be merely
a matter of spiritual parentage; it had become a property right.

5

The protection of literary, dramatic and musical property

Many textual interpretations confirmed by many judgments
were necessary before a satisfactory definition of literary property
was arrived at. The French law of 1793 applied to 'writings of
all kinds', but the expression was so vague that it could be made
to include literary tasks set to schoolboys or theatre programmes.
Is was agreed that in order to be entitled to protection a literary
work must be a product of the mind. But, after all, the task-work
of a schoolboy can be the production of an eager young mind
intent on translating Livy or demonstrating some geometrical
theorem. And a theatre programme can demand skill, taste and
reflection from the man who draws it up, and they are all at-
tributes of the mind.

What is then a production of the mind? Where written work
is concerned it means a text which reflects the personality of its
author. But what is a reflection, and what is a personality? To
understand the meaning of a reflection we must be acquainted
with the reality which is reflected. A reflection is not a definition;
it is merely the adventitious repetition of that reality. And what
of the personality of the author? Is it possible to recognize the
individual emanation of the author from the text of a museum
catalogue or from a guide book?

It is easy to see the difficulties which faced, and still face, those
whose task it is to interpret the law. To begin with, it was necessary to ignore the literary value of the text to be protected, and
thus the editor of a commercial hand-book and the author of
an income-tax guide were placed on the same level as a d'Annun-
zio or a Steinbeck; quite rightly, too, because both the hand-book
and the guide are productions of the mind just as *The Child of*

Pleasure and *The Grapes of Wrath* are. No distinction is made between the author of a text-book on gardening and the author of a treatise on philosophy. The translation is granted the same protection as the original work; the annotations are protected equally with the annotated text. The compiler and the creator are placed on exactly the same footing. The law takes no account of the critical spirit; it is not drafted to satisfy a Carlyle or a Sainte-Beuve. It is concerned only with written texts and not with their merit or their purpose. Written text as such is protected by law. The law concerns itself with the .text itself and not with the idea of which it is the expression. The text may be that of an almanac, a book of cookery recipes or an official year-book; provided that its form is such as to bear the impress of its author's personality it is entitled to the protection of the law. It goes without saying that such protection does not apply to the price-list of a business house, to a publicity prospectus or to a telephone directory. Thus in order to be outside the protection of the law of copyright a text must lack all originality; it must have neither individual face nor form, neither heart nor soul. But even in a concert programma it will usually be possible to find something or other which expresses the personality of the man who drew it up.

To tell the truth it is not at all easy to discover any form of written text outside the provisions of the law of copyright, which even goes so far as to include compilers and anthologists, who can hardly be said to be the authors of the collections they publish, though they are treated as such whilst the real authors disappear in the shadow of those who have edited, dissected and arranged their work. No law is more generous or extends to a greater number of beneficiaries; and no law is more democratic. The genius and the mere artisan of letters are both taken under its wing, and Paul Claudel counts no more in its eyes than the author of a rhyming dictionary.

The law completely ignores the idea which has inspired the writing. Plagiarism is none of its business. Its general tendency is to regard ideas as the property of whoever takes them up and passes them through his own brain to the world. Their materialisation in the form of written signs is all that comes under its jurisdiction. Einstein, for example, first established the principle of relativity, but only the works in which he personally sets out the theory and comments on it are his own in the eyes of the law. His discovery itself has given rise to a great variety of publications over which he has no rights whatever.

The law sets such store by the protection of literary property that it is extremely punctilious with regard to property rights in a title. The title must be an essential part of the work protected; it must give the work an individuality, render it, so to speak, a juridical entity. At the same time, however, the title must not be one which has been common property in the libraries of the world for ages. For instance, if two contemporary authors both publish a work entitled *Iphigenia,* or perhaps *Daphnis and Chloe,* neither is in a position to reproach the other. But authors are notoriously sensitive, and one might publish a work entitled *Eve and Adam,* or perhaps *Juliet and Romeo,* and, because he has changed the usual order, feel that he is entitled to proceed against any other author using the same inversion. But in its wisdom the law has determined that a title shall not be regarded as a product of the mind unless it is essentially part and parcel of the work it has been used to identify, and that an author shall not produce a title and demand protection for it unless the title is accompanied by the publication of the book whose title it is, or is given a publicity which it is impossible to ignore. However, if an author uses a title which is liable to be confused with the title of a book which is already published, and if that title is given to a book which is similar in subject to the general theme of the already published book, then the author in question himself encroaches on the literary property of another and is liable to the process of law. Thus if an author published a novel entitled *Poil de Navet* dealing with the fate of a child ill-treated by his family, then he would lay himself open to proceedings on the part of the heirs of Jules Renard, the author of *Poil de Carotte.*

And this brings us to a consideration of fraudulent representation in literature.

Literary plagiarism is robbery camouflaged by one or two personal touches on the part of the robber designed to conceal the origin of the ill-gotten goods and to deceive the reader. Fraudulent representation is plain robbery. The law ignores plagiarism and leaves it to public opinion to condemn the plagiarist, but it provides sanctions against fraudulent representation. When an author introduces borrowed material into his work without quoting the source he is guilty of plagiarism. There is the well-known case of Alexandre Dumas who, in his haste to provide impatient editors with instalments, included whole chapters of Walter Scott without arousing the suspicion of the average reader. Dumas was probably tremendously amused at the deception and regarded his large-scale borrowings as little more than a practical joke. The case of Virgil, who borrowed entire verses by the poet Quintus Ennius and incorporated them into the text of his own *Aeneid*, would have been a more serious matter but for the fact that Virgil openly acknowledged the robbery and boasted that he had 'rescued the pearls from the midden of Ennius'. Many contemporary authors have been deceived by their own memories and led quite innocently to introduce the words of others, forgotten but still present in their unconscious minds, into their own work. But these are venial errors, and though they may border on plagiarism they have nothing in common with fraudulent representation.

Fraudulent representation necessarily involves the possibility of confusion between two works. An example taken from the history of literature is that of Leonardo Bruni d'Arezzo, a famous Hellenist and Latin scholar of the early fifteenth century, a man whose knowledge and judgement had won him the highest reputation. When his work *De bello italico adversus Gothos* was published twenty years after his death it was seen to be practically nothing but a translation of volumes V, VI and VII of the *Historiae* of Procopius, the Byzantine historian. Here we have a clear case of fraudulent representation. But there are still baser examples. For instance, an author receives a manuscript from a beginner asking for his judgement; he declares later that he has lost it; he leaves it in a drawer for some time and then publishes it under his own name almost untouched. That, of course, is downright robbery.

What about parody? Does that come under a similar head? Not at all, and it is even something of an honour for an author to find his work parodied. If it is really true that the *Batrachomyomachia*, a well-known parody of the *Iliad*, is actually the work of Homer himself then it is pleasant to think that an author should be able to criticise his own work so severely, even to the point of cruelty, but the tradition which ascribes 'The Battle of the Frogs and the Mice's to a brother of Queen Artemisia seems more credible. Not many authors have made fun of themselves! it is a form of heroism rarely met with amongst creative artists. The *Cid* of Corneille, Racine's *Andromaque* and Voltaire's *Zaire* have all been parodied at one time or the other. English, Spanish and Italian literature all have their parodists. Shakespeare himself has been parodied. Both the poems and plays of Victor Hugo have been parodied. Such is literary fame.

Another consequence of literary fame is for an author to find himself quoted. An author whose talent is recognized and who is regarded as an authority will almost certainly see his words reproduced in the form of quotations in critical essays, in literary textbooks, in theses, in anthologies and, quite generally, in places where it is flattering for an author to find his work quoted.

At the same time he has no rights over these quotations, because as soon as his work has been published, i.e. given to the public, everyone has the right to express his opinion of it in word or writing and to support his judgement by quoting, more or less at length, from the work he is praising or criticising. Most authors are only too glad to see themselves quoted at length in anthologies, text-books and, above all, dictionaries. That is one of the little weaknesses of the creative artist.

Up to the present we have discussed the rights of authors in connection with their books or pamphlets, but it makes no difference whatever if the work is in the form, say, of newspaper articles. The rights of the journalist are the same as those of the novelist, the philosopher, the historian and the scientist. And how could it well be otherwise? The journalist turns his hand to all kinds of writing, and the newspaper which prints his work is something like a miniature encyclopaedia dealing day after day with a great variety of problems: home and foreign politics, science, sociology, economics, law, literature, the fine arts, agriculture, industry, commerce and so on. Whether they are dailies or weeklies, periodicals have a multifarious character which gives them a special position in the law relating to literary property. For one thing, a title, just like the title of a book, enjoys no protection unless it is accompanied by text. A title cannot be reserved indefinitely, and the length of time during which it may be so reserved varies in the law of different countries, after which it may be taken by any one who wishes to use it provided that its previous usage has been definitely abandoned. And for another, editors of and contributors to a periodical are just as much authors as those who write books, and their rights are protected in just the same way. The permission of the author of an article, or perhaps that of the periodical in which it has been published, must first be obtained before the article in question may be reproduced elsewhere. Further, text entitled to protection must be a product of the mind of its author and not a mere news item or a simple piece of political, financial or sporting information, etc.

Of course, it is quite true that from the pen of certain journalists even a news item takes on a form which is so personal that one can well refer to it as a product of the mind. There was a period in France when a leading daily published news stories which were so skilfully condensed into a few lines, and so elegantly phrased that they were really epigrams worthy to rank with those in which the Greek poets of Alexandria were accustomed to comment on the events of the day. In this case the writer's style was as good as a signature. He certainly had rights in such work, but he never made use of them. He was far too amused at the exercise of his talent to bother about obtaining any payment other than that from the newspaper to which he contributed the daily fruits of his genius for brevity. This authentic successor to the court poets of the Ptolemys was Félix Fénéon, who was also well known as a leading art critic at the beginning of the century. It is no easy matter to give a personal touch to a brief report of a common assault, a robbery, a fire or a street accident, and young journalists, 'cub reporters', are put on to such trivial matters in order to sharpen their talents.

Newspapers are, in fact, nurseries of literary talent, and many great writers, both in Europe and America, began their careers working for them, writing short news items on the minor events of the day, and so on, and there are few schools better able to encourage the gift of observation and the talent for literary composition.

The life of the individual and the life of the nation are both becoming more and more like a novel. The press, the wireless — and now television — bring the outside world into our private lives with a wealth of detail and a variety of incident which stir the emotions in the very best and most effective tradition of our contemporary imaginative authors. The press in particular has greatly increased our curiosity and enhanced our impatience. Every day in every house in both town and country men's eyes are glued to newsprint and their ears are cocked for the wireless news, eager to lap up the next instalment in the great novel of life. Newspapers are read today as Dickens, Balzac and Washington Irving were read formerly. A month's reading of a morning newspaper with an evening newspaper in support is equivalent to reading a long imaginative work in thirty chapters. Do the journalist's rights as an author like any author need any further justification?

A curious chapter in the story of literary property is that which deals with letters and the respective rights of the writer on the one hand and the recipient on the other.

The technical device of fictitious correspondence has been very popular in literature. French literature for example has the *Provinciales* of Pascal, the *Lettres Persanes* of Montesquieu, the *Nouvelle Héloïse* of Rousseau, the *Lettres de mon Moulin* of Alphonse Daudet and the *Amitié Amoureuse* of Madame Leconte du Nouy. In English literature Samuel Richardson's *Clarissa Harlowe* consists of letters supposedly written by that unfortunate young lady to her friend Miss Howe. And the *Religious Letters* written by Gogol during his stay in Rome also belong to the same school.

We have mentioned these fictional works in connection with real correspondence in order to indicate the popularity of the epistolary form, which is still more attractive when the letters in question were written by men and women who have found a place in the affection of posterity. No form of literature is more spontaneous, more impulsive and less deliberate than the letter, though some letter writers have unfortunately written with an eye to future publication rather than for the exclusive benefit of their correspondents. Madame de Sévigné was after literary success when she spread herself out in her letters to her daughter, and it is no use Mérimée's trying to appear so sensitive and tender in his *Lettres à une Inconnue,* because we are never in doubt that in writing them he was thinking more of posterity than of the *inconnue.* This sort of thing makes the reader a little embarrassed and ill at ease; it smacks too much of deception, even trickery. But how agreeable, sometimes even moving, are the letters taken from the box or drawer in which they have been piously kept by the recipient and given to the world after the death of their author! How much should we know of Cicero the man and of the private background to his public life but for the 380 letters he wrote to his friend Titus Pomponius Atticus, letters which have come down to us just as they were dictated in all the impulsiveness of his spirit and the warmth of his heart? And there are other letters of Cicero also extant, some 900 in all. They cover the everyday life of Rome under Catilina, Pompey, Caesar and Octavian. They represent the story of a man's life, a great work of literature drawn direct from the wellsprings of life. The 9,000 letters of Voltaire are of a different kind, full of sharp gibes, profound reflections, lamentations, attitudinizing, confidences, maulings and caressings, and quite as much gall as honey, the whole representing a rich moral, political and literary harvest ontstanding even in his vast literary performance.

There is no doubt whatever that letter-writing is just as much a literary form as novel writing or memoirs, and the writers of letters have just the same rights in their work. But the difficulty begins when we come to consider the rights of those to whom the letters were written. A letter is like a gift made to the one to whom it is addressed; once it is in his hands it is indubitably his property. If he pleases he can tear it up or throw it in the fire. It ceases to be his property only if the author has specified that it shall be destroyed, or if is written in specific confidence, in which case its contents may not be communicated to any other person with impunity. The military authorities, for instance, attach great importance to the superscription 'secret' which they put on certain letters and documents both in times of war and peace, and we know from experience what dramatic consequences can follow from the deliberate, or even accidental, communication of the contents to others. Certain love-letters are just as secret, and to divulge their contents can produce equally dramatic consequences.

The law recognizes that the recipient of a letter is the lawful owner of the letter as such, but that the right to publish its contents is reserved to the author himself. It is not often that the correspondence of a well-known man is published during his life, and it is usually his heirs who take the responsibility for posthumous publication, and it should be stressed that neither during the letter-writer's life nor after his death has the recipient any right whatever — in French law at least — to publish the contents of such letters. The legal position with regard to a letter is the same as that of a manuscript: an author may take it into his head to present the manuscript of an unpublished work to a friend, a collector, or even a museum. In such a case the friend, collector or museum would enjoy property rights in the manuscript as such, but none at all in its text. By a strange paradox there have been cases in which authors, having written letters and omitted to keep copies, have approached the recipients with a view to publication, only to find the owners of the letters unwilling to communicate the text or lend the letters, insisting on their right to retain them in their possession as their absolute property. Now if the authors in question had kept copies, or were able to remember the texts, then they could have published without recourse to the recipients and drawn a profit from the venture in the ordinary way.

The publication of letters often proves a valuable source of income. The heirs of famous writers have drawn unexpected revenues from the publication of their letters to friends, often quite trifling affairs. In France we have seen the market swamped with letters written by Marcel Proust, some of them consisting only of a few words in reply to an invitation to dinner, or accompanying a gift of flowers. We have also seen the publication of letters in verse written by Guillaume Apollinaire to a young lady he was attached to during the years of his military service. More than 800 years have passed from the time those half-passionate, half-prudent letters passed between Héloïse and Abélard until the publication of the love-letters of Victor Hugo and Juliette Drouet, and in that long period French literature has been enriched with innumerable tender documents. Those of Julie de Lespinasse addressed to the Comte de Guibert, published incidentally and rather touchingly by his widow, will always be read. And readers will return again and again to those of Chateaubriand to Madame Recamier, to observe the varied moods of a heart constantly a prey to new passions.

A lover has, of course, the ordinary rights of an author in his love-letters, but it will never be considered admirable or desirable that he should make use of them for the purpose of publication.

'Confidential journals' and 'intimate diaries' fall into somewhat the same category as such letters, but nevertheless they are often published and the heirs of men who have recorded their most secret thoughts and acts have frequently not hesitated to assert their rights in them. Not many authors have such a taste for

the public confessional that during their lifetime they publish
the 'journals' which record both their joys and sorrows, the nights
of sleeplessness which have tortured them, the number of cigarettes
they have smoked in a day, or the mood for work they found
themselves in on waking. The 'Journal' of André Gide, which,
incidentally, did much to win him the Nobel Prize for literature,
is from this point of view a monument of physiological confidences. Up to the present nothing of its kind — and certainly not
anything published during the life of its author — has ever been
so frank. Day after day the reader is permitted to observe the
author wrestling with his headaches, his lack of appetite, his tired-
ness, his laziness or, on the contrary, an over-abundance of vitality
which occasionally leads him into singular aberrations. And all
of it is treated at great length in the daily jottings of the great
French author. But such is the objectivity of the law on literary
property that the description of a stomach ache, once published,
may well bring to the voluble sufferer more than enough to pay
the fees of the doctor called in to relieve the pain. Frankly, it is
rather comic to see an author making money out of a stomach
ache which troubled him only for a few moments of a long life.
However, the law is so anxious to ensure that authors are not
robbed of their just due that even this is possible.

Incidentally, the style of these diaries and journals is generally
poverty stricken; what is usually called a telegraphic style from
which the personal pronoun and all the refinements of good
writing are banished. In the *Carnet* of Benjamin Constant, which
is extremely laconic, we read: 'Business with Charlotte in Geneva
(February 1811) ... Madame de Staël brings me back to Coppet ...
Struggle with my father, Charlotte and Madame de Staël ... Miserable life ... Charlotte unsuccessful in everything in Lausanne ...
Dinner with Madame de Staël at d'Arlens ... Scenes ...' Taine,
who quotes these entries, adds: 'These few pages of the journal
referring to Benjamin Constant's love life tell us more about it,
even in their summary form, than all our speculations.' That is
very true. Coupled with what we know of the extreme sensitiveness
of the Swiss writer such laconic and tragic entries as 'Miserable
life ... Scenes' do tell us more than the longest explanations. That
is why it is only right and proper that an author should have full
rights in his journals and diaries. The public has always been
greatly interested in any intimate notes of this kind; consider, for

instance, the great success of Tolstoy's journal, and that of the Genevan philosopher Amiel, and of the *Carnets* of Maurice Barrès. However, it is not to this kind of egocentric note that we must look for his historical or biographical anecdotes. We know more about Louis XIV from the *Journal* of Dangeau than from the *Memoirs* of Saint-Simon because Saint-Simon pushes himself into the foreground at every opportunity whilst Dangeau writes with laconic succinctness and objectivity. Dangeau's note on the death of Corneille has often been quoted: 'That good fellow Corneille is dead. He was renowned for his plays. He has left a vacant place at the Academy.'

The servants of great men have sometimes kept diaries. The entries are often naïve, but at the same time they provide material for the psychological studies which it is now the fashion to devote to great men. The recollections of Constant, Napoleon's valet, have contributed something to our knowledge of the character and nature of the French Emperor. Thus there is no reason why a valet should not become an author and enjoy all the advantages of his new rôle. And there are many other kinds of people who keep diaries: actors and actresses, sailors, explorers and soldiers (For example the *Cahiers* of Captain Cognet and the innumerable diaries kept, often by simple soldiers, during the 1914-18 war). Prisoners of war have kept their diaries, ordinary convicts too, including men condemned to death. They all enjoy the protection of the laws relating to literary property.

The law is vigilant. Like Argus it has a hundred eyes, and half are always awake whilst the other half sleep. It watches over everything that comes in black and white from the press, and its criterion is the part played by the mind and the imagination. It is as just as it is discerning, and it does all honour to its noble and generous origin by granting protection only to such works as are products of the mind and the imagination and stamped with the personality of their author.

But what about literary creations which are given to the world verbally? Speeches, lectures and sermons for example have something of both a work of art and a work of literature, and the law protects them all as soon as they are printed. That goes without saying. However, it is possible to conceive a case in which a listener has such an excellent memory that he is able to recall almost word for word something he has listened to and that he then steals the thoughts or words of an orator or preacher and uses them for his own financial benefit. Or, for example, an auditor could take down a university lecture in shorthand or in stenotype. In both cases he would become liable to the original author if he delivered the text again in public or if he caused it to be printed, broadcast or otherwise reproduced. The only exception made in French law applies to political speeches, legal pleadings and indictments. Speeches delivered in parliament and at meetings of municipal councils, or at official meetings and ceremonies, are presented to public opinion; they are 'published' by the fact that they are pronounced for the use of public opinion, which has the right to judge them and approve or reject them. By the same token the press has the right to reproduce them in whole or in part without reference to their authors and without the payment of any fee or royalty. It would be a different matter, however, if an individual chose to publish them in a collection or to include them as a whole in any literary work for his own profit. Legal pleadings and indictments may be reproduced without fee in legal publications and in the press, but the same freedom is not granted to publishers or compilers.

French literature is particularly rich in sermons and legal pleadings. Bossuet, Flechier, Bourdaloue and Massillon in the seventeenth and eighteenth centuries, Dupanloup, Lacordaire and Ravignan in the nineteenth were the notable French preachers, whilst forensic eloquence is represented by the great advocate Patru in the seventeenth century (incidentally, Patru made such an engaging speech of thanks to the Academy on his election that its members subsequently decided that in future all newly-elected members should address a speech of thanks to them for their election), and by de Sèze, the defender of Louis XVI, Berryer, Lachaud, Jules Favre and Henri-Robert. Parliament has its eloquence, too, and here we think above all of William Pitt, Fox, Robert Peel, Disraeli and Gladstone, all past masters of the sublimest form of human expression. The protection of the spoken word is wholly justified by the brilliance which such men have added to it, and the law grants it freely, protecting the rights of the author even in the public reading of his words. Some writers have made money by reading their books in public. Charles Dickens, for instance, gave a series of readings in the United States at which Mr Pickwick, Nicholas Nickleby and Barnaby Rudge earned him large sums of money. French law goes so far as to forbid the readings of a book to a public audience, even if it is a non-profit-making venture, without the permission of the author.

Thus, as we have seen, literary work, whether written or spoken, is very well protected.

Translations enjoy just the same protection as the original works. Once he has come to an agreement with the author, or the author's heirs, on the point, a translator enjoys the sole rights in the text of his translation. There are great translators just as there are great writers. Whilst remaining faithful to the meaning of the original text, their translations are stamped with the impress of their own taste and informed with their intimate knowledge of the author's thoughts. Baudelaire, for instance, translated Edgar Allan Poe's *Tales of the Grotesque and Arabesque,* and the translation was a masterpiece. As a relaxation André Gide translated Tagore and Conrad. In all languages there are celebrated translations of Homer, Dante and Shakespeare. Unquestionably, translation is a form of literature all its own, and in consequence it deserves the same consideration and the same advantages as original work.

What we have said above concerning written work applies equally to theatrical work, except that the performance of a play gives its author special rights. The playwright enjoys double rights: rights in the publication of his play and rights in its performance. The writing of a tragedy, a comedy or a simple sketch is only the beginning; after that it must be staged and given an appropriate setting, and actors must interpret it. Thus in addition to the author's rights there are the rights of the producer, the director, the actors, the designers, the costumiers, and even the Government and the local municipality perhaps. A play like the graceful and ethereal *Pelléas et Mélisande* of Maeterlinck advances to its ultimate production in a cloud of agreements contracts, estimates, bills and vouchers of all sorts which would certainly detract from its poetic appeal if the audience had to think of it all whilst watching Pelléas celebrating the lovely hair of Mélisande. Fortunately, however, no one has to bother about it all except the producer and all the other back-stage personalities — and occasionally the author. It is a hard job to materialize the emanations of genius in the form of pecuniary rights, but, after all, life, in the words of Joyce's Dedalus, is 'a swirling torrent of muddy water on which the apple trees strew their delicate blossom'.

In France, where the theatre has enjoyed the steadily growing favour of the public since the middle ages, the rights of playwrights were defined and established by law even before those of the poets and philosophers. A law promulgated in July 1791 provided that 'dramatic works may not be presented in any public theatre with- out the formal written consent of the author, his heirs or assigns.' Like the other laws of the French Republic, this was a strict enact- ment and it provided for the confiscation of the receipts of any producer whose enthusiasm, impatience or dishonesty might lead him to produce a play without the consent of the author, to whose benefit the confiscated sum was then applied.

What is 'presentation' in the eyes of the law? It is the represen- tation of a literary work by living characters moving, speaking or singing on the stage, creating the illusion of movement and con- versation in real life, in short, an attempt to reproduce from an author's text sometimes the humour, sometimes the pathos of past or present everyday life, lending it perhaps the veil of fairy- like enchantment or the arabesques of the dance. In order that there shall be 'representation' in the eyes of the law there must be a performance in public. Representation stands in the same relation to a play as publication does to a book or execution to a piece of music. If the piece of music involves living characters singing or dancing then it is represented and not executed. For instance, Beethoven's *Pathetic Sonata* is executed, whilst Mozart's *Marriage of Figaro* is represented. The only exception to this rule concerns pieces of music with choirs; despite the presence of living persons on the stage, or around the organ of a church, such pieces are said to be executed because the choristers are not characters On the other hand, a ballet is represented although it is not ac - companied by song, because the dancers on the stage are characters. In short, a representation is a spectacle; it can be silent if it is mimed, with one voice if it is a monologue, or with lifeless char- acters if it is performed by marionettes.

The theatre is as old as mankind itself, and following up our study of the rights of the author we can say that there were authors even before man adopted the artifice of speech. Amongst the first wandering groups of primitive men there were undoubtedly some better endowed than others with the art of gesture and grimace. They made pantomime and they danced before man was able to fashion stones or trap animals. Man has a natural inclination to act. He uses all the resources of a fertile imagination to express his feelings and convey them to his public. If he is sad or in pain he groans, sheds tears, moves his lips wildly, throws his arms into the air or lets them fall to his sides; and if he is filled with joy he shows it by a series of rapid expirations accompanied by a rapid jerking of the shoulders, bending of the knees, stamping of the feet, the pressing of his hands to his ribs, and generally by a contraction of the muscular system not far removed from a convulsion. It is not difficult to believe that such violent movement and loud cries to express emotions are a survival from the days when man was unable to express his already rich and varied emotions and sensations in words. Human society has always evolved from day to day as though on a stage; it plays a part without knowing it, and if men love the theatre so much it is because they see in it a reflection of their own behaviour.

It should be clearly realized that an author can exercise his property rights only in respect of a public performance of his work whether the audience pays to witness it or not. If, for instance, someone arranged a performance of, say, Edmond Rostand's play *La Samaritaine* in his home to an audience of friends, Rostand's heirs would have no recourse against him and it would not even be necessary to ask their permission. But if, on the other hand, some charitably inclined person, struck perhaps by the symbolic title of the piece, wished to arrange a performance in his home for the benefit of some charity then he would first have to obtain permission.

Today composers in particular are very sensitive and vigilant in respect of their rights. *O tempora, O mores!* We are far removed from the days when they abandoned themselves freely to their inspiration with no other aim than to express the innermost urges of their souls and without expecting any greater reward than to observe the pleasure it gave to others.

On a café terrace two street singers, accompanied perhaps by a guitar, give the customers a song or two from their repertoire, then, cap in hand, they go from table to table to collect their reward. Very likely they have sung one or two popular song hits all the rage at the time. But if an official of a musical rights society happened to be passing he would be perfectly within his rights if he approached the two performers and demanded royalties on behalf of his clients the composers, for in the eyes of the law there has been a public performance.

July 14th is the National Day of France, and on that day French people make merry and dance almost everywhere; in the towns they even dance on the streets and in the squares. Small orchestras instal themselves on specially erected platforms at appropriate points and play dance music to the happy crowds. But day of national rejoicing though it is, the composers still demand their royalties on every waltz, fox-trot or rumba played.

For two or three days at a time travelling fairs fill the village squares and urban fair grounds with their menageries, roundabouts, shooting galleries and swings, and a discordant barrage of music assails the ear of the visitor. But even in all this noise and confusion it is very unlikely that the composer's musical rights go under.

Even when carillons are ringing out gaily from church belfrys musical rights have to be paid to the composer of the tune performed, unless the musical copyright happens to have lapsed.

Societies for the collection of authors, playrights and composers royalties maintain a highly-efficient network of control in order to keep track of the many ways in which the public makes use of the work of their members. Their officials are constantly on the alert, and they seem possessed of a special sense. They study the newspapers, check up on the programmes of celebrations and festivals, and — it goes without saying — nothing that is sung or spoken on the screen, on the wireless or on gramophone records escapes their attention. When we read the solemn proclamation in the Universal Declaration of Human Rights that 'Everyone is entitled to the protection of the moral and material interests deriving from any scientific, literary or artistic work of which he is the author' we may rest assured that it is more than the expression of a pious hope; he is not merely entitled to but he is assured protection — at least in all countries which recognize the right of a creative artist to dispose freely of the product of his mind.

An anecdote is told which effectively illustrates the care with which the rights of creative artists are looked after by the appropriate societies. One day a poorly-dressed man presented himself at the office of a benevolent fund attached to a French society of composers, asking for assistance and saying that in better days he had been a member of the society as a song writer and had always paid his subscriptions regularly. 'My work met with no success,' he declared sadly, 'and I have fallen on evil days so that now I have no roof over my head and don't know where my next meal is coming from.' The treasurer of the benevolent fund was about to give him a small sum of money when suddenly he paused. 'What did you say your name was?' he inquired. The applicant repeated it. 'Wait here just a moment, will you?' said the treasurer and he left the room. A few minutes later he returned with the chief accountant of the society who greeted the poor fellow with the words: 'So there you are at last, Mr so-and-so. We've been looking for you for years. We've written you letter after letter, but they've always come back marked: "Gone away. Address unknown." We've been in touch with your friends, but they didn't even know whether you were dead or alive.'

'If it's about my overdue subscriptions,' said the suppliant nervously, I'm afraid ... '

'Nothing of the sort,' interrupted the chief accountant, 'We've just deducted them from your account, and by this time it's become quite a big one. Didn't you know?'

The unfortunate — or shall we now say fortunate? — man then learned that one of his last songs had enjoyed a great popular success, had been sung everywhere and even used on gramophone records, and that all the time the society had been collecting his royalties, which now amounted to several hundred thousand francs. The society knew what the composer himself did not know.

This is the sort of work performed by the Société des Gens de Lettres de France, which was founded in 1836 by Victor Hugo, Balzac and a number of other authors, and it keeps numerous agents at work both in France and abroad to look after the interests of its members whose work is used in the press or on the wireless, etc. In the same way the Société des Auteurs Dramatiques collects royalties for its members on the public performance of their works no matter where or when. One French playwright, arriving by aeroplane from Paris in the capital of a South-American State, discovered to his surprise that one of his plays was being performed there. He had known nothing about that windfall, but the local agent of his society had not been idle, and the sum which was immediately placed at his disposal as royalties enabled him to spend an unexpectedly luxurious time there.

In the same way the Société des Auteurs, Compositeurs et Editeurs de Musique maintains a network for the protection of its members' rights all over the world.

Yes, everyone has the right to the protection of the moral and material interests resulting from any product of the mind of which he is the author. It was right and proper that this should be solemnly proclaimed in the Universal Declaration of Human Rights so that thereafter no one could plead ignorance of this fundamental truth.

6

The protection of works of art

At first the danger of any encroachment on the property rights of a painter, a sculptor, an engraver or an architect seems remote. They are all creative artists whose particular work is unique, born of a combination of hand and brain with the assistance of a technique whose special application is all their own. The rôle played here by the tools and the materials is quite different from the rôle of the pen or the typewriter in literary performance. We speak with admiration of Turner's palette, Cézanne's brushwork and Dürer's incomparable burin. Rodin's chisel, we say, was the equal of Michelangelo's, and we compare the pencil of Ingres with the grafting knife of a clever horticulturist. There is an artisan side to the practice of the fine arts which gives an undeniable character of authenticity to the subsequent work.

The law protects creative art here just as it does in literature. It takes no account of the materials or of the degree of artistic talent involved. The designer in a porcelain factory is just as much protected, and by the same token, as a Renoir. In the eyes of the law a landscape gardener has the same rights as a Bonington or a Sisley. There are men everywhere who are what we call 'Sunday painters' in France, painters like Rousseau for example. Is there anything which lacks the impress of personality more than their work does? They stolidly copy exactly what they see before them. If they set out to paint a tree they put in each branch and each twig and each separate leaf. If they paint a face they give it two eyes, a nose and a mouth, but the eyes are not made to see, or the nose to breathe, or the mouth to smile. Nevertheless, there are people who collect their work, just as there are people who collect pictures fashioned laboriously out of feathers or human hair. Now these men also enjoy full legal rights in their work although the part played by creative art in its production is reduced to such a minimum as not to be readily appreciable.

The unwillingness of the law to discriminate between undoubted talent or genius and mere artisan skill is a moving tribute to its respect for the human personality. We are thinking here of those thousands of modest artists all over the world who spend their lives in minor artistic tasks such as the illustration of school books, the designing of chocolate-box covers, the painting of commercial signs, the illustrating of prospectuses and catalogues (and some of the catalogues issued by the big stores really are works of art), the menus of restaurants, calendars and Christmas cards. Clearly, such things have an artistic value and carry the impress of individuality, and in the course of time they often become eagerly sought after by collectors. And in museums devoted to popular arts and crafts we are already beginning to see some of those popular decorative panels representing hunting scenes of all kinds, the boar hunt, the stag hunt and the deer hunt, which used to — and often still do — decorate the walls and windows of French delicatessen stores, and in Esthonia I have seen decorative panels in fishmongers' shops representing the great variety of fish sold there. These still lifes have a very definite artistic value in the eyes of conoisseurs, and it is a matter of course that their authors should enjoy protection in the same way as famous painters or engravers.

What protection do they need? Protection against imitation which amounts to forgery. The fraudulent imitation of a work of art is a forgery. During the lives of the painters there were forged Corots and Courbets, just as today there are forged Utrillos and forged Matisses. An artistic 'fashion' invariably produces forgeries. A work of art done 'in the manner of' an artist and signed with his name is equally a forgery, and the injured artist has the right to prosecute the forger. But if the artist is dead and all rights in his work have lapsed then the forger can be prosecuted only in the ordinary way for false pretences. The story of the false Vermeers which deceived even the experts a little while back is well known. The forger took good care not to copy any particular picture; instead he painted new pictures in the style of Vermeer. His efforts were then accepted as authentic Vermeers, and art circles congratulated themselves on the discovery of previously unknown works by the great master. What legal resort is there against such a forger? Vermeer's rights lapsed three hundred years ago. Anyone who desires to copy his pictures may do so; anyone who desires to imitate his style may do so. However, the collector who has bought a forged Vermeer represented to him as authentic can prosecute the vendor for false pretences in much the same way as a man who has been persuaded to purchase a bar of lead covered with gold leaf on the representation that it is a bar of real gold can prosecute the swindler. Further, thanks to the fact that most countries recognize the moral rights of the artist in his work his heirs can take anyone to court who damages his reputation even if all material rights have lapsed.

The rights of the artist can be most effectively protected in connection with the reproduction of his work. No one is entitled himself to reproduce or to have reproduced any work of art by engraving, protography or any other process, without the consent of the author or the author's heirs even if the work in question is materially his own property. A man who owns a canvas of Van Dongen may not have it reproduced in an art magazine, for example, without the consent of the artist even if the picture is a portrait of himself. When a man buys a picture the rights that he thereby acquires are limited. He has bought the actual canvas itself, but no part of the painter's talent, and its reproduction would probably serve to illustrate a judgement on the artist; favourable or unfavourable, it is of no account, a judgement which touches the person of the artist. 'We are best protected by our talents' wrote Vauvenargues. However, the owner of a painting, sculpture, engraving or drawing, has the right to exhibit it publicly without informing the artist. Once he has purchased the work of art in question he may exhibit it where he likes, even in a public gallery or museum.

As we have seen, there are many complications involved, and we have dealt with some of them because they excellently illustrate the care taken by the law to protect the person of the artist and his talent, and to see that no one may besmirch his reputation by fraudulent imitation. In practice it does not often happen that artists are unwilling to permit the reproduction of their work, by engraving or photography; and generally they are only too anxious to see their work brought before a wider public.

Certain countries, including France, grant an artist special protection by a modern version of the *droit de suite*. For example, if an artist sells one of his works for a modest sum at a time when either he is unknown or his genius is unrecognized, and subsequently sees it sold publicly for a sum so great as it be altogether out of relation to what he originally received for it, then the law provides that a proportion of the purchase price shall be paid as compensation to the artist or his heirs. However, this right is not applicable to private sales. This *droit de suite* is a moving example of the consideration and understanding shown by the law to the artist. Forain, a great black and white artist whose cartoons and their texts are still fresh in the memory of the French public, once did a drawing calculated to touch the conscience of the country. It depicted a scene at sales room in which an auctioneer was knocking down a picture at a price big enough to thrill the assembled public, whilst in a corner stood a poorly-dressed woman with a shawl over her head and a thin, sickly child at her side. 'But mummy,' the child is saying, 'that's one of daddy's pictures.' Forain's drawing is said to have done not a little to secure the passage of the modern *droit de suite* in France.

The law takes such care to protect the rights of the artist that it even extends its provisions to those works of art which are known in the world of fashion as 'models'. Such 'model' dresses and hats are protected in the same way and for the same reason as all other works of art are protected, and that is only right and proper. The designing of a dress is creative art, and material which is made up to the design of a fashion artist is an expression of the creative spirit. To see a hat being created in the hands of a modiste is to realize that between the modiste and the sculptor there is only a difference of materials. Any illict reproduction of the resultant hat would be fraudulent, and the person responsible would soon find himself in the courts.

And finally there is architecture, one of the noblest of the arts, and one to which we owe some of the greatest masterpieces which have magnified mankind. It is an art of design, and from the design spring power and grandeur.

The architect is not a builder, except in his mind. Fénelon has expressed it very well: 'The man who erects a column or sets up a wall is merely a builder, but the man who conceives the whole building, having arranged all its proportions in his mind, is alone the architect.' It was in this way that the temple of Rameses II at Luxor, the Propelaeum of the Acropolis at Athens, the Cathedral at Chartres and the Capitol at Washington came into being. They are amongst the most wonderful examples of creative art. From the primitive pile dwellings of the lake cities to the breath-taking Mosque of Cordova, from the igloos of Kamchatka to the Palazzo Vecchio at Florence, the evolution of architecture has kept pace with the sublime development of the human spirit.

It is a strange thing that at a time when the names of great painters and sculptors were known to all, the names of the great architects, mere master builders as they were then called, remained in obscurity. At a time when the names of Cimabue and Giotto were on everyone's lips, no one bothered about the names of those great men who designed the Gothic cathedrals, glorious flowers of architecture and the Christian faith whose beauty has never been exceeded. The Renaissance directed the attention of cultured men to the beauties of the past and developed the sense of the decorative and the luxurious in civil architecture; the names of such men as Serlio, Vignole, Inigo Jones and Francisco de Mora then became well known, no longer as master builders but as architects.

Like the writer and the musician, the architect enjoys exclusive rights in his work; no one may copy it and no one may construct a similar building, even if the materials used are different, and, finally, no one may reproduce the work of an architect without his permission either as a drawing or a photograph if the reproduction is intended to serve as the subject of a study or for the purposes of instruction.

Like the writer and the musician, the architect may work in peace, secure in the knowledge that the law will protect the fruits of his talent against all encroachments.

7

*The protection of photographs and films, and of broadcast
and televised work*

Pictures play a more important rôle today then ever before in
the dissemination of news and as a means to fix in permanence the
fugitive scenes which pass before our eyes. Whether they are
photographic stills or motion pictures they recreate the past; they
allow us to see things which happened too far away for us to
see in person; they allow us to see, and even to hear, people
who are dead. Whether photograph or film they are different in
one respect from the painting or the drawing in that they result
from the collaboration of an artist with a mechanical apparatus.
But as the painter choses his motive and uses his brush, so the
camera man studies the landscape, the thing or the person he
intends to photographs, arranges his composition and sees that his
light is suitable before exposing the film or plate held ready in
his camera to record the luminous message of the outside world.
  Photography has been an art from the beginning. Some of the
photos taken towards the middle of the last century by the early
masters of the art display greater poetic vision than most of the
pictures painted in the same period. What could be more drama-
tically beautiful than those series by photos taken by William Brady
during the American Civil War showing troops in bivouac in the
first light of the dawn preparing for battle, or more mournfully
realistic than the long lines of ambulances carrying away the
wounded? No signed painting by an artist ever surpassed the
psychological realism of those famous photographs of Abraham
Lincoln, conveying all the rugged nobility of his features to the
beholder. Many of the more intimate aspects of nineteenth century
history are known to us today only through such photographs. Far
from being crude and cold images, they are eloquent and evoca-
tive, and they appeal not merely to our understanding, but also
to our most complex emotions. In short, they are works of art,
and the rights of their authors are protected by law in the same
way as the rights of painters or engravers. We call them photo-
graphers or camera men as though they were mere technicians,
but they are artists. No one has more understanding for the quality
of light or can use it to better effect. In their hands the art of

portraiture has borne new and brilliant witness to man's genius for harnessing the inertia of material things to his own spiritual vitality.

The protection which the law accords to the producers of photographic works is thus amply justified. No one may reproduce their work without permission.

All this applies equally to the art of the film. However, the film is born of both the photograph and the theatre. It is the work of a number of people and not only of one. It is simultaneously a work of art and a dramatic work — and often a musical work as well. It is published, performed and executed. Thus it is a compound of many rights: those of the producer, the scenario writer, the dialogue writer, the actors, the cameramen, the sound technicians, and sometimes of the author whose novel or whose play has served as the basis for the scenario. Faced with such a multiplicity of interests the law has first to determine the destination of the creative rights. But who is the creator of such a complex work of art? Is it the producer? Or the writer of the scenario? Or the writer of the dialogue? Or the camera man? The producer can hardly claim the title. After all, Balzac's publisher never dreamt of claiming the authorship of *Le Lys dans La Vallée*. Nor does the Director of the Metropolitan Opera in New York claim to be the composer of *Boris Gǒdonov*. Now as the producer obviously isn't the author can it be the scenario writer? Hardly, because without the work of the dialogue writer which gives dramatic life to the scenario the writer of the latter would never see his work projected on to the screen. What about the camera man then? He is often a genius, and surely, seeing that the film is above all a series of moving pictures, he is the man who plays the leading rôle in its production? But how much would his art be worth without the collaboration of the producer, who provides the funds, of the scenario writer who gives him the framework in which he must operate, and of the dialogue writer who gives it tongue?

In such a conjunction of material and artistic activities as the production of a film the problem of rights is a complex one. The law in its wisdom recognizes the rights of all who take a creative part in it and contribute to its ideas.

As far as the author of the novel or the play which serves as the basis for the scenario is concerned, he has merely granted publication rights in another form, but just as he retains the right to determine the conditions of publication or performance where the publisher and the theatrical producer are concerned, so he also retains certain rights of control over the making of the film. If he takes an active part in the production of the new work of art whose original theme he has provided, then he becomes a collaborator and enjoys all the advantages that implies.

Television, which has developed from the theatre, the cinema and the wireless broadcast, and which represents nothing more than the production of oral and visual entertainment in the home, is in exactly the same position with regard to the law for the protection of artistic and literary property as that of the three arts of which it is the synthesis.

Similarly, author's rights in the talks, prose and poetry texts, plays, music and song broadcast to the listening public by wireless are formally protected by law all over the world.

8

The moral rights of the creative artist

We have seen the care with which the law protects the rights of the author in his works; we shall now see how it protects his person against all damage to his honour and reputation. This latter protection is the moral right of the creative artist.

We should like first to clear up a misunderstanding which has put Europe and America at loggerheads. This moral right is unfortunately neither well established nor properly understood, and the responsibility for this falls on certain authors who have allowed themselves to be so blinded by their desire for gain that they have too easily forgotten just how much of themselves, of their heart and soul, they have put into their work. It makes them indifferent to the way in which their work is often mutilated and deformed when it is 'adapted' for the screen or for broadcasting. Honour is not a commodity and it should not be treated as though it were. The moral right is the noblest and most disinterested aspect of the rights of the creative artist. It should not be debased with impunity.

We are anxious to convince the public that in thus defending the moral right of the creative artist we are also defending its own rights. The honour and the reputation of the creative artist should be as precious to those who enjoy his work as they are the artist himself.

After all, the law aims at protecting a work of art from distortion, mutilation and profanation. In demanding that the work of art itself shall be treated with respect, it affirms that its author is also entitled to respect.

The law protects the person of the author. In the eyes of the law a creative artist is a man with an honour and a reputation to preserve, a man entitled to keep his creations free from all distortion and debasement. The law is the expression of this moral right. Once an author has given the world an idea, whether in the form of a poem, a tune or a picture, how could he remain indifferent to the danger of its subsequent debasement or distortion at the hands of others by changing its form or perverting its meaning? The creative artist is the master of his work as long as it remains in his hands; no one can rob him of it, publish it, exhibit it, produce it or execute it without at the same time encroaching on the personality of the author. Even after his death the publication of works he has left behind unpublished may sometimes damage his reputation. We know the eagerness with which the general public awaits the 'previously unpublished' work of great writers, and we know how often mediocre or unfinished work has seen the light of day just because some forgotten box or drawer has revealed manuscripts which were never intended for publication by their author. Sometimes, of course, the find is a happy one. This was certainly the case with Diderot's masterpiece *Le Neveu de Rameau*, whose manuscript came into the hands of Goethe and was translated by him into German. The French public first made its acquaintance indirectly through a retranslation from the German.

The widespread recognition of the moral rights of the creative artist today makes it possible for him to defend himself against any encroachments on his intellectual and moral personality. Publishers, and particularly producers, have often arrogated the right to 'adapt' an author's work. The producer finds a scene too long to suit him, so he cuts it; an actor doesn't like his lines, so he alters them; the play seems too depressing, so it is given a 'happy ending'. What a gross outrage it would be if a producer, deciding that

Shakespeare's *Hamlet* was too sad, changed it so that Ophelia recovered her reason, or never lost it, married the Prince of Denmark and lived happily ever after! No, Shakespeare will remain master for ever of Ophelia's destiny, and Cervantes has laid down the adventures of Don Quixote for all time. No one has the right to give any other meaning to a work of art than the one its author has already given it. The expression on the face of Maya belongs to Goya just as the final chorus of *Tannhäuser* belongs to Wagner. Certain producers adapting a novel or a play for production as a film have a tendency to interfere with its action, pleading the special requirements of the screen as their excuse. During the lifetime of an author it is usually easy enough to get him to agree to changes, and as long as copyright has not lapsed there is no great danger of any very serious mutiliation. But what about those masterpieces which no longer enjoy the protection of the law? A nation is entitled to defend the memory of its great artists and writers, and in a number of countries there is a growing body of opinion which believes that the State should now intervene to uphold the respect due to the great works of art and literature of the past which are at the moment at the tender mercies of anyone who cares to lay hands on them. Italy, for instance, is justly proud of being the fatherland of the immortal Dante. Should not the Italian people through their Government have the right to veto any 'adaptation' of the *Divine Comedy* which obviously damages the reputation of their great poet?

Public opinion has often expressed its disapproval of the 'retouching' of sculptures and architectural monuments under the guise of restoration. In the nineteenth century this sort of restoration was a positive mania: statues whose heads had been damaged by the effects of time or the malice of man were given new heads, or new noses or chins. Why, there was even a suggestion that the Venus de Milo should be provided with arms... Feudal ruins, much of whose beauty resided in their tragic dilapidation, were turned into shining new chateaux, with well scraped walls and newly carved decorations, but unfortunately the workmanship of the nineteenth century artisans was not on the same level as that of their feudal predecessors, and the inexhaustible patience of those old workmen had given place to the hurried tempo of modern times; even the tools were no longer the same. Our twentieth century shows a greater respect for the work of the past; it preserves as far as possible what still exists of that work, but it does not attempt to refashion what is lost.

This respect for the beauties of the past is even extended to nature; upholding the moral right of nature, so to speak. Societies for the protection of the countryside, etc, have been formed and they now keep a jealous eye on our natural heritage to preserve it from all vandalism: the lovely view at the bend of a river, a noble forest, a natural chaos of rocks. The movement began in the United States and spread rapidly. By the creation of their National Parks the Americans became pioneers in the struggle to preserve our mountains, valleys, lakes, waterfalls and woods in their pristine beauty. New Gardens of Eden have been recreated in this way, natural paradises protected from the malice of men where bird, beast and tree are safe from the gun, the trap and the axe. From the United States the recognition of this moral right of nature has spread throughout the world, and now the cedars of Lebanon and the gentle giraffes of Uganda have the same right to follow the laws of their own development without interference as the sequoias of California and the bears of the Rocky Mountains. If a plane tree overshadowing a fountain in some public square is beautiful in the eyes of men, its beauty has its own rights. If water plunges in a silver cascade from a high rock throwing a shower of jewels into the sunlit air, man is now inclined to leave its beauty untouched rather than dam its waters or guide them through a power-plant turbine. As the author of the plane tree and the waterfall, nature is recognized as the creator of works of art, and by that same token she now enjoys protection like other creative artists.

That is the nature of the moral right.

Let us conclude our study of the rights of the creative artists as set out in the Universal Declaration of Human Rights with these few examples, which will, we hope, appeal both to the heart and the understanding.

It is to be hoped that on the basis of the facts and ideas set out in these pages public opinion will unite to demand the signing of a universal convention to protect literary, artistic and scientific works. Amongst all the expressions of man's creative activity works of art are best calculated to create those bonds of mutual understanding and those common ideals without which the world brotherhood of man will always remain a vain hope.

REX WARNER

Freedom
in literary and artistic
creation

FREEDOM
IN LITERARY AND ARTISTIC CREATION

1

Introductory

It is, of course, impossible to define precisely the conditions necessary for, or even favourable to, the creation of art and literature. If we look back into the past we shall find great work done in sickness and in health, in war and in peace, under enlightened governments and under tyrannies, in prison as well as at liberty. So that it might seem that, fundamentally, the only absolute necessities for the production of great art are genius in the artist and sufficient health and liberty of body to use the hand or the tongue.

Yet, clearly, the question deserves further discussion, even though we must admit the impossibility of precisely answering it. Some conditions at some times are certainly better than others. And in our own days many will have been forced seriously to consider the warning of Tacitus. 'It is easier to destroy culture than to bring it back again.'

In the times which Tacitus had in mind, as in our own times, what destroyed culture was a centralised and despotic government operating by means of informers and of secret police. Yet it would be too simple to conclude from this that art and literature can only flourish under a democratic régime, too simple and also too complicated, since today governments with widely different principles are constantly announcing the purity of their own brands of democracy. Tacitus himself, for all his republicanism, declared that the emperor Nerva had contrived to combine dictatorship with liberty, and it would certainly be a mistake to claim that the kind of liberty which literature requires can only exist under some specific political system.

Yet this subject of politics is one that must be discussed. It is, I believe, on the fringe of our main subject and not, as many writers would say, either fully embracing it or else at the very centre. Yet, though I do not believe that politics, as such, have more than an accidental importance for writers and artists, we must admit that, if we are to advocate any reforms in the treatment of the arts, we shall be immediately confronted with the problem (a very paradoxical one) of the relations of the State to its creative workers. The old liberal view was that, so long as the police did not interfere with a writer's productions, so long as his person was safe from arrest if he expressed unpopular views, then that was all that was to be expected in a civilised State. The writer should be allowed to adopt any political creed that appealed to him, or need have no political creed at all. The State should simply obey the direction of Milton, who wrote: 'Give me the liberty to know, to utter and to argue freely according to conscience, above all liberties.' This rather negative avoidance of interruption was all that the writer asked for from the State: the State's real business was elsewhere, in the organisation of trade and industry, in sanitation, in military or legal affairs.

True that this conveniently unaggressive theory of liberalism has never been carried into practice in any one country for any long period. Even in England between the wars the police did interfere with the productions of writers, amongst whom were James Joyce and D. H. Lawrence. And both in war and peace the government of every country in Europe has denied the right of publication to various groups for various political reasons.

I am not arguing here whether these suppressions were right or wrong, justified or unjustified. Obviously the prosecutions of Flaubert, Joyce and Lawrence were unjustified, and it was a sign of a healthy public opinion that in these cases the police appeared in the end ridiculous. In other cases there are strong arguments for and against police action.

But, apart altogether from the question of how far, if ever, the liberal ideal of liberty was put into practice, what is true today is that in very many quarters the liberal ideal or theory is wholly discredited. We hear now constantly of the duties of the writer towards the State and of the duty of the State towards the writer. These duties are variously defined, but in general it is true that, over much of Europe, the writer, so far from having to complain, as he often did in the past, that his work is unrecognised or neglected, now finds himself in the full glare of official publicity, the recipient or perhaps the victim of all kinds of governmental encouragement. And both writers and governments proclaim that in these happy circumstances, true freedom of creation has at last been achieved.

I think that the arguments in favour of such systems must run, more or less, as follows. Basically it is assumed that the State, operating by methods which, however they differ among themselves, are invariably described as 'democratic', is beneficient and progressive. The writer is a citizen, like anyone else. He has special gifts and a special part to play, though again opinions may differ as to what precisely his special gifts are and what is his exact rôle in the common advance. It must be assumed, however, that he is willing to co-operate in the obviously desirable aims of his elected government. Since he will naturally wish to help, both he and the government are enriched by the subsidies paid to him and the assistance offered to him. Once he has shown his ability, he will be free to cultivate it. The State needs and appreciates his work. The artist needs and appreciates the State.

Thus the writer may be enrolled almost into the civil service. It is claimed that for him this will constitute not only economic, but spiritual freedom. He will be free to pursue his art without the need for earning his living by doing, in addition to his real work, one or more of the extra jobs that writers in most countries have to do in order to support themselves and their families. And the very fact that he is working consciously and happily with his fellow citizens, that he is esteemed by them, that he is part of a team, will free his mind from many complexes and inhibitions which afflict his fellow writers in countries where writing is not accepted as one of the tools and adornments of government and where publishing is always commercial and often vulgar. His early struggles will be devoted simply to showing the competent authorities whether he is able to write well. Once he has succeeded in doing this, he will be spared the humiliations of touting for extra jobs, writing pot-boilers (as Balzac did for ten years), keeping an eye on the market for films when he is writing a novel, and all the other necessary degradations. Freed from such necessities, his native talents will blossom more richly. He will have achieved security, both economic and spiritual, and without security writing must be, in our days, either haphazard, commercial, embittered, vulgar or, finally, non-existent.

Such views as the above are widely held and deserve consideration. Two main questions are, I think, involved: first, is it good or desirable for the State to secure the glad, ungrudging support of its writers? Secondly, is it good or desirable for a writer to secure the glad, ungrudging support of his State?

On these questions I can write, not as a political theorist, but only from personal belief and experience. Still, some slight incursion into political theory seems, at the beginning of the argument, necessary.

The modern State, whether we like it or not, and for whatever reasons, certainly gives more to and demands more from its citizens than ever before. The liberty to spend one's money in one's own way, the liberty to fight or not to fight in a war, the liberty to choose some wholly distinctive method of education for one's children — all these and many other individual liberties have gone. In England, at any rate, one is not even allowed to take one's own life, and though a successful attempt to do so will indeed frustrate the police force, an unsuccessful attempt will immediately call down on the offender the penalties of the law.

Most of these modern deprivations of personal liberty are assumed to be justified by increasing somehow the general sum-total of liberty. It is admitted that, ideally speaking, people should be allowed to consult their own consciences and tastes with regard to fighting or abstaining from fighting in a war. Yet to acknowledge this right fully might result in the even greater deprivation of personal liberty which would follow an enemy conquest of a nation whose forces were not fully employed. Thus it is with the best of intentions that the modern State deprives us of our personal and our anti-social liberties.

Members of the United Nations have subscribed to various articles all emphasising the individual dignity and worth of every single human being under the sun. This is assumed to be common ground between Christian and Communist, Arab and Hindu, — that the human individual is of fundamental importance.

Now we have seen that the modern State, always with the best of intentions, proceeds constantly by curtailing some individual liberties in order to promote, either immediately or at some future date, others. This process involves the existence of an acknowledged and general aim, and one imagines that, theoretically, most States would declare that their general aim was the implementation of the Universal Declaration of Human Rights, though one imagines that few States could reasonably suggest that within their borders the provisions of this document are fully carried out. Yet in different ways most States do either aim or pretend to aim at the increased welfare, security and full development of their citizens. Governments are conscious of this, and insist upon something almost in the nature of gratitude. In Article 29 it is laid down: 'Everyone has duties to the community in which alone the free and full development of his personality is possible.'

The wording is vague. It is not clear whether 'the community' means the State in which a person happens to be born or a possibly self-chosen State or some other organisation such as a Church or a club. Also it is possible to infer from this article that if the community does not assure 'the free and full development' of one's personality (and what community does?) then one has no further duties to it. Still, though the phraseology of this article is certainly unfortunate, it would be fair, I think, to assume that it expresses the simple fact that where a State is occupied with our welfare as individuals, we ourselves must acknowledge that we have duties towards the State.

Obviously our duties must be to assist the State in helping us, in ensuring 'the free and full development' of our personalities.

How can a writer do this, benefiting both himself and his own State? Of course he has to fulfill the ordinary duties of a citizen, paying his taxes, obeying the laws. In so far as he is a writer, differing in this respect from other citizens, I should suggest that his duty will be more often to oppose and to criticise than to praise and support a State organisation. Here I am attempting to approach the subject from the point of view of the State rather than of the writer. Consequently the word 'duty' may be permitted.

The State has, on the whole, to operate in terms of statistics. In estimating the needs of its citizens for housing, education or nutrition, it is bound to consider wide areas and great masses of people. The effects of its exertions on the single person in a particular place must escape, nearly always, the attention of its legislators. The writer and the artist, on the other hand, are always concerned with the particular instance. They may generalise, certainly, but never along the lines of statistics. Their material is always of that kind that cannot, under any circumstances, be mathematically expressed. Thus it would seem that the activities of the writer and artist should supplement or even contradict the activities of the State, rather than that they should coincide with or gladly support these activities.

There is another point of at least equal importance. We have learned that power corrupts and that absolute power corrupts absolutely. In many modern States effective power is now, for one reason or another, concentrated and centralised to a degree unknown in earlier times. And, while the machine extends its dominion, there is a tendency to believe that the machine exists in its own right, to exalt the means and forget or only dimly remember the ends. Is it not therefore in the interest of any State which deserves to call itself progressive to be equipped always with an opposition? Should not this opposition be encouraged? Is there not still truth in the paradox of Socrates who at his trial had the face to suggest that, so far from being condemned to death, he should in the best interests of the city be kept for the rest of his life at the public expense and given free license to disseminate his overwhelming criticisms, since these, he said, were directed to one end alone, 'to make men better'?

May I be allowed to quote from an essay which I wrote some years ago on this subject? [1] Today and always, it seems to me, literature must make the same claim as Socrates made for himself. It should be treated with honour by the State, even subsidised, and should be not only allowed but expected to criticise the State in every way. For this is its public service and it is a service which, in these times, seems almost more than ordinarily necessary, since today there exists, together with a general desire for the elements of a good life, — food, work and peace (and also a general belief that these elements are attainable) — an extreme vagueness as to how these good things are to be secured and what, in the end, is to be done with them.

This is what may be called the political task of literature — to hold the mirror up to nature, to show men how they live and what is meant by their own words and manners, to investigate everything under the sun, to retain the tradition of the past, and to explore the future, to instruct, to criticise, to delight, to create and to reveal. In these activities, as in all others, the writer may be greatly helped or greatly hindered by the society in which he lives. The more he can co-operate with this society, the happier, as a rule, he will be. Yet, though his work is conditioned by his social group, it is not determined by it. And there is a sense in which it is true to say that his work must be, whether he is con-

---

1 'On Freedom of Expression' in *The Cult of Power*.

scious of it or not, always disruptive of any State organisation. For his loyalties as a writer are to something wider and deeper than any State can be. His view of individuals must be closer and more intimate than the view taken by statesmen; his estimate of general principles must be wider and more far-reaching than is possible for a particular legislator. In the ordinary affairs of life he will, like everyone else, look for and admire efficiency. But efficiency can never be for him a reason for existence. And this view of his must penetrate the State itself if the State is not to be a mere machine or ossification.

So much for what, in my opinion, ought to be the general attitude of the State towards its writers and artists. As for the particular means it may employ to encourage art and writing — education, scholarships, subsidies, etc — it will be more convenient to discuss these when we come to consider the question from the point of view of the writer or artist himself. Certainly one must admit that few, if any, States are today prepared to foster within themselves what is, or might be, a disruptive or revolutionary principle. Such an idea must seem to many honest statesmen, particularly in periods of crisis, a plain contradiction to common sense and security. Yet still I should suggest that to adopt any other attitude, however necessary it may appear, is a sign of weakness and of incompleteness. The men who condemned Socrates were honest men; but is was Socrates whom they condemned, thus depriving Athens of a civilising force far greater than that represented by his democratic accusers. A state that was really based on truth and justice would accept unhesitatingly the words of Milton. 'And, though all the winds of doctrine were let loose to play upon the earth, so truth be in the field, we do injuriously by licensing and prohibiting to misdoubt her strength. Let her and falsehood grapple; who ever knew truth put to the worse in a free and open encounter?'

I should suggest that in so far as a state approximates to its own professed ideals of truth and justice, so it will welcome the free play of 'all the winds of doctrine', will abolish censorships and will even go out of its way to make possible the publication of minority opinions.

And now, having briefly discussed the principles with regard to freedom of creation which, it seems, the State should, in its own interests, hold, let us consider the question from the point of view of the writer or artist himself. What are or should be the claims he makes from the State? Does he want to be helped at all? Does he acknowledge any duties other than those of the tax payer or the conscript? Has he, as a writer or artist, consciously any specific contribution to make to what is called 'society'?

Many of these questions are, and must remain, personal. It is quite obvious that different people would answer them in different ways. Nor is it certain that an answer given in intellectual terms and in good faith by a writer would really correspond with the deeper principles of his creative activity.

So far as the more general of these questions go, my own attitude must be fairly clear from what I have written already. One would not have suggested that the State should grant freedom of opposition without oneself wishing to claim the freedom to oppose. But I am far from suggesting, as some have done, that a conscious revolutionism is or ought to be part of the make-up of a writer. There is no reason whatever for a writer to be 'political' in any sense and many reasons against his being so. The freedom which I think he should claim is not so much freedom to oppose (though he should claim this) as freedom from the necessity of giving support. As has been said already, his aims are different from those of statesmen. He studies what is individual and remarkable, not what is calculable or average. This being so, his 'opposition' is likely to be not premeditated (though it may be so), but more often, in a sense, accidental.

Personally I am in agreement with the general view, without accepting all the particular conclusions, expressed by the English novelist Graham Greene, in a discussion on this very subject published in 1948 under the title of *Why do I write?* [1] This short book of letters between Graham Greene himself, Elizabeth Bowen and V. S. Pritchett (all distinguished contemporary novelists, and each very different in style and outlook from each) is interesting from many points of view, in particular perhaps in the fact that on basic principles a large measure of agreement is found between these widely different novelists. I shall refer to this discussion again. Now I wish merely to emphasise Graham Greene's demand

---

[1] *Why do I write?* An exchange of views between Elizabeth Bowen, Graham Greene, V. S. Pritchett (published by Percival Marshall).

for one special right, the right of the author to be disloyal, to be disloyal not only to some abstraction such as 'society', but to particular groups (political, religious or other) within society. He writes 'I would emphasise once again the importance and the virtue of disloyalty. If only writers would maintain that one virtue — so much more important to them than purity — unspotted from the world. Honours, State patronage, success, the praise of their fellows all tend to sap their disloyalty. If they don't become loyal to a Church or a country, they are too apt to become loyal to some invented ideology of their own, until they are praised for consistency, for a unified view. Even despair can become a form of loyalty ... Loyalty confines us to accepted opinions: loyalty forbids us to comprehend sympathetically our dissident fellows; but disloyalty encourages us to roam experimentally through any human mind: it gives to the novelist the extra dimension of sympathy.'

There is a kind of bravado in the use of the words 'loyalty' and 'disloyalty', but the meaning is clear enough. It is claimed that the writer will not be able to write well unless he is able to stand apart from and outside his society or his group. He may owe allegiance to society or to group in all other matters, but not in the matter of his art. Here he must use an individual and possibly a 'disloyal' vision and sympathy: otherwise he will be blind, conventional or both. It is interesting that, of the three English writers who took part in the discussion from which I have just quoted, Graham Greene, being a Catholic, is the one most committed to a particular intellectual and spiritual loyalty. He is also the one who claims with the greatest force, the right to be, so far as his writing is concerned, 'disloyal'. The other two novelists do not dissent from him, though they express themselves differently. V. S. Pritchett writes, 'I doubt if any writer who has ever lived has lived in harmony with the group into which he was born or which he has joined or into which he has drifted ...' He also regards it as a necessary condition for good writing that the writer should be able to look both ways. 'It seems to me,' he says, commenting on the views expressed by Graham Greene, 'that this ambivalence — what you call disloyalty — will be a clearer and clearer duty as the world becomes planned, organised and socialised, and will be inevitable if the world goes to pieces.'

Elizabeth Bowen employs the word 'conflict' in preference to 'disloyalty' or 'ambivalence'. She writes 'I do think conflict essential, — conflict in the self (a never quite dislodgeable something to push against), and an if anything hyper-acute sense of every kind of conflict, and every phase of any kind of conflict, in society.' And in what she regards as the most unlikely event of 'a conflictless Better World' she claims that 'The artist — particularly the writer, as the most comprehensible — will take on the stature of a Resistance leader.'

It is unnecessary, I think, further to amplify these opinions. I should suggest, in concluding this part of the argument, that neither from the point of view of society, if society is really concerned with the free and full development of its individual members, nor from the point of view of the writer, if he is genuinely concerned with truth, is any kind of regimentation or direction desirable, and that one of the chief freedoms which a writer or artist should claim is freedom from interference or suggestion in his art from outside groups, however much he may be, in matters that do not concern his art, attached to these groups.

2

Some Particular Problems

We must now approach the subject in a more practical manner and discuss the question of how precisely the writer or the artist can be freed from conditions which are held to hamper his liberty of creation. Here again it is impossible to lay down rules that will suit everyone. Literary and artistic creation has appeared under widely differing conditions and what has proved to be one creator's meat has often been another's poison.

Even on the question of education there will be differences of opinion. Some will go so far as to say that it is better for a creative artist to have no education at all than the kind of education which can restrict or corrupt the mind, better a Boeotian indolence than the discipline of Sparta.

Such a view seems to be exaggerated, and I do not think that many writers and artists would themselves wish to be cut off from the possibilities of learning. They are indeed often less likely to be corrupted by this process than are many others. One has frequently heard people say (and sometimes with a kind of self-exculpatory pride) 'Shakespeare was ruined for me at school'. But such people are seldom writers. For them no schoolmaster, however bad, could 'ruin' Shakespeare. It is fair therefore, I think, to claim that among the conditions favourable to literary and artistic creation is the free and easy accessibility to every one of the great works of the past. As for methods and systems of education, there is room for great differences of opinion. A writer, I think, will usually select what he needs and fall avidly upon it. He is more likely to suffer from deprivation, if there are not enough books, than from a surfeit, if there are too many.

Literacy, therefore, and even a certain degree of learning seem to be either necessary or advantageous to most writers and artists today. Not all governments are yet able to ensure even these minimum conditions for all their citizens, but all governments would claim that they are advancing in this direction.

Education, therefore, we conclude should be, ideally speaking, free for all. More difficult questions arise when we come to consider the conditions of life for writers and artists once their education in school or college is over. Many of them have obviously been inspired by foreign travel. Should foreign travel be made easily available to them all? If so, at whose expense? Many have profited in the past by being able to devote themselves entirely to their art. Is this a necessary condition for the best work? If so, can it or should it be provided for all or for some? How should it or could it be provided? By State subsidy? By private patronage? By increasing the prices of books and pictures? By what means?

Such questions are exceedingly difficult to answer, but they are the subject of our discussion. In attempting to find answers to some of them I shall have to consider the conditions prevailing in England and to look at these conditions from the point of view of an English writer, since I have neither the requisite knowledge or the experience of other countries and other arts. Even in this limited field generalisations are difficult enough.

Let us begin by disposing of some rubbish. Many people (usually those who are neither writers nor artists themselves) will positively extol the advantages of abject poverty for any practitioner of the arts. They will point to the struggles of Balzac in his early youth, and claim that it was this hard life that enabled him to write the *Comédie Humaine*. They will say much the same things of Dostoievsky and will even approve, on rather abstract grounds, of his imprisonment in Siberia. Though they will seldom pursue either suffering or poverty themselves, they will affirm that for artists both poverty and suffering are essential.

Such views and arguments are blind and inaccurate. Suffering, God knows, comes to almost everyone who is not wholly insensitive; but suffering is not confined to the poor. Poverty, moreover, can corrupt just as easily as riches, though in a different way. It has certainly debased more people than it has elevated. And, so far as writers are concerned, a simple examination of biographies would show that from Aeschylus to André Gide by far the greater number of good European writers have been, on the whole, not badly off. Nearly all have enjoyed long periods of leisure; nearly all have been able to devote themselves, for long periods of time, exclusively to their work.

This state of affairs, in England at least, no longer exists. Not that it is necessary for a writer to starve. If, as is usual, he is a person of some education, there will be plenty of opportunities for him to secure what is called 'gainful employment'. He may teach in a school, work on the B.B.C., join some cultural organisation like the British Council, work in a publisher's office, in advertising, in the civil service, in films. But he will not, unless he is among the very few successful dramatics or best selling novelists, be able to live by his real work, which is creative writing.

It may be said that this is no new thing — that at no time have very many creative writers been able to live by their own exertions in their particular field. It is true that not many have at any time been able to live in any luxury by writing, yet, until, quite recently, quite a number have at least been able to live without spending their time and energy on pursuits outside their own chosen work. On this subject I cannot do better than quote V. S. Pritchett, writing in the discussion from which I have quoted already. He says: 'At one time a novelist might devote most of his time to his art and, if he were esteemed, live modestly on the earnings of his work. A small private income often helped him along, the cost of living was low, taxation hardly existed; in other words society subsidised him without realising it was doing so. If he had some other occupation it was nominal; its hours were easy; the pace of business was slow. Even a poor wretch like Gissing could live somehow by his work alone; and though the system was sometimes niggardly it did not prevent a man from writing for years on end. In some cases — the case of Crabbe, for example — patronage made it possible for him to write.'

Pritchett goes on to say: 'This happy condition of affairs has vanished, since the huge rise in the standard of living, and the huge booty that the State collects in taxation. The State has abolished the private income and has put nothing back in its place. The State is abolishing private saving and has turned what was once a virtue into a useless vice. To speak for myself, I might after twenty years of writing, have expected to live on my income as an imaginative writer. I could not possibly do so.'

Now this fair and accurate statement, made by one of our leading imaginative writers, raises several questions. I do not think that many people would dispute the accuracy of Pritchett's account of the position of a writer in England today. There would be many, however, who would insist that the position is far from desperate. 'Why,' such people might ask, 'should a writer expect to be allowed time and money for the pursuit of what is, after all, a luxury?'

To this question we can only reply that the work of the creative imagination is not an unnecessary luxury, but something essential to society. If this point is not granted, the discussion is at an end.

Suppose, however, that this point is granted, it may still be maintained that a writer may actually produce better work, work springing from a fuller experience, if he is compelled to earn his living, not by his art, but by joining with his fellow-citizens, who are not writers or artists, in their different activities. If, it may be said, he is isolated from them, privileged or cossetted, he will become less capable of understanding their problems and expressing their natures, he will tend to retire into some ivory tower of his own and will cease to confer on society the benefits which society has a right to expect from him.

This argument deserves consideration. It will be readily granted that a total isolation of the writer from the society in which he lives is likely to be a bad thing both for society and for himself. But is there, in the modern world, much likelihood of this happening? The whole process of education and growing up is bound to bring a writer into the closest contact with his fellow men and women. Society, through all the media of laws and regulations, of mass education, and entertainment, leaves him less and less alone. If any ivory towers exist today, they are neither numerous nor easily accessible.

We need not then contemplate, under any foreseeable conditions, the likelihood of a total separation of the writer from his fellow men. The question we have to answer is simply this one: will a writer be helped or hindered in his writing by doing some 'ordinary' job, whether teaching, coal-mining, journalism or what not?

Such a question is impossible to answer in clear and precise terms. Yet I think that most writers themselves would certainly claim that they would be, on the whole, capable of doing better work if they were able to earn their livings by the pursuit of their art. While some experience of the economic struggle is obviously valuable to a novelist, for example, too prolonged or intense an experience of this kind may end in a drying up both of energy and of inspiration.

My own view is that it is just and reasonable to deplore a state of affairs such as that described by V. S. Pritchett. I think it is true to say that the atmosphere was a better one for writers in the days when there were more small incomes, more personal independence and less public obligations. It can be argued, I think, that both justice and efficiency have been served by the vast encroachments of national and international organisations. But it is difficult to see how, up to the present time, either art or literature have benefited from the new economic régime.

That both governments and individuals are conscious of this situation is evident from both action and discussion. There have long been various prizes awarded to writers and artists and designed to make their work easier as well as more honourable. And in many countries the 'intelligentsia' constitute a recognised class which is treated with care and respect, at any rate so far as the material conditions of life are concerned.

I should suggest that the aim is a good one, that it ought to be possible for an imaginative writer of ability to live on the proceeds of his own work, and that he himself is likely to be the best judge as to whether or not he should, for longer or shorter periods, devote himself to some wholly different sort of work. I should suggest too that, of all the advantages of a small income to a writer, by far the greatest is independence. Equally injurious to him are the necessities of following a political line and of securing financial success by deliberately 'giving the public what it wants.' [1]

I shall assume, therefore, that in most cases a writer is helped rather than hindered by the possession of sufficient money to keep himself and his family in reasonable comfort without the need of spending his time and energy on occupations which have nothing to do with his art.

Is it possible for any means to be devised by which some writers or all writers should be in this happy position?

To this question we can reply at once that of course it is possible. Just as a modern State may subsidise the shipping or the sugar industry, so it may, if it thinks fit, subsidise the production of books and pictures. Even the maintenance of public libraries and art galleries is a form of subsidy. And in countries with Communist governments the subsidisation of art and literature goes much further than this. In some, at any rate, of these countries it seems evident that subsidisation by the State has also meant control by the State in the sense that attitudes and opinions which are frowned on by the government are not allowed to be expressed at all, or only with great difficulty, by those in receipt of State aid. We have already examined the arguments in favour of such a system, and I have expressed my own opinion, which would be, I think, shared by the vast majority of English writers, that no amount of economic security is worth the sacrifice of liberty to choose, without outside interference, one's style, one's subject and one's treatment of it. I would go even further than this and would agree with Graham Greene in exalting the virtue of 'disloyalty' in a writer.

For my own part, therefore, I must logically oppose any form of State subsidisation which gives the State the right or the opportunity to dictate to writers the manner or the substance of their writings. Does this mean that one must oppose any and every plan by which the State or some State-supported public body might attempt to subsidise literature and art?

I do not think that this necessarily follows, and here I should

[1] Though here, too, it should be pointed out that there are no hard and fast rules. Milton followed a political line, and Dickens often deliberately gave the public what it wanted. In both cases it could be maintained that their work gained in value from the courses which they took. Yet these courses were dictated if by necessity at all, by a psychological rather than by an economic necessity.

disagree with Graham Greene who, in his discussion of some of the suggestions put forward by V. C. Pritchett, writes: 'You may well ask, have you no plan, have you not one constructive suggestion to make? And my answer is quite frankly, None. I don't want a plan for literature. I don't want a working party, however high-minded or benevolent, to study the standard of life among novelists and decide on a minimum wage. Even if by a miracle the State could be excluded from such a plan, I still don't want it. A plan can be taken over later by other authorities. Nor can a craft be trusted to legislate wisely for itself.' And he concludes: 'No, our life is too organised already. Let us leave literature alone. We needn't worry too much. Man will always find a means to gratify a passion. He will write, as he will commit adultery, in spite of taxation.'

The conclusion is, no doubt, true. Yet it is also true that conditions can exist when the satisfaction of a passion is either difficult or impossible. Nor does the very difficulty of such a satisfaction necessarily produce an added exuberance or refinement. It is a matter of historical fact that in some states of society conditions for the production of literature and art have been more favourable than they have been in others. And it does not appear that these favoured periods have been characterised always simply by a lack of 'organisation'. Indeed even today, and even in 'capitalist' countries, an elaborate organisation exists by which books and works of art are sold or presented to the public. It would appear that Graham Greene, if not wholly satisfied with the existing organisation, is prepared to accept it as a lesser evil than what might be feared from any kind of 'planning'. He is even opposed to the administration of any sums of public money by authors themselves in the presumed interests of their fellows. As for a committee of authors appointed to use a fund of money wisely to encourage and support the deserving, he asks: 'But who is to chose the authors? In any one generation how many authors could you name whom you would trust to show discrimination or even common integrity?'

Here again it seems to me that he overstates his case. All men make mistakes; very many are dishonest. Yet some methods of administration are better than others, and, for my part, if there were a large sum of money set aside to encourage and relieve authors, and if this sum of money was at the disposal of a committee consisting of, to name no others, Pritchett, Elizabeth Bowen and Greene himself, I should be fairly confident that such a committee would do a great deal more good than harm.

There is indeed already in England a large body of opinion committed to the view that the ordinary process of supply and demand is not the ideal atmosphere for the production of literature and art. This is shown by the activities of such bodies as the Arts Council and by the increasing numbers of scholarships and grants of one kind or another. True that the plays and books and writers and artists who profit from these public or semi-public organisations may not be the most deserving. Justice, absolute and exact, is, we must agree, impossible. Yet some of the most deserving have certainly profited; some valuable work has been made possible which might otherwise never have appeared. Nor are the vagaries and prejudices of committees any more unreliable, biased, or simply wrong than are the vagaries of the market — a fact that can readily be verified by examining a list of the best-sellers of, say, ten years ago. The plain fact is that, while many writers in the past have succeeded in producing early in their careers works which have become immediately popular and which have at once brought them monetary rewards, many other writers have not produced such works till late in their lives and have not become popular until after their deaths. Such people have, in the past, none the less been able to devote themselves to their art, sometimes through the possession of a private income, sometimes through patronage. These two means of support have, in most of Europe, either ceased to exist or begun to disappear. It does not seem unreasonable to propose that something should be put in their place.

I should suggest, therefore, that we should reject the extreme view — that nothing whatever should be done to encourage or support writers and artists except for what is done through the normal channels of trade. The other extreme view — that writers and artists should become an acknowledge part of the State machinery and, as such, subject to State control in their art, has been already rejected, powerful as are the forces making for such a condition of affairs both in Europe and Asia.

We have now to enquire whether anything can be done to secure greater freedom for the artist without the risk that, in the process, the artist may become spiritually or intellectually subservient to the State or to any other organisation which supports him.

Let us admit at once that the dangers of political control or censorship are immense. Such a control seems to be about the one thing that might finally make creative writing impossible. Moreover in these days the exercise of such a control can be far more thorough and efficient than ever it was in the past. Just as in a thoroughly centralised State a popular revolution is almost unthinkable, so is the dissemination of art and literature which may be held damaging to the régime.

Yet it remains true that there is a great difference between a total and a partial intervention of the State. It would be, I should suggest, a sign of enlightenment rather than evidence of dictatorship if a modern State were to devote a considerable part of its resources to the support of art and literature, so long as the support was given with no political motive and the resources were administered by people whose main concern was with the excellence and the integrity of the art and literature itself. No doubt committees would have to be formed, and no doubt their decisions would frequently be wrong, and always disputed. This does not mean that their work would not be valuable. Such committees have for many years in many countries of Europe subsidised opera and the theatre. I fail to see why the same principle should not, in the present crisis, be applied to literature and to painting.

There would be, no doubt, all kinds of variations in the application of the principle. In 1911 in England the poet Rupert Brooke advocated a plan by which several hundreds of writers, painters, and musicians should receive £ 500 a year from the State. (The equivalent of this sum today would be at least £ 1,200 a year). He imagined a future in which municipalities would support the arts in their own areas. [1]

Some, including V. S. Pritchett, have less confidence in the enlightenment of Town Councillors than Rupert Brooke had; but with the general principle Pritchett and many others are in

---

[1] Such a policy of decentralisation has had many advocates. E.g. in his preface to *Prometheus Unbound*, Shelley writes: 'If England were divided into forty republics, each equal in population and extent to Athens, there is no reason to suppose but that, under institutions not more perfect than those of Athens, each would produce philosophers and poets equal to those who (if we except Shakespeare) have never been surpassed.' The present trends of world history seem to make such a solution singularly unlikely.

agreement. He well describes it as follows: 'The State has destroyed the private income which directly or indirectly has been the economic basis of our culture; the State must replace what it has taken. There would be a large number of failures; but the one or two successes would wipe them out.'

It is impossible to examine in any detail the various methods that might be employed by an enlightened State (and by 'enlightened' I mean one that would encourage excellence and 'disloyalty') to subsidise its writers and artists. Pritchett himself makes several interesting suggestions in the discussion to which I have been referring. He writes, for instance: 'What I am in favour of is this: not one kind of subsidy, but many kinds. I am, for example, in favour of subsidies for limited periods of time. A writer might be subsidised at thirty-five, but not again till he was fifty-five, at twenty-seven and then at forty-five and so on; according to what he could write and his general situation as a writer.' Indeed one would commend always the utmost amount of flexibility in such planning, the greatest possible concentration on individual needs.

There are some purists, not, as a rule, writers themselves, who will maintain that already we suffer from a glut of writing, a little good, much bad or indifferent. Subsidies, such people might say, might serve merely to increase the supply of what is already in excess. In fact, I should say, the tendency might well be in the opposite direction. Many writers today are forced, in order to support themselves, to write too much or to write too carelessly. Many novelists have been told by their publishers that, if they wish to secure sales, they should write at least one novel a year; and many are conscious that, in writing less than this, they will write better. What they fear most of all is a situation in which for sheer lack of money either they will not be able to write at all, or else will have only the odds and ends of their time to devote to writing. It is from this fear that a subsidy should be able to deliver them.

Nor would such subsidies interfere with the ordinary activities of publishers and of booksellers. Indeed, much as one may regret the methods of some publishers and the ignorance of many booksellers, I should be strongly opposed to any plan that was to dictate to the book trade what it was to publish and sell. On this matter the arguments of purists are really dangerous. I recall, for example, a conversation which I had in Berlin with a member of a foreign cultural mission in whose country the State had a more or less complete control of publishing. He was horrified at the condition of the book trade in England. 'Your railway bookstalls,' he said, 'are full of worthless literature. Think of the amount of paper and print, the number of hours of work that have gone into the production of so much writing that is of purely ephemeral importance. In my country, on the other hand, you will find the shops full of volumes of Shakespeare, Tolstoy, Balzac and the classics. The other books simply do not exist. What my people read is worth reading, and they enjoy it. Whereas in your country I have heard that even bishops take their chief delight in the reading of detective stories, which must necessarily exalt crime and violence.'

How far this picture of a whole nation devoted solely to the study of great literature is accurate, I am in no position to judge. But I should most strongly oppose any plan that might be made to reform my own countrymen in this direction. Liberty of choice between good, bad and indifferent literature is in itself a good thing. [1] And so far as contemporary literature is concerned it is impossible for anyone accurately and in all cases to determine which is which. Even if such a complete classification were possible, I do not believe that the 'good' author would greatly benefit by the total elimination of the 'bad'. And, of course, in point of fact, when the State exercises a real control over publishing, it is almost certain to regard as 'good' those authors who are obviously in agreement with its main aims. Such a state of affairs, as we have suggested already, is either very dangerous or absolutely fatal to literature.

I should claim, therefore, that, both from the point of view of the writer and from that of society, publishing should be as free and as unrestricted as possible.

True enough that publishers as well as writers have their problems. Many publishers who would wish to produce more experimental or unusual writing are deterred from doing so by the belief that the market is not yet ripe for work in which they

[1]   Again to quote Milton, who over and over again in his *Areopagitica* and other writings, emphasises the importance of the diffusion of all kinds of opinions, — 'A man,' he writes, 'may be a heretic in the truth; and if he believes things only because his pastor says so, or the assembly so determines, without knowing other reason, though his belief be true, yet the very truth he holds becomes his heresy.

have faith themselves. The more reputable publishers will take a risk in publishing books which they consider good, even if they do not anticipate immediate sales; or, very often, they will finance good contemporary writing from the profits made on writing which, in their opinion, is, though saleable, much less valuable. Yet of course only the bigger publishers are materially able to take such risks or to adopt such methods for financing work in which they believe. There seems to be no reason why, in appropriate circumstances, some part of the subsidies which we have recommended for authors should not be used to assist publishers also, as an indirect means of assisting the authors themselves.

All these, however, are questions of detail. In each country different needs will be felt, different methods of organisation be found desirable. Here I am only concerned with the advocacy of the main principle — that in these days some form or forms of subsidy for the arts is necessary, if these arts are to thrive as they have done in the past.

3

Conclusions

We are now, perhaps, in a position briefly to summarise some of the conclusions which we have reached or suggested.

We began with the assumption that art and literature are valuable to society. This is not an assumption that is often challenged. Every country is rightly proud of its own great writers and artists. Nearly everyone will admit that the civilisation to which he belongs has been to a considerable extent determined and inspired by its art and literature. Most people will agree that the preservation and continuance of this tradition now and in the future is a thing to be desired.

Next we arrived at a conclusion which would be by no means so generally accepted. We enquired very briefly into the ways in which art and literature have shown themselves beneficial to society. Much of this we overlooked. All those refining, deepening and sharpening influences on the mind; all the added perceptiveness, the inspirations, the glimpses into the unknown or the dimly realised; all the delights, pleasures and disciplines of the arts were scarcely mentioned. Since our main subject was the liberty of the creative writer or artist in the modern world, we emphasised in particular one aspect, one requirement which seemed essential. This we called, using Graham Greene's word, 'disloyalty'. And we insisted that, of all freedoms, the most valuable and essential one was the ability to stand apart from any political or religious organisation, to survey the world from a standpoint different from any that is conventional. This view was not expressed in an exaggerated form. It was never suggested that all writers should be conscious revolutionaries or that they should be devoid of either political or religious convictions. What was suggested was that the sphere in which they work is beyond politics and different from religion. We therefore concluded that any dictation or control exercised over writers and artists by political or religious bodies was bound to be both dangerous and constricting.

Next we began, again in very general terms, to enquire into the positive needs felt by writers and artists. We agreed that, in nearly all cases, education is a positive advantage and again we emphasised the need for a wide rather than a restricted education. Ideally speaking, education should be free for all and should include accessibility to the books, pictures, music and works of art of the world.

We emphasised also the need for leisure and pointed out that at the present time it seemed to be becoming increasingly difficult for writers and artists to live by their work alone. It was admitted that powerful arguments exist against the paying of any subsidies to writers and artists. Direct subsidies from the State might lead to that very control which has been already described as something dangerous; indirect subsidies, proceeding from committees of authors, from universities or from any other source might have their own disadvantages in parochialism, in corruption, in inefficiency. Nevertheless it was suggested that, with certain reservations, subsidies of one kind or another would produce an atmosphere of greater freedom for writers and artists. Education, then, leisure (and by 'leisure' I mean 'time in which to work freely') and freedom from outside censorship, control or dictation seem to be the chief demands which writers and artists have to make on the societies in which they live.

And here we are again confronted with the main paradox that lies at the heart of all this argument. It is State intervention that has, in the last century, changed the face of Europe and altered, among other things, the condition of writers and artists. In the long run it seems to be only State intervention that can effectively restore those conditions of adequate leisure and security which have, in most countries, now ceased to exist. There may still be a few individuals capable of helping the arts from their own resources (Mr Somerset Maugham in England provides one example of this). But on the whole the problem is too big to be dealt with by individuals, and the resources of individuals are diminishing to the point when little or no surplus income is available for such purposes. Independent or semi-independent bodies such as Universities can certainly achieve much, but they too are often or usually dependent on the support of the State. Finally, then, though with the utmost reluctance, it is to the State that we must look. And we must expect from this modern, central-ised, immensely powerful State qualities which have seldom been shown in history by such organisations. We must expect, in fact, from politicians humility and from legislators a readiness to sus-pend judgment. True that in such humility there must be the elements both of pride and of confidence, the fine pride and confidence of a Milton who is not afraid to 'let truth and false-hood grapple', who disdainfully rejects the notion of putting ideas into people's heads rather than allowing them to choose and to reflect upon a variety of ideas. A State capable of such generosity must be really strong and really based in fact upon the wills and aspirations of a great people. For we are demanding the final test of strength which is the admission of weakness. We are claiming that the State should, when power is in its hands, not use this power in certain directions, owning indeed that it cannot pretend to omniscience, and that, even for its own perfect develop-ment, it requires the aid and even the opposition of forces that are not either national or political, but rather individual or universal. We are demanding a state within the State, supported by the State; and perhaps the demand may seem excessive, the prospects of magnanimity remote.

Yet here, as in other directions, the outlook is by no means hopeless. Many States will maintain, with varying degrees of sincerity, that freedom of expression in literature and the arts is

among their most cherished aims. Can we not hope that some at
least of these States will adopt a method of paternalism that is,
in the best sense, fatherly? For a good father will prefer his son
to be an independent being rather than an imitation of himself.
Not that this analogy is wholly acceptable, since, if we were to
press it further, we should find that just as, in the paradox of
Oscar Wilde, nature is constantly imitating art, so many States
are the children of the arts which they foster. 'Poets,' says Shelley,
are the unacknowledged legislators of the world.' We claim that
they should be acknowledged as such, but that the means and
processes of their legislation should be left to the poets themselves,
should be, as they always have been, in spite of critical inquiries,
shrouded in a kind of mystery, should never be, under any circumstances, subjected to the judgment of governmental commissions,
however well intentioned, or of statisticians, however mathematically accurate.

BART BOK

Freedom of science

FREEDOM OF SCIENCE

1

Introduction

Scientists are citizens and, in common with other people, they like their rights and freedoms. The scientist in his research laboratory desires freedom in the selection of research topics. He wants a minimum of direction and he should be allowed to talk freely about his research work. He should have access to the publications of other workers in the field and he should have the right to publish freely the results of his own investigations. If conditions make it necessary that there be certain restrictions on his freedom of communication, he wants to know beforehand what these restrictions are, and he should be free to reject research opportunities which do not guarantee to him the minimum requirements of freedom which he considers essential for his works. The scientist should have the right to communicate freely with his colleagues in his own country and abroad and he wants to have no restrictions put upon his freedom of travel and of correspondence.

Scientists are citizens and they want to exercise their rights as free citizens. They should be free to participate in the cultural and intellectual life of the community. They should be allowed to participate in their government and, if this seems necessary, to criticize it. As citizens, scientists are prepared to accept the duties and responsibilities of citizenship and they are well aware of the fact that they must earn the right to be free men and women. They ask for some special dispensation because science, pure and applied, is so uniquely important to the welfare of the world and because advances in science are so critically dependent upon freedom.

The community which restricts the freedom of its scientists as citizens will lose in the end. In modern society, government at all levels is constantly faced with policy decisions involving complex scientific and technological matters. Wise decisions must rest in part on the advice of civic-minded scientists, and useful advice will hardly be forthcoming if scientists are not free to exercise their civic responsibilities.

Twenty years ago the problem of freedom of science did not seem very acute. The atomic bomb, jet-propelled, guided missiles and biological warfare were still to be found only in imaginative novels and occasionally in the comics. We still had to learn by experience how totalitarian States can restrict and pervert science. Then came the 1930's with the growing menace of Naziism. We saw how a government, bent on conquest and world domination, silenced the cultural and intellectual leaders who refused to give up their freedoms. In the war years of the 1940's we saw how science had to be used to forge the weapons without which it would have been difficult — or perhaps impossible — to defeat the enemies of freedom. The peace which followed did not bring a feeling of security. Nations that had worked well together toward the defeat of the common enemy grew distrustful of each other's motives and we seemed soon far from the hopes of universal and permanent peace that were felt in the world in the spring and summer of 1945. The average non-scientist had good reasons to become suspicious of modern science, which had produced horrible weapons of war, and there came a wave of distrust of the men and women who practised these strange arts — the scientists.

The Universal Declaration of Human Rights comes to us at a time when it is very necessary for all citizens to re-examine the basis for our traditional rights and freedoms, including the freedom of science. Scientists must study the Declaration, not only because it is their duty as citizens to do so, but also as a simple matter of self-preservation. Intelligent non-scientists must do likewise, for free science can flourish only in a community that is sympathetic to it. The Declaration must be made the basis for study and for arguments, for freedom should be something that is thoroughly alive in the minds of men. It is the primary function of this article to provide a background for one phase of the great debate on rights and freedoms: we shall present here once more the case for the freedom of science.

We have perhaps stressed too much in these first paragraphs the gap that may seem to separate the scientists from the non-scientists. Freedom of science is not separable from political and economic freedom, and freedom of science is at most only a part of the much broader area of intellectual freedom. A businessman, an industrialist, a technician, a worker, a farmer, a government official, or anyone who reads today about an attack upon a scientist's right to speak as he wishes, or to travel freely, may wake up the next day to find himself criticized and maltreated in very much the same fashion.

A non-scientist may find it difficult to appreciate the scientist's extreme concern with freedom unless he has a fair understanding of the methods and motivations that are basic to a scientist's work and of the nature of the contributions by science to society. We shall have frequent occasion to refer to these matters in the body of the article, but it seems worth while to present here some preliminary general comments.

Science works basically for peace and the better life and not for war. The really important contributions made to society by modern scientific and industrial laboratories have been that they have eased our tasks of daily living, that they have provided us with means of communication so effective that the traditional boundaries between nations and between continents are fast losing their meaning, and that they have given us the medicines and drugs with which we can fight the diseases that weaken us. For every death in war attributed to science, there are hundreds of lives saved by modern science. Basic scientific research, done freely, and without in most cases any thought of future application, is the foundation upon which modern technology is built. It seems almost commonplace to repeat it here, but electrical technology, as we know it today, had its foundation in very simple laboratory experiments carried out by curious individuals like Michael Faraday and Heinrich Hertz. The thinking of these men had in turn been greatly influenced by the work of those who came long before them, like Isaac Newton, who studied the gravitational attraction between the sun and the planets, the earth and the moon.

Scientists as well as non-scientists are apt, however, to over-stress the effects of science upon the material advancement of the world; the human and cultural values of free science should not be overlooked. While the presumed or real social usefulness of a given field may play a part in the planning of one's researches, the principal motivating power of scientific research continues to be just plain curiosity. The scientist can only give free rein to his curiosity if he is accorded the freedoms of which we have spoken above. Curiosity and a spirit of adventure are invaluable assets for human progress; without them the world would be dull and uninteresting. The opportunity to participate in scientific research, in the exploration of the unknown, provides us with an ever-present and expanding frontier of the mind. In our search for scientific truth, we make the fastest progress by allowing the human mind freedom to explore in a spirit of adventure.

We must, in presenting our case, make some distinction between basic, or pure, research and applied research, or development. Basic research deals with the laws of nature in their most elemental form and advances in basic research add to our stockpile of knowledge. Applied research takes the results of basic research and applies them to the development and construction of machines and instruments with practical uses, or in the development of socially useful techniques and procedures.

It is not always possible to make a distinction between a research scientist and a research engineer. The functions of the two overlap to a considerable extent; we find not infrequently a good engineer working for a shorter or a longer time as an expert research scientist, and *vice versa*. The scientist and the engineer both do their best work if they are engaged upon a project which holds their wholehearted interest. Pride in the usefulness of his work is to the research engineer what curiosity is to the pure scientist. This does not, however, imply that a good engineer is not just as curious as his colleague on the other side of the fence, or that the pure scientist derives no joy from the contributions he makes to the building of the imposing overall structure of scientific thought and accomplishment.

Basic and applied research both require an atmosphere of freedom for their proper development. Basic research cannot survive for long under a system of restrictions in the freedom to practise it. Applied research may continue to be productive for some time after restrictions go into effect, but in the end it too will become sterile because of the lack of a continuous flow of new basic ideas.

There is one final aspect of scientific research that we should mention at this point. In the search for truth, dishonesty is unthinkable and, if a scientist were foolish enough to be dishonest in the presentation of his basic observational data, or in his analysis, then he would find that in the end he would surely be detected and exposed by his colleagues. In the code of the scientist there just is no room for dishonesty. Other more complex areas of human endeavor would gain if they could take to heart the object lessons of science. In the codes of business practice and of politics, there is need not only for the adaptation of the methods that have been used in scientific research, but also for the moral standards which long ago were accepted by scientists everywhere.

Is freedom really essential to scientific advance? Could science not advance equally well, if scientists were given all the necessary material support while being restricted in some of their freedoms? Scientists feel sometimes a little impatient when these questions are asked and they tend to brush them aside. One cannot, however, deny that such questions are being asked with increasing persistence in recent years, especially by those who would like to see scientific research closely coordinated with military needs. We shall try to answer these questions in the pages that follow, but we must point out here that science advances most effectively by confronting one point of view with others opposed to it. Under the fascist regimes and under fascist occupation the suppression of the freedom of discussion had a deadening effect on scientific advance.

How can we preserve the freedom of science? Scientists must be made to realize that their freedoms can only be retained if they are willing to protest vigorously against all attempts at infringement of these freedoms. They must learn to take no freedom for granted and they should not relinquish their efforts to make it known publicly that without freedom society can never hope to obtain a maximum return from the individual scientist and from science as a whole. Scientists can not accomplish this task alone. They need the sympathetic support from non-scientists in all walks of life and in all professions. The freedom of science cannot be maintained unless there is in world opinion a climate favorable to it.

2

Our Cherished Freedoms

Article 19 of the Universal Declaration of Human Rights reads:

'Everyone has the right to freedom of opinion and expression; this right includes freedom to hold opinions without interference and to seek, receive and import information and ideas through any media and regardless of frontiers.'

Article 19 strikes at the heart of what is meant by freedom of science. Other articles supplement it, notably Article 12,

'No one shall be subjected to arbitrary interference with his privacy, family, home or correspondence, nor to attacks upon his honour and reputation. Everyone has the right to the protection of the law against such interference or attacks.'

and Article 13,

1.   Everyone has the right to freedom of movement and residence within the borders of each State.

2.   Everyone has the right to leave any country, including his own, and to return to his country.'

supplement this.

As a group these three articles give expression to the scientist's desire to be free to write, to speak and to publish as he wishes, to distribute his published results freely and to have access to the publications of others, to travel to distant parts, to attend meetings and to speak without restriction about his work. From the scientist's point of view, these three articles are important since they state clearly the minimum rights that must be guaranteed if there is to be freedom of communication.

We have tried to show in the introduction that it is wrong to think of scientists as a group of citizens distinct and different from the rest of us. To be effective in his work, the scientist needs as much as anyone a guarantee that he will be accorded the rights expressed in Articles 20-26 of the Declaration. These include the right to freedom of peaceful assembly and association, the right to take part in the government of his country, the right to social security, to free choice of employment without discrimination, the right to rest and leisure and to an adequate standard of living and the right to an education.

Article 27 is especially important to the scientist. Paragraph 1 reads:

1.   'Everyone has the right freely to participate in the cultural life of the community, to enjoy the arts and to share in scientific advancement and its benefits.'

If this Article had been written twenty years ago, it would, to the majority of the world's scientists, have seemed like an admirable statement, but it would not have been considered by them as especially significant for the scientist. In recent years there has been a wide questioning of the scientist's right to free participation in community activities. In the days of the atomic bomb, scientists are supposed to be much more careful than nonscientists in choice of organizations that they join or in the popular causes that they wish to espouse!

Paragraph 2 of Article 27, which reads as follows,

2.   'Everyone has the right to the protection of the moral and material interests resulting from any scientific, literary or artistic production of which he is the author.'

deals with such matters as copyright and patents. With regard to copyright, the scientist's problem is not different from that of any other author and generally it is less acute. The right to the individual's personal material benefits from a discovery, the right to a full financial return on a patent, is one of great importance, especially to the workers in the applied sciences and engineering.

Rights and freedoms are meaningless unless they entail certain duties and responsibilities. We shall speak about these more fully in the concluding section of this article, but we do well in closing this chapter to quote here the first paragraph of Article 29:

1.   'Everyone has duties to the community in which alone the free and full development of his personality is possible.'

3

Threats to the Freedom of Science

Towards the end of the nineteenth and the beginning of the twentieth centuries, the organization of scientific research was far less complex than it is today. In the United States basic research was largely confined to privately endowed universities. The first large industrial research laborotories were developing, but these had not yet reached the importance that they have today. The government's involvement in research undertakings was a relatively minor one. In Europe, scientific research was mostly done in government-supported universities, but, on the whole, scientists were free from extensive supervision and direction. Society accepted gratefully whatever scientific research had to give and there was little attempt at direction or pressures from outside. The scientists did all of their own planning.

As a student, first at Leiden and Groningen in Holland and later at Harvard University, I am privileged to have had a front seat in the auditoriums in which were announced many of the theories and discoveries that were to prove of tremendous social significance fifteen to twenty years after they were first made. How did science advance in the days before we had operational research and large-scale projects?

We were fewer in numbers then, than we are today. As a junior member at Leiden of the Ehrenfest-de Sitter school of physicists and astronomers, it was my privilege to be present at meetings and colloquia where men and women like Niels Bohr, Albert Einstein, Arthur Compton, Lord Rutherford, Madame Curie, Lise Meitner, Warner Heisenberg and the young giants of physics talked about their work, and at other meetings in which Arthur Eddington, Harlow Shapley and Henry Norris Russell spoke of their ideas on the universe. I remember sessions around the fireplace or at the beer table, and walks through the woods and along the beach, which were scientifically fully as effective and more productive than the elaborate panels and committee meetings to which we travel today by Pullman and by aeroplane. In those days scientists had all the freedom they wanted and, while they might have grumbled about the lack of material support given them for their work, they knew that they were free to work and think as they wished.

Some of my readers might accuse me of sentimentality in trying to relive the 'good old days'. Please, do not misunderstand me. As a scientist, I cannot help but be proud of the increased stature which science has gradually assumed in society. But before we consider the complexities of today, we do well to pause briefly in the past and remember the time when the greatest scientific minds of each decade were left free to do the work for which they were trained, without undue interference and without being forced to spend a large fraction of their time in administrative and organizational tasks.

Advances came then largely through the free and unrestricted interchange and communication of ideas between workers in a field. Let us suppose that a man or a woman made a scientific discovery, or developed a new theoretical approach. It frankly did not matter much if the discovery or the theory seemed of great moment to the world at large, but it was important that, to the scientist who actually did the work, there was somehow nothing like it in the entire universe. Being free to write and speak about the new development as he or she wished, the author was almost sure to arouse the interest of one or more colleagues. Their reactions to the new development might differ. One might be favourably impressed and another annoyed, but what really counted was that the new idea was being talked about in the profession and that before long it had become a subject for critical study by workers in the field all over the world. The scientist who had originally developed the idea might feel elated or depressed about the reception given to his work, but he was not likely to feel as though he were working in a vacuum.

Perhaps I have written the above paragraphs too much in the past tense. Today scientific research in many fields still follows to a considerable extent the pattern that I have outlined, but there is no denying that the growing trend towards organization of science does not encourage the free and unrestricted interchange of ideas.

The differences between scientific research as it is practised today and as it was fifty years ago are probably largely the result of the following circumstances:

1. Modern technology and industry are dependent upon the results of pure scientific research, supplemented by carefully-planned programmes of development, most of which must be

executed and directed by highly competent trained scientists. The
giant modern industrial laboratory is very much the outcome of
twentieth century science.

2.   The communist revolution presented us with the attitude
that the sole purpose of science is to serve the interests of the
common people and that there is no science 'divorced from politics
anywhere in the world'. In communist countries the progress of
science was to be fostered, but science became in some respects an
instrument of the State.

3.   In the non-communist countries, the governments have had
to assume increasing responsibilities for the social welfare of their
people. Increased governmental participation in conservation of
resources, power development, agriculture, transportation and
health has made it necessary for these governments to depend increasingly upon the advice and assistance of scientists.

4.   World War I suggested and World War II demonstrated that
science and technology are all-important to modern warfare. The
modern military establishment resembles in many ways a giant
laboratory for research and development.

5.   Modern science is elaborate and expensive. An effective cyclo-
tron can no longer be built by one or two men with nothing but
simple laboratory equipment available to them; the price of a
powerful new telescope may easily be in excess of one million
dollars.

6.   Experience with planned research programmes executed by
carefully selected teams of experts have demonstated that in certain
areas of science, especially in medicine and in applied science,
knowledge can be advanced rapidly by teams of research workers
operating according to a carefully designed master plan.

One immediate consequence of these trends towards bigness,
towards organization and planning, and towards social and military significance, is that society will naturally seek ways of controlling and guiding the young monster, with, as an almost inevitable result, restrictions in the freedom of science. The idea of
the patent, which had originally been designed to protect the individual inventor and to prevent secretiveness about inventions,
was perverted to the extent that it has become more conducive to
monopoly than to the thriving of a competitive capitalistic society.

The scientist in an industrial laboratory can never be completely
free in the selection of his topics of research and even the large

university laboratory has become so complex that there had to be an increasing emphasis on organization and direction. In a communist society, scientific research is subject to planning from above, with social and political considerations frequently of greater importance than the interests of pure science; scientists who do not conform with political directives are in danger of being discredited, dismissed from their positions and even purged. In noncommunist countries, the trends of governmental and military control are also generally restrictive in nature. To the political and especially to the military leaders, the scientist's desire for complete freedom of communication of ideas seems unreasonable and unless these leaders understand from long and intimate association just how science operates they are generally not in sympathy with the scientist's appeals for complete freedom.

Scientists of the present day cannot take it any longer for granted that they will be permitted to enjoy all of the traditional freedoms. In a society in which certain restrictions of freedom are unavoidable, there will always be a tendency to impose the maximum restrictions. We are not living in a benevolent Utopia in which the scientist, in his traditional ivory tower, has his freedoms handed to him on a silver platter. No, if, as scientists, we want our freedoms, we must learn to fight for them.

While it is important that scientists and non-scientists alike should learn to recognize threats to the freedom of science in any form or guise, we cannot present in a brief essay a complete catalogue of existing threats. For illustrative purposes, we can, however, single out two broad areas of conflict which are indicative of the existing dangers. For the first of these, we select the great genetics controversy in the Soviet Union; for the second, we analyze the implications for the freedom of science of the current security regulations and loyalty investigations in the United States of America.

In the genetics controversy we are concerned with the radically different viewpoints held by Trofim Lysenko and his Lamarckian school of Soviet geneticists, and by the great majority of geneticists of the Western Democracies. Lysenko has vigorously attacked the classical view, associated with the names of Mendel and Morgan, and he claims to have shown that environment plays a much greater rôle in genetics than had been thought to be the case in the past. Until recently there were in the Soviet Union itself many vigorous dissenters to the views held by Lysenko, but these voices appear now to have been stilled and Lysenko has declared that his theories have the official approval of the Central Committee of the Communist Party and of the Academy of Sciences of the USSR.

We have every reason to believe that in the Soviet Union and in Eastern Europe there still exists considerable opposition to the new trend, because the scientists of the Soviet Union and of Eastern Europe have been traditionally in the forefront of scientific advance and because they have shown by their past scientific accomplishments that they respect and use the scientific method.

The principal issue from the point of view of freedom of science is that the Soviet Government and the Soviet Academy of Sciences have seen fit to condemn officially and on ideological grounds the classical theories of genetics, and that they have directed the geneticists of the Soviet Union to be guided in their researches by 'progressive Michurinite biology', which is the term used in the Soviet Union to indicate the Lamarckian approach. No scientist, however friendly he may feel toward the Soviet Union, can ever tolerate this policy. For it is the basis of all true science that the results of experiments are the supreme arbiters in controversies and that political or doctrinaire concepts should have no place in scientific argument. Impartiality and freedom from bias are the very root of scientific inquiry. Science totally loses its bearings if the government can lay down rules with regard to permitted and forbidden directions of scientific thought. What has happened recently in the Soviet Union in the field of genetics will almost inevitably lead to the imposing of similar restrictions in other fields. There are already signs that physics, mathematical probability and cosmic evolution are being subjected to ideological tests.

Let us now accept, on the most favourable hypothesis, that there exists a truly scientific controversy in the field of genetics and then analyze certain aspects of this controversy directly related to the Universal Declaration of Human Rights.

What, with due regard to the principles of the Universal Declaration of Human Rights, should first of all be the attitude of the Government of the Soviet Union? It may be assumed, again on the most favorable hypothesis, that the political leaders of the Soviet Union have themselves examined with care the reports prepared by Lysenko, that they have obtained competent scientific advice, and that they have come to the conclusion that it is to the best interest of the advancement of science and of the welfare of the people that the fullest support of the State be given to the research of Lysenko and his followers. It is then certainly the duty of the State to support to the limit the experiments of Lysenko and his school.

A wise government should, however, realize that what seems 'absolutely true' in science at a given time, is frequently shown within a decade to have been a poor guess, and that the absolute and final opinion of today will almost certainly be replaced within a century by something very new and different. It is therefore a wise scientific policy not only to permit to the opponents of the favoured theory every form of freedom of investigation and publication, but, further, to provide them with even more than the minimum support which they require to continue with their work. Such a policy has a double advantage. First, it would guarantee to the minority the opportunity to carry on without disturbance. Second, it would provide the favoured majority with a steady incentive to do its very best work; science advances through the shocks of opposing views.

In the Western democracies, the non-conforming geneticists of the Lysenko school should be able to do their work alongside the classical geneticists. Here too, it should be realized that science flourishes on controversy. Our universities should not discourage competent teachers of biology who wish to test the Lysenko point of view from carrying out their experiments and from making their voices heard.

There is nothing in the Universal Declaration of Human Rights which declares that clashes between opposing views should not result in heated and, if necessary, violent argument. It is the essence of freedom that everyone is entitled to an open hearing in the marketplace, but that, in return for this privilege, he listen to criticism and that, in good time, he must answer his critics.

If great controversies are approached in a spirit that on all sides complete freedom of science must be preserved, then they must almost inevitably lead to increased activity in the field of the controversy, with science benefiting in the end on all counts. Under no circumstances can we tolerate attempts to suppress views, to restrict activities or experimentation, and to compel the abject following of an officially-recommended line of thought.

Let us now turn our freedom-telescope upon the Western Democracies, especially upon the country of which I am proud to be a citizen, the United States of America, and analyze the nature and significance of the restrictions imposed upon the publication and the discussion of results of scientific research falling under the security regulations set by the Military Establishment.

The Government of the United States, democratically elected and expressing the will of the American voter, has decided that it is in the best interests of world peace and stability that the United States be at all times prepared to resist military aggression; the American people feel that they are entitled to adequate insurance against a repeat of 'Pearl Harbour'. To protect the national interest, scientific research in certain areas has been declared *confidential* or *secret,* and special procedures, known as *security regulations,* have been established to ensure a distribution of the results of these researches within the limits set by the United States Governments. Scientific papers published under these regulations are referred to as *classified material.*

First of all, it should be understood by readers outside the United States, that classification does not apply to free research done in the universities, that industrial research is subject only to the traditional patent restrictions, that practically all non-military governmental research is published freely, and that only a portion of the scientific research done for the Military Establishment is subject to classification. To the best of the knowledge of the author there are, for example, no security regulations in effect with regard to research in the field of astronomy, though certain related fields are affected. In a field like physics, increasing attempts are made to release for free publication the results of researches that do not immediately bear upon national security. Scientific papers which at first are marked confidential or secret, are frequently *declassified* for free publication within a relatively short period.

It must be understood further that no scientist is forced to work on a classified project. Many contracts made with the Military Establishment have a specific clause that the results of the research done under the contract may be published freely; several universities in the United States have refused to enter into contracts with the Military Establishment or with other Departments of the

Government unless this is specifically stated to be the case.

The fact remains that there are some large areas of science in which research is of a confidential or secret nature. From an immediate — and basically shortsighted — point of view, it is in the interest of the contractor, the Military Establishment, to impose rather tight restrictions. As long as security regulations of any sort exist, the person whose work is affected by them should try to argue for their elimination whenever they seem unwarranted.

Unnecessary security regulations are imposed for many reasons, sometimes deliberately, but most frequently because it is the decision requiring the least thought from the person who imposes them. Bureaucratic convenience is probably the most potent force working for security regulations. An army officer or a Government official will find it generally very much simpler to stamp a paper, reporting on a research which he does not understand, as *confidential* than to listen to the arguments of experts favouring declassification. The most responsible parties are in this case the scientist who did the research and the director of the laboratory in which the work was done. They must not rest until the results of the research are given the widest possible circulation consistent with national security.

It would be a healthy development if the procedure could be reversed, by leaving it to the security officer to demonstrate the need for classification before an impartial board, which should have among its members at least one scientist expert in the field under consideration.

Classification is in a way the partial or total hiding of the results of scientific research and there is no denying that classification procedures will generally work against the best interests of science. The most obvious consequence of classification is that a given scientific paper will be accessible to only a relatively small circle of scientists and that most workers in the field are denied the privilege of reading and studying it. It is difficult for nonscientists to realize how depressing can be the thought that there may exist scientific data and analyses relevant to a project at hand and yet inaccessible to a scientist who wants to work in the field. The scientist who is not accorded the privilege of sharing in the secrets is only too apt to become sterile and discouraged and he may readily change his field of research to one in which no secrecy exists. When indiscriminately applied, security regulations may be highly detrimental to the area of research to which they refer, for an area of research in which security regulations are in effect will not so readily tempt the investigator outside the magic circle as one free from restrictions of any sort. The government which imposes restrictions, presumably for the reason of wanting to go ahead faster in this area than its competitors, may find research-advance retarded when exactly the opposite is hoped for.

The agency which imposes security regulations should be made fully aware of the risks which it assumes by doing so; in many cases the person who does the research on the project, or the responsible scientific director of the project, are the only ones in a position to make clear to the non-scientists in charge of security what these risks actually are. It may be that public education, rather than protest, is the strongest weapon available to the scientist who wishes to protect his own interests and that of the area of research in which he is working.

Security regulations and secrecy flourish under unstable world conditions and when there exists an extensive lack of trust between nations. The fear of attack from without is almost surely accompanied by a fear of attack from within and this last fear produces widespread searches for disloyal citizens. The almost inevitable result is a series of so-called *loyalty investigations* by legal and extra-legal bodies within each country. The term 'loyalty investigation' has a double connotation. No government can be denied the right to check on the reliability of its employees and one cannot find fault with fair and routine loyalty investigations leading to *security clearance* for secret or non-secret gevornmental work. Much harm can, however, be done by loyalty investigations which are in effect witchhunts, designed not only to discredit the individual who happens to be the victim, but generally aimed at suppressing through fear the free expression of opinion by others. Any public body which institutes investigations of this sort, be it the British Empire, the Soviet Union, or the United States of America, assumes a heavy responsibility. An investigation, or group of investigations, instituted to protect the nation from unnecessary harm, may readily boomerang and prove to be against the best interests of the country which undertakes it.

At present little is known about the procedures employed in loyalty tests in the communist nations and of the nature of the punitive actions that have accompanied them. The known cases of purges of scientists in the Soviet Union have, however, aroused a profound indignation. No one who believes in the principles of the Declaration of Human Rights can keep silent when, following the disappearance of one of the Soviet Union's most famous astronomers, the former Director of the Poulkova Observatory, Dr B. P. Gerasimovicz, all references to his work were omitted from textbooks and scientific papers for more than ten years. Even a man who may stand convicted in the eyes of his nation and his government has the right to recognition for his scientific work.

The nefarious results of loyalty investigations upon the freedom and advancement of science are probably in clearest evidence today in the United States, where scientists are free to comment on the actions of their government. The most spectacular investigations have been those by the House Committee on Un-American Activities, which has at times viciously attacked and smeared certain distinguished scientists, whose absolute devotion to the principles of true Americanism cannot be doubted. There has been a loud chorus of protest against these unwarranted attacks and the scientists who were involved have emerged from the ordeal with increased stature in their professions. The fact that men like Dr Harlow Shapley and Dr Edward U. Condon have defended themselves successfully against all attacks, does not however prove that loyalty investigations really do no harm.

The relatively glamorous and well-publicised cases of dismissal as a result of an investigation into the loyalty of an individual are the most dramatic proofs of the existing threats to the freedom of science. And yet in a way they do not represent the most serious threat. The greatest danger lurks in all probability in the vague threat of possible attacks upon one's loyalty, or the simple threat of bad publicity, which frightens the more timid scientists and hurts most of all those who cannot afford to protest.

The simple threat of loyalty investigation may already lead to the dismissal of the victim. If the scientist is employed by a small private institution, the administration of which considers itself vulnerable to outside criticism, then the simplest procedure is frequently, under one pretext or another, to get rid of the troublemaker. Or, if he is employed by a large State-supported institution, under continuous close scrutiny by a not-very-well-informed and frequently suspicious legislature, then he may find again that the mere threat of an investigation leads to a loss of his position.

Let us examine the r ot uncommon case of the young scientist
with a family, who is eager to exercise his right of participation in
his government by joining a liberal political organization. A few
words from a kindly dean or department chairman may suffice
to show that by doing this he is jeopardizing his chances of rapid
promotion or a better job. Hardly more than one out of ten will
go through with his plan to join when it is obviously the better
part of wisdom not to do so. The fear of exposure and bad publicity has in some cases been so intense that some scientists have
foolishly denied their past affiliation with causes that are not
popular with the investigating body. The decline in recent years
in the membership of organizations dealing with the social responsibilities of scientists shows that many of the younger generation
of scientists in the United States have come to realize that it is
'safer' to stay within the narrow boundaries of one's chosen field
of research than to enter byond them. Society will again be the
loser, for it will not profit to the fullest by what the scientists can
contribute.

We have thus far placed the greatest stress upon the problems
facing the individual. The institutions which employ scientists
have a special duty to see to it that those who work for them
enjoy the greatest possible freedom. By and large, the heads and
trustees of institutions at which one or more scientists have been
under attack, have shown themselves to be courageous champions
of the freedom of science. The large privately-endowed universities
and technical schools have an especially enviable record. They
have realized that their strength lies in attracting teachers and
research men competent in their chosen field who, conscious of
their duties as citizens, explore far and wide and who know that
their institutions will back them when they have the courage to
speak out according to their convictions. The institution which
can guarantee its scientists the maximum amount of freedom of
expression will benefit in the end for, given the choice of employment between two institutions, the scientist will generally
choose the one which guarantees him the greatest protection of his
rights, even though this may involve a sacrifice of salary.

Freedom of conscience, of assembly, of association and of speech,
all of these have a meaning only if the atmosphere of the community is one which fosters freedom. In a way it is a mistake to
speak of the freedom of science, or of intellectual freedom, as

distinct from political and economic freedom. We cannot build a wall around our institutions and thus protect them from all outside influences and, similarly, we cannot build a wall around a particular freedom and guarantee it, while denying other basic freedoms. The special problems which confront the scientist may be somewhat more clearly outlined than the problems encountered by other members of the community, but in the end the same issues will have to be faced by all. A community which guarantees to its scientists the freedom to exercise the rights of the Declaration will almost certainly be a community sympathetic to all of the principles of the Declaration.

4

Internationalism, Peace and The Freedom of Science

Through the United Nations we are all participating in an experiment, the purpose of which is to discover ways in which the nations of the world can learn to live in peace while they continue to operate as separate political entities. The primary aim of the United Nations is not so much the avoidance of war as the aggressive promotion of world peace. Since a lasting peace can be had only in a world where there exists a genuine desire for international cooperation and friendship, it is pertinent to ask how the freedom of science bears on internationalism and world peace.

We must begin by reminding our readers about the way in which science operates and the nature of the contributions from science to society. Most science has its beginnings in one or a series of experiments. The results of apparently very dissimilar experiments may point to basically similar correlations between observed data and these in turn lead to some of the basic laws of nature, such as the laws of gravity, of electricity, or the theory of the chemical bond. Science thus helps us to understand the world we live in. This is, however, by no means the end of the story. For on the basis of the derived laws it is possible to create certain new experiments and not infrequently we are given to a certain extent control of the forces of nature.

It is well to note here that science by itself is neither good nor evil and that the effect of science upon humanity depends wholly on the way in which we make use of the power given to us. In other words, science is impersonal and whether or not the results which science produces will be beneficial to mankind depends upon the way in which the results of scientific work are applied. Many scientific inventions have both good and bad consequences and sometimes there may be considerable difference of opinion as to whether the end result is either good or bad. For these reasons it is not possible to say simply that science has had either a bad or a good influence upon internationalism. The only statement that we stand ready to defend is that science exerts at present a profound influence on peace and internationalism. To illustrate the point, we shall examine briefly two examples of scientific developments that have affected international relations and which presumably will continue to do so for years to come; both are feats of science and of engineering, the first, the aeroplane and, the second, the advent and application of research in the properties of the atomic nucleus.

Aeroplanes are most wonderful tools of peaceful communication between nations. And yet, very much the same planes which carry our businessmen, scientists and political leaders in times of peace, bring death and destruction through the bomb they deliver in wartime.

The science of the atomic nucleus and its practical applications presents us at present which a most complex picture. On one hand we are faced with the almost unbelieveable destructive power of the atomic bomb, on the other side we have the promise of a new and untapped source of power, unequalled by any other source yet developed. Should we call a halt to all of our nuclear research until the world is ready to make intelligent use of the new power that is given it? Every one of us knows that we should not stop progress and it is doubtful if we could, even though we might wish to do so.

Much as we may hate war, the moral issues of the use of science in war are far from clear-cut. Let us consider once more the atomic bomb. In the United States an overwhelming majority of the people holds that the use of the atomic bomb over Hiroshima and Nagasaki was justified because it helped to shorten the war and because for every human life destroyed in this bombing the lives of hundreds of soldiers were saved on both sides. On the other hand, we find that the use of the atomic bomb was considered an immoral war crime by large groups outside the United States and by many inside the United States. The use of science in war cannot be condemned on an absolute basis. Those among us who consider themselves the strongest supporters of the United Nations, would, I believe, be grateful for the modern scientific weapons of war if the need should arise to break the power of an aggressor intent upon destroying the foundations of the peaceful world which we are trying to build under the United Nations.

Science loses its impersonal character as soon as the issue of the freedom of science is brought into the argument. If the results of scientific research are freely available, and if the avenues of world-wide communication are kept free and open, then scientists, with the aid of men and women in many walks of life, can use science to help create an era of international good will. The fruits of science, freely exchanged, can assist in the building of a world in which hunger and privation are eliminated.

Intellectual freedom and freedom of communication are essential for the creation of a spirit of cooperation and mutual understanding among the peoples of the world. Free science makes a fundamental contribution toward world peace and world government through the support which it provides to the many rights and freedoms embodied in the Universal Declaration of Human Rights. The observance of the principles of freedom of inquiry and of freedom of thought in science is a constant challenge to anything in politics or in the cultural realm which tends to be dogmatic or absolute.

We have thus far dealt with science and the freedom of science and we have not referred to the scientists themselves. Scientists are citizens and I doubt that, on the whole, they are either very much better or very much worse citizens than the rest of us. Scientists are human beings whose primary social function it is to work to the best of their ability for the advancement of science, almost irrespective of the uses to which their discoveries might be put. It has been said that scientists cannot and should not be expected to foresee the consequences of their work and that they can influence only in very minor ways the uses to which their discoveries are put; I rather disagree with this point of view. A scientist who ponders the social consequences of his work is in a very much better position to arrive at valid conclusions than a lawyer or a politician who lacks the background for an understanding of the basic developments underlying the discovery. A scientist should not try to be omniscient, but in his own special area of activity he should be able to evaluate more clearly than his fellow citizens. As an example we consider again the application of nuclear research, especially as far as it deals with the peaceful uses of atomic energy. Here is an area in which progress depends to a great extent on the readiness of the expert scientists in the field to take a leading part in the long-range planning. If this planning is to be done on a world wide scale, it must be done in a spirit of freedom of inquiry.

Internationalism in science is at present subject to many forms of control. International barriers to the freedom of science are imposed because of fear of war, of political involvement, or of a possible loss of political advantage. Not infrequently they result from the narrow-mindedness and provincialism of those in power. Scientists know from everyday experience how close we are to one world of science and they have, therefore, a special responsibility of working for the removal of all unnecessary barriers.

The free interchange across national boundaries of men and ideas is basic to the advancement of science. History shows that science advances generally by stepwise procedures and that every new development is built on the discoveries and theories that came before it. Because of the basically cumulative character of science, almost every field owes its development to the work of men and women from many different nations. One does not need to go very far back in the history of science to prove this, for in every area of scientific research the present state of knowledge has a truly international background. Let me illustrate the point with an example drawn from my own field of research and consider the nationalities of the men who contributed most significantly over the past fifty years to the increase of our knowledge of the Milky Way System.

During the first fifteen years of our century, the principal advancements in our knowledge of the structure and motions of the Milky Way were made by the Hollander, Kapteyn, the British, Eddington, the German, Schwarzschild, and the Americans, Pickering, Schlesinger, Campbell and Seares. Methods were developed for the wholesale measurement of stellar brightnesses, spectra, motions and distances, and the first evidence was forthcoming to show that stellar motions were not distributed in a purely random fashion. The period between 1915 and 1920 was that of the American, Shapley, who succeeded in showing that our sun was located far from the center of the system. In the decade that followed, the Swedish astronomer, Lindblad, the Hollander, Oort, the Swedish-American astronomer, Strömberg, and the Canadian, Plaskett, changed our whole outlook upon the motions of stars in our Milky Way System. In 1930 the Swiss-American, Trumpler, building in part upon the earlier work of the German, Wolf, the American, Barnard, and the Swedish astronomer, Schalen, gave proof of the existence of a layer of obscuring matter close to the central plane of our Milky Way System; his results were confirmed and extended by the work of the American trio, Stebbens, Huffer and Whitford, and by a host of other investigators. Subsequently attention was focussed upon the study of the dynamics and evolution of our Milky Way System, with important contributions by the Indian astronomer, Chandrasekhar, working in America, the Soviet astronomer, Ambarzumian, the American astronomer, Baade, who was born and educated in Germany, and many other astronomers from all over the world.

The story of the astronomers has its counterpart in every field of scientific research. No significant advance in medicine, for example, is the product of research by nationals of only one country. Perhaps the most dramatic demonstration of the international character of science was given in the war-time studies leading to the large-scale release of the energy of the atomic nucleus through the atomic bomb. At Los Alamos American scientists were working side by side with their colleagues from many European countries, notably with some of the world's most distinguished refugee physicists from Germany and Italy.

Science cannot be worldwide unless it is free. In most fields of research advance would have been stifled if there had not been a continued interchange of men and of opinions. Since a wide exchange of knowledge has traditionally been helpful to the advancement of science, scientists must ever be on the watch against threats to the freedom of international communication.

Non-scientists often find it difficult to imagine how strong can be the bonds growing out of common interests between scientists of totally different national backgrounds and living at opposite ends of the world, but working upon researches in the same general area. We notice this especially where relatively few scientists are involved, as in astronomy, and I would like to use once more an example from my own field of research. I have never had the opportunity to visit the Abastumani Observatory in the Georgian Republic, where several of the staff astronomers are working on problems very similar to those with which I am struggling from day to day. In many ways, I have more in common with them than with some of my colleagues at Harvard University. For in our researches on the colours of distant Milky Way stars, we have had to battle against very similar obstacles, such as technical difficulties in photographic or photoelectric photometry, a lack of colour standards and of spectral types of faint stars. I am sure that Milky Way astronomy would stand to gain by close friendly cooperation between the Harvard and Abastumani astronomers. But would not the world at large benefit as well by such international friendships? I think that the answer to this question is 'yes', for, through the establishment of intimate contacts between scientists of different nations, we are laying in a perfectly natural way the foundations for widespread contacts of peoples of different lands, contacts which, in the end, must help to make the peace secure.

It is a very fine thing to write in general terms about how free science may contribute towards internationalism and world peace, but these generalities are of no value unless they can be the basis for specific action. Fortunately we have in UNESCO an organization dedicated in large part to this very purpose of facilitating international communication in all forms. The promotion of the freedom of science is more particularly the function of the Natural Sciences Department of UNESCO. What are the specific problems with which UNESCO should concern itself?

UNESCO is not primarily an operating agency. Its functions are to stimulate, to facilitate, to initiate, and to assist international organizations in carrying out more effectively the work that they have undertaken to perform. It is part of UNESCO's philosophy that freedom alone does not suffice, but that it must be supplemented by opportunities to undertake the tasks which we are given the freedom to do. It is meaningless to give scientists the freedom to attend international meetings, unless ways and means can be found to overcome difficulties caused by the high cost of living, or by currency restrictions, which may block the most able scientists from attending meetings of their international professional organizations. Freedom of publication is meaningless unless publication media are provided and unless these publications are promptly distributed on a world-wide basis. International communication is to some extent already blocked if a scientist is not permitted to publish either his full paper, or at least a comprehensive abstract, in a language which is read and understood by the majority of his colleagues in the field.

International communication in science has been fostered in a great variety of ways. At the professional level, international congresses, and especially the international scientific unions, have proved their worth over the past thirty years. The majority of the international congresses have not generally been active between meetings, which take place every two to five years, but the international scientific unions operate on a more continuous basis. The more active unions have, for instance, commissions of experts, the members of which exchange views by correspondance during the time between meetings. Some unions sponsor one or more specialized bureaux or projects and during the past five years specialists of several countries have met at small technical symposia under union sponsorship. The primary aim of the international unions is of course the advancement of the science which they represent, but indirectly they have made significant contributions to international relations. They might have accomplished more, were it not that, because of the professional character of the unions, the older scientists in each field enter more into the unions' affairs than the younger ones. This is in many ways deplorable, since the causes of intenationalism and world peace need active support from the younger generation.

Exchanges of scientists, young and old, but especially in the younger group, are promoted through an extensive existing system of international exchange fellowships. UNESCO has recently tabulated close to twenty-thousand individual fellowships opportunities, many of them open to scientists. Everything possible must be done to increase the numbers and the quality of these international exchanges. The holders of these fellowships should not only undertake to perform the specific tasks for which their fellowships are granted, but they should use their opportunities to acquaint themselves with the ways of life and thought of peoples in foreign lands, and, upon their return home, they should consider themselves responsible ambassadors of good will in the cause of internationalism.

To give meaning to visits to foreign lands, such visits must be preceded and followed with sympathetic study of work done in other countries and, if possible, with extensive correspondence. In addition, there are always foreign visitors to be welcomed. Those of us who have travelled abroad know how much students appreciate little gestures of friendship and welcome, especially during the first days after arrival in a new place. There is hardly a lonelier person than the boy or girl of eighteen to twenty years of age, holder of a fellowship, who has just arrived in a foreign country where he or she will spend a year. A small kindness may at that time make all the difference in deciding the student's outlook upon people of other lands, and a student who is totally ignored cannot help but build up a certain resentment against the country that he or she is visiting.

Another major way in which scientists participate in the free communication of ideas is through publication of their scientific papers in journals accessible to workers in the field anywhere in the world. Unfortunately there exist at present serious barriers to the prompt world-wide circulation of scientific literature. In many fields the scientists from the Western Democracies have great difficulties in obtaining the latest papers published in the Soviet Union and *vice versa*. An efficient international scientific postal service continues to be one of the real needs of our times.

In most of the larger fields of science, like medicine, biology, chemistry and mathematics, the number of published articles has become so great in any one area that the scientist who wishes to remain abreast of what is happening in his field must resort to the practice of reading only abstracts of most of the papers in his field. The preparation and world-wide distribution, preferably in more than one language, of these abstracts presents one of the most difficult problems in international scientific relations. It is clearly in the interests of good international relations that UNESCO should sponsor the publication and distribution of comprehensive abstracting journals.

It is obvious that international communication in science cannot operate effectively without a good measure of freedom of science. The rights and freedoms guaranteed in the Universal Declaration of Human Rights are basic to good international relations in science. International congresses and meetings of the international unions lose much of their meaning if excessive restrictions upon the issuing of passports and visas exist. In recent years such restrictions have gradually been tightened until the success of many a scientific venture is jeopardized by the nonissuance of a passport or a visa to one or more of the participating scientists.

The world-wide sharing in the advances of science should include as far as possible the free sharing of technical knowledge and of the tools required for the application of science to human needs. The primary responsibility rests with the Economic and Social Council of the United Nations and the Specialized Agencies, notably, again, UNESCO. With a rapidly increasing world population, and with our resources being exhausted in part, it becomes imperative for the nations of the world to use science to the fullest in the solution of their social and economic problems. World peace will not be secure unless we succeed in finding ways of maintaining and, for most parts of the world, improving, the standards of living. We must find ways to overcome the barriers which obstruct effective mutual assistance among the United Nations in such matters as reconstruction of war devastated countries, in the exchange of information on technical processes and of resource techniques, and in the protection of nature. To be truly effective such a programme should be supplemented by an extensive programme of fundamental education, which should penetrate into the most remote and underprivileged areas of the world.

To this point we have principally stressed the immediate and practical benefits which the world may expect if we permit science to operate within the framework of its traditional freedoms. There are, however, certain intangible ways in which free science contributes to the creation of a climate favourable to world peace. We must here again distinguish clearly between science, the impersonal large body of verified facts and the correlations between these which we generally call the laws of nature, and 'free science', which is the same science now made alive by the personalities of the free investigators, which creates in an adventuresome spirit, and the basic attitude of which is one of curiosity and of doubt.

Science, free or otherwise, will in the end almost surely lead to 'one world'. It does not necessarily follow, however, that this world is going to be a pleasant one, the kind of world in which we like to think that our children and grandchildren will grow up. Without freedom, this 'one, world' might well resemble in many ways the *Thousand Year Reich* which Adolf Hitler envisioned and which the United Nations were forced to oppose by fighting World War II. The chances for a free world, one in which the individual is given the opportunity of leading a full life, are however much better if science is allowed to make its contributions to society in an atmosphere of responsible freedom. Free science can be a strong ally in the common effort to achieve the 'one world' of the Universal Declaration of Human Rights.

It has been pointed out many a time, most forcefully in recent years by Harlow Shapley, Harold C. Urey and Arthur H. Compton, that scientists come closer than any other group of individuals to being world citizens. This is not specially to the credit of scientists, since it is brought about by the natural one-worldness of their field, but it does place upon scientists certain definite responsibilities. In the words of Compton: 'scientists are prototypes of world citizens.' As long as science is free, scientists are almost automatically joined in a world brotherhood and it is fervently to be hoped that the scientists of the world will realize that in the Universal Declaration of Human Rights lies the promise of a guarantee for their cherished freedoms and that it is their responsibility to join the forces that must lead in achieving the universal adoption of the Declaration. As citizens we are all free to express our preferences with regard to our desired forms of national government and of world government, but these questions need not divide us when we join in the world-wide campaign for the adoption of the Universal Declaration of Human Rights. We may compromise with regard to the political and economic systems under which we live, but no compromise is possible when we are called to the defense of our basic rights and freedoms.

5

Implementing The Declaration —
Towards A Charter For Scientists

The Universal Declaration of Human Rights is issued at a time
when the freedom of science is under attack from many sides.
Scientists have reason to be grateful to the drafters of the Declaration, for we have been given an inspiring restatement of basic
principles to guide us in the fight for the freedom of science.
While the strength of the Declaration lies in its general applicability, the scientists, like any other group of people in our society,
must give thought to ways of implementing the Declaration and
they should try to put into words just how certain Articles of the
Declaration affect them.

As scientists we do well to realize that in the fight for freedom
of science we must strike a balance between defence and offence.
Our principal defence consists in being ever watchful for un-
justifiable infringements of our freedoms and of protesting
promptly and vigorously whenever the occasion calls for a protest.
As part of our offence we must demonstrate repeatedly, and by
example, that freedom of science has paid off in terms of scientific advancement and that free science has a big contribution to
make towards the creation of a meaningful peace and towards
responsible world government. The advance of science without
freedom must in the end lead to the enslavement of science, no
matter what may be the nature of the economic or political system
that poses restrictions.

It is worth repeating once more the truism that the facts of
nature know no ideological boundaries. In the days of the Inquisition, Galileo fought the fight for the freedom of science and
Bruno was burned at the stake because of his refusal to accept the
Church's dogmatic attitude with regard to the Copernican theory
of the solar system. Even in our enlightened twentieth century we
have seen the spectacle of religious fundamentalism refusing to
accept or consider the unprejudiced verdict of scientific experiment, and quite recently we have seen how totalitarian governments have found it impossible to tolerate in their countries scientists whose basic philosophy is that no single theory remains
unchallenged and unchanged for long. To these threats scientists

have invariable replied that the growth of science and of civilization is stunted as soon as we abandon the principle of freedom
from dogma.

We have seen in the earlier chapters that largely because of the
growing importance of science in society, the outside world attempts to control and direct the development of scientific research.
We need not enter again into the motives for this course of action,
but we should recognize that besides fear and greed, or a shortsighted desire for power, there may exist an honest desire to advance civilization by leading science along clearly defined paths.
Unfortunately science does not advance in this fashion; science
remains to a considerable extent accidental and the opportunities
are often not realized until the research stumbles upon them by
accident. At certain stages of development — especially in the
area of technology — there is room for planned research and for
operational research, but in much of our basic research we shall
continue to work by the use of seemingly wasteful methods, with
the individual scientist or institution doing the planning.

Freedom implies an attitude of responsibility in the person who
profits by it. While science certainly has important contributions
to make to society, it cannot by itself give us the key to the solution of the complex problems of society. To be an effective practitioner of freedom, a scientist must be sensitive to the ever-present
need for guidance and he must be especially careful not to confuse
freedom with an unwillingness to cooperate.

The Universal Declaration of Human Rights is like a call to arms
to all men and women of good will. What opportunities are there
for enlistment? Since in this article we are very much concerned with science and scientists, I wish to take advantage of the
opportunity given to me and make certain very specific proposals
about the way the individual scientist can participate in the fight
for freedom and the good life. I propose that every scientist should
deliberately set aside one afternoon or evening a week — say three
to six hours — to give thought to the broader social implications
of his own work and of that of his fellow scientists and further
that, depending on his personality and inclination, he should in
some way make known the conclusions at which he arrives.

When scientists are approached with request for participation in
some socially significant activity, their excuse for refusal is fre-

quently that the cause is one thoroughly deserving of support, but
that the individual who is being approached is too busy with his
or her own work to join. I have much sympathy with this point,
but I would retort that in a period of world crisis like the present,
the hope of survival lies in political and social action by the individual. It almost seems as though the time has come that we
must all try to be good scientists on Monday, Tuesday, Wednes-
day, Thursday and Friday, save the world on Saturday, and recu-
perate on Sunday!

The choice about how to proceed with the discharging of one's
social responsibilities is very much in the hands of the individual
scientist. Some may find it more satisfactory to join organizations
formed expressly for the purpose of study and action on the social
implications of science. Others may prefer to work through their
professional scientific organizations and still others may prefer to
work through community groups in which the scientists are at
best a small minority.

The most important individual decision is that of the choice of
the area, of areas (preferably not too many), for one's extra-profes-
sional activities. We should apply to this choice the same sort of
judgement which, as scientists, we employ in the selection of a
research topic. Special competence may play a rôle in our decision,
or we may turn to a topic apparently passed over by others. An
astronomer, for example, will generally have considerable experience in the field of international relations, but he would normally neither be a very much interested, nor an especially effective
member of a group inquiring into revision of our patent laws.
An atomic scientist may join the astronomer's study group on international relations, or he may wish to examine the problems of
the possible usage of nuclear energy as a source of power in under-
developed areas. Or, instead, he may decide that what his community needs most is popular education in the basic physics of
the atomic nucleus. An engineer or industrial scientist may join
in the nuclear physicist's project for the study relating to under-
developed areas, or he may wish to undertake the patent study
which failed to arouse the interest of the astronomer.

Some scientists, just like many other citizens, have a hearty
dislike for joining voluntary organizations; they may prefer study
to action. From serious study and contemplation they will form
opinions which in their total effect may do more good to the

world than all the committees work taken together. As long as there is freedom of expression, a single intelligent individual can wield great power for the common good.

For many scientists education is an important professional activity. Those scientists who are good teachers and speakers will find popular education a rewarding field for extra-curricular activities. Much of the existing popular fear and distrust of science and scientists comes from lack of understanding. The need for popular education on basic nuclear physics has already been mentioned and every field of science can present its own list of topics for mass education. The scientists who participates in popular education will generally discover that his science benefits by contacts with a great variety of people.

To date the emphasis has largely been on the popularization of the results of scientific research and, while any form of science education is to the good, an overstressing of the results may develop an 'amazing story' attitude in the listener and may not contribute to his understanding of the basic aims and methods of scientific research and of the spirit in which this research is done. Mass education should be only a part of our total educational effort. The most urgent need of the moment is perhaps for a programme aimed specifically at our political and economic leaders, among whom we find often a tragic lack of understanding of science coupled with, at least in some cases, a strong desire to learn.

The United Nations and the Specialized Agencies are very much in need of sympathetic support from scientists. Several of these Specialized Agencies are to a large extent concerned with problems in pure and applied science and they depend heavily on the voluntary support from scientists outside the organization; UNESCO offers a wide area of activities for scientists who wish to contribute to international understanding and to world peace. We noted in the preceding chapter that science seems to move us more and more towards a unified world. This implies the need for some form of world government and it is not surprising that scientists are playing leading parts in the various movements towards world government. Scientists who are aware of the potential destructiveness of modern scientific warfare can probably make a greater contribution by working positively for world government than by the negative approach of fear propaganda. It has been suggested that scientists might well take the lead in conditioning the public mind for the acceptance of constitutional world government.

It would be helpful if, to supplement the Declaration, there were to exist several Charters of more limited scope. A Charter for Scientists would, for example, be a useful adjunct to the Declaration. In recent years there have been sporadic discussions about such a Charter and some tentative drafts have actually been proposed. The author of this pamphlet was privileged, as a member of the Committee on Science and Its Social Relations (C.S.S.R.) of the International Council of Scientific Unions, to participate in the drafting of one such Charter at a conference in Paris in June 1948. This particular draft was admittedly a first attempt prepared for the purpose of arousing public interest, as the C.S.S.R. explained in its official announcement. I was given the assignment of publicising the Charter in the United States and of soliciting comments for use in subsequent drafts. It would be out of order for me to propose here a new version of the Charter, but it may facilitate future discussion and debate if, in closing this article we reproduce the draft Charter of the C.S.S.R. and analyze briefly its principal faults and deficiencies. Upon my return from the Paris Conference of the C.S.S.R., I showed the draft Charter to a group of friends in the Boston and Cambridge area. They pointed to a certain looseness of wording and organization in the official C.S.S.R. draft, and, accepting many of their suggestions, I submitted the draft Charter for consideration to American scientists in the following form:

In consideration of the prominent place which science holds at present in society, and of the rapid transformation of the world through the application of science, and in consideration further of the fact that scientists can obtain and use information not readily available to others, the scientific worker has certain obligations towards society over and above the ordinary duties of citizenship.
It is therefore the duty of every scientist:
a) to maintain a spirit of honesty, integrity and cooperation;

b) to examine searchingly the meaning and purposes of the work that he or she is performing, and, when in the employ of others, to inquire into these purposes and to evaluate the moral issues that may be involved;

c) to promote the development of science in the ways most beneficial to all mankind and to exert his or her influence as far as possible to prevent its misuse;

d) to assist in the education of the people and of governments in the aims, methods and spirit of scientific research and to keep them abreast of scientific progress;

e) to promote international collaboration in science and to work for the preservation of world peace.

In order to be able to fulfill these obligations, scientists must claim certain rights, the principal ones of which are:

a) economic security and the right to participate freely in all activities permitted to the average citizen;

b) the right to obtain information about the purposes for which assigned research projects are being done;

c) the freedom to publish the results of his or her researches and the utmost possible freedom to discuss work in progress with other scientists.

The Charter for Scientists differs from the Universal Declaration of Human Rights in that the Charter stresses the duties and obligations of scientists. Several of our friendly critics have drawn our attention to the omission of one or more articles dealing specifically with the contributions of science to world government and with the obligation of scientists to emphasize the human and cultural values of science. The first omission can be rectified by the following modification of Article (e):

e) to promote international collaboration in science, to work for the preservation of world peace and to contribute towards a spirit of world citizenship.

With regard to the second point, we can probably do no better than to incorporate verbatim one of the four points of the general recommendations by the Natural Sciences Panel at the Boston (September 1948) meeting of the U.S. National Commission for UNESCO, which reads:

f) to emphasize and develop the human values associated with science and technology.

Some of our correspondents, while agreeing to the spirit of the first half of the Charter, expressed doubts about the need of giving to these points the formal status of a Charter. I reject this objection, since in the complex world of today there are many scientists who look for guidance that can come from a well-written common code of the profession. It may be many years before we can hope to achieve the universal adoption of the Charter by scientific societies, by nations, or by international bodies, but in the meantime the mere existence of a Charter focusses attention upon the need for consideration of its basic premises. I can see tremendous gains if individual scientists in considerable numbers were to decide solemnly and voluntarily to attach their signatures to the Charter.

There were many strong, and to some extent justified, criticisms of the second part of the Charter, the articles dealing with the rights that scientists must claim in order to be able to fulfil their obligations to society. After a year of reflection, I can see that we lacked in wisdom when the last three articles were formulated. It has been pointed out to us that scientists should have no claims to economic security, other than those accorded to all citizens. Serious objections have been made to the inclusion of the right to access of information about the purposes for which the work is being done and of the rights of the freedom to publish and of the freedom to discuss the results of one's work. It has been pointed out to us that the military could not possibly employ a research scientist who subscribed to these two articles and that it was unrealistic to expect industries in a competitive society to grant to their research scientists these specific rights and freedoms.

As one member of the C.S.S.R. who assisted in the drafting of the Charter (and I must make it clear that I am speaking solely for myself) I acknowledge the partial validity of the objections and I would be prepared to cast my vote for a modified version of the second part of the Charter. And yet, I do not regret that we stated these rights in the form that was adopted in Paris; we were perhaps aiming at an ideal rather than a practical solution of the difficult problems that scientists are facing today.

In a modified version of the Charter it may be desirable to omit altogether the reference to economic security in Article (a) of the second section of the Charter, provided that it be understood that scientists, like all citizens, are entitled to the economic rights of the Universal Declaration. Article (b) could be softened by insisting only upon the right to obtain *general* information regarding the purposes for which assigned research projects are being done; scientists must, however, insist upon the privilege of knowing the basic aims of the research projects in which they are asked to participate and no one should undertake to work on a project which he believes to be socially or morally wrong. The major objections to Article (c) can probably be met by a slight change of wording and the addition of one further clause:

c)   the freedom to publish the results of his or her researches, as well as full freedom to discuss work in progress with other scientists, except where these privileges may have to be restricted for socially or ethically justifiable reasons.

In the end it will probably prove to have been all to the good that the C.S.S.R. by its somewhat precipitate and idealistic action focussed attention not only upon the need for a Charter, but also upon some of the main unsolved problems of the day. The battle for freedom of science is half won if we learn to recognize and isolate the principal threats and dangers. We have now as guides for battle the Universal Declaration of Human Rights and the feeble and untried weapon of a Charter that is yet imperfect. May the discussion proceed.

Biographical notes

GERMAN ARCINIEGAS

Born at Bogotá, Colombia in 1900.

Author:

El Estudiante de la Mesa Redonda (Pueyo, Madrid, 1932); *America, Tierra Firme* (Ercilla, Santiago, 1937); *Los Comuneros* (A.B.C., Bogotá, 1938); *Jiménez de Quesada* (A.B.C., Bogotá, 1939); *Los Alemanes en la Conquista de América* (Losada, Buenos Aires, 1942); *Biografía del Caribe* (Sudamericana, Buenos Aires, 1945); *Este Pueblo de América* (Fondo de Cultura, México, 1946).

English translations:

The Knight of El Dorado (Viking, New York, 1942); *Germans in the Conquest of America* (MacMillan, New York, 1943); *The Green Continent* (Knopf, New York, 1944); *Caribbean, Sea of the New World* (Knopf, New York, 1945).

Public life:

Minister of Education of Columbia (1941–1942 and 1945–1946); Chargé d'Affaires, of Colombia, Buenos-Aires, 1940; Vice-Consul of Colombia, London, 1931–1932.

Academic life:

Prof. of Sociology, Universidad Nacional, Colombia; Visiting Prof. Columbia (New York) 1943; University of Chicago, 1944; Mills College, California, 1945; University of California, 1945; Columbia University, 1948–1950.

Honours:

Member of Academy Colombiana de la Lengua and Academia Colombiana de Historia.

Correspondent of Academia de la Lengua Española, Academia de Historia Argentina, Academia de Historia de Venezuela, Academia de la Lengua de México and Honorary Associate of the National Institute of Arts and Letters, United States.

JEAN PIAGET

Professor Piaget was born in 1896 and received his Doctorate in Natural Sciences at Neuchâtel. He studied psychology, sociology and philosophy at Neuchâtel, Zürich and Paris before accepting a Chair of these three sciences at Neuchâtel University where he lectured between 1925 and 1929. In that year he went to Geneva and thence to Lausanne where he still holds the Chair of Psychology and Sociology. Other distinctions have been showered upon him. He is a Director of the Institut Rousseau and the Bureau International d'Éducation. He holds honorary Doctorates from the Universities of Harvard, the Sorbonne, Brussels, and Rio de Janeiro. He is a corresponding Member of the French Society of Psychology, the Roumanian Academy of Sciences and those of Montpellier and New York. He has been an Assistant Director General of UNESCO, President of UNESCO's Swiss Commission and led the Swiss delegation at the General Assemblies of 1948 and 1949.

His many publications have been translated into almost as many languages including English, Spanish, Polish, Czech, Turkish and Swedish.

LYMAN BRYSON

Professor of Education, Teachers College, Columbia University New York, N.Y.

Born, July 12, 1888, Nebraska, USA.

Academic degrees: MA, LL.D., L.H.D.

Special Consultant on problems of international understanding, UNESCO, 1947. President, Institute for Inter Cultural Studies, 1949. Vice-President, Annual Conference on Science, Philosophy, and Religion, 1949. President, American Association for Adult Education, 1944—1946. Fellow, American Association for the Advancement of Science. Chief, Bureau of Special Operations, Office of War Information, 1942. Counsellor on Public Affairs and Chairman, Invitation to Learning, (Broadcast Program), Columbia Broadcasting System.

Publications:

Adult Education, The new Prometheus, Science and Freedom, etc. As an educator, has been concerned mostly with the sociology of mass communications and adult education. As a broadcaster, carried on, for twenty years, commentaries and discussion programs having to do with literary, social, and political questions, has also done a good deal of lecturing and forum leading in many parts of the United States.

His first international experience came at the end of the first World War when he spent five years, first with the American Red Cross and then with the League of Red Cross Societies, studying educational conditions in Europe and Asia. In 1922, he was secretary of the International Health and Welfare Conference held in Bangkok, Siam.

Taught in the universities of Michigan (his alma mater), California, and Columbia, and have lectured in many others.

MAURICE BEDEL

French writer born at Paris in 1883.

He studied medicine, submitted a doctor's Thesis on Periodic Obsessions at the same time as he published his first literary work *Le Cahier de Phane* (poems). After extensive travels in Europe and Africa he wrote his first novel, *Jérome 60 Latitude Nord* (1927) which gained him the Prix Goncourt and was the subject of heated exchanges between Norway and the author. Applying his gift of malicious observation to the study of political behaviour in France and abroad, he had a series of resounding successes with *Molinoff, Indre-etLoire* (1928), *Fascisme Au VII* (1929), *Philippine* (1930), *Zulfu* (1932), *La nouvelle Arcadie* (1934), *L'Alouette aux Nuages* (1935) and *Le Laurier d'Apollon* (1936). As an essayist he is the author of *Monsieur Hitler* which aroused considerable interest when it appeared (1927), and *Géographie de Mille Hectares* (1937) which is judged to be his masterpiece. Further works are *La Touraine* (1935), *Berthe au Grand Pied* (1943), *Traité du Plaisir* (1946) and *Dessin de la Personne Humaine* (1947).

He was President of the Société des Gens de Lettres de France in 1948-49.

REX WARNER

Born in 1905 and took his degree at Oxford in Classics and English literature. I have taught these subjects in schools in England and in Egypt. During the war, when teaching in London, he was a member of a Home Guard Anti-Aircraft Battery. After the war became Director of the British Institute at Athens, and later still, in 1948 was attached to the Technical University in Berlin.

His first works, *Poems*, and a novel *The Wild Goose Chase*, appeared in 1937 Since then he has written other works, *The Professor*, *The Aerodrom*, *Why was I killed?* and, last year, *Men of Stones*. Has also written a book of essays *The Cult of Power*, and translated various Greek plays into English verse (also some modern Greek poetry).

His works have been published in America and translated into French, Italian, Spanish, Czech, Swedish, Norwegian, Danish, German, Polish and Bulgarian.

BART J. BOK

Born at Hoorn (Holland), April 28, 1906.

Studied in University of Leiden and University of Groningen (Holland).

R. W. Willson Fellow in Astronomy, Harvard University, 1929 —33; now professor and associate director of Harvard College Observatory; Member American Astronomy Society; American Association Scientific Workers;

A.A.A.S., Sigma Chi.

Author: *The distribution of the Stars in Space* (1937); *The Milky Way*, 1941 (with Mrs. Bok); *Basic Marine Navigation* 1944 (with T. W. Wright).

Chairman of the Commission for Unesco of the U.S. National Research Council.